Antony McCammon studied at Marlborough College, the Sorbonne and McGill University. He has had a career in international banking and environmental studies and has travelled widely. He was British Honorary Consul in Zürich for eleven years.

THE
HONOURABLE
CONSUL

A Story of Diplomacy

Antony McCammon

The Radcliffe Press
LONDON • NEW YORK

Published in 2013 by The Radcliffe Press
An imprint of I.B.Tauris & Co. Ltd
6 Salem Road, London W2 4BU
175 Fifth Avenue, New York NY 10010
www.ibtauris.com

Distributed in the United States and Canada Exclusively by
Palgrave Macmillan
175 Fifth Avenue, New York NY 10010

ISBN: 978 1 78076 302 6

A full CIP record for this book is available from the British Library
A full CIP record is available from the Library of Congress

Library of Congress Catalog Card Number: available
Printed and bound by CPI Group (UK) Ltd, Croydon, CR0 4YY

Contents

PART II : AND WHAT IT LED TO   173

List of Illustrations

Foreword

In recent times, the office of the honorary consul has not had the best press - Graham Greene's eponymous book, with its descriptions of a man who had come down rather in life and who was seeking solace in drink and self-pity, combined with Hollywood stereotyping, have helped to give a negative colouring to many people's perceptions of the office, and of those who fill it. But even at the time he was writing, Greene's description of the honorary consul and his world was becoming outdated - in the world of the modern honorary consul, it has passed firmly into history. Antony McCammon's shrewd, vivid descriptions of the realities of modern consular life show the full extent of those changes and the extraordinary range of duties and responsibilities which the modern honorary consul has to fulfil.

It may be useful to set some context. Most honorary consuls are not career officials - they are locally-engaged staff, usually, but not always, with the nationality of the sending country. They usually work outside the capital, either in smaller cities, or in cities that are distant from full-time diplomatic missions, or in cities with a large resident or transient population of foreign nationals, where a government believes that some form of representation is desirable. An honorary consul, who is appointed to fill such a representational office, may well combine the job with his or her regular employment - which is usually, but not exclusively, in the commercial sphere. The appointment is generally looked on as a considerable honour, bringing a great deal of social prestige, which, for many governments, justifies the low honoraria granted for what can often be more than a full-time job.

In very general terms, honorary consuls have responsibility for the welfare of citizens of the appointing country within their designated consular area. In alphabetical order, a normal day may include one or more incidents under any of the following headings: accidents, arrests, demonstrations (whether compassionate and sympathetic, as with the death of the Princess of Wales, or hostile, as with recent policy in Iraq and Afghanistan), drugs, football hooligans, hospitalisations, imprisonments, lost documents, lost passports, money laundering, notarisations, riots, royal visitors, terrorism, theft, VIP visitors and overarching it all, the attendant bureaucracy of form filling, and liaison, with London, with the Embassy and with the local authorities. The honorary consul will not only need to be able to deal with all of those types of incident, and do it firmly but sympathetically, bearing in mind all the emotional charges that are inseparable from such happenings. He or she will also need to ensure that all those concerned are kept fully informed and up to date with all developments: from those involved in the incidents, to their next of kin, wherever they may be, and all the officials who need to know, both local and national. That liaison work often requires more stamina than dealing with the incident itself. But the best recommendation I can give to those wanting to know what honorary consuls do is to read this book!

The average honorary consul is, in fact, not at all an average person. To do the job successfully, an ideal candidate needs to have the broadest possible background and experience, preferably in a line of work which has involved close contact with the public and with officials. It may be ageist to suggest it, but it seems that such experience is most usually found in those closer to the end of their careers than in those closer to the beginning. In an ideal world, the candidate will also have worked in a variety of different countries, and be familiar with different languages, customs, traditions and ways of working. Above all, he or she will need to be approachable while keeping detached, be friendly while remaining strictly professional, be firm while respecting individuals and their individuality, and be tolerant and patient in difficult and trying situations. A certain taste for adventure - in the sense of pushing slightly on occasion to see whether the rules do in fact have some elasticity, which could help resolve an issue - does not come amiss.

When, in the late 1990s, the Consulate General in Zürich was closed, and its functions were transferred to the Embassy in Berne, it was decided that as Zürich was the commercial and banking capital of Switzerland an honorary consul was needed to represent Her Majesty's Government's interests in the city, the canton, and in an extended consular area in northern and eastern Switzerland. In Antony McCammon, the Embassy was fortunate in finding a candidate who fulfilled so many of the 'ideal' qualities required for the job. His memoirs of his time as the 'Honourable Consul', as his Latin American friends described him, show the unique gifts and character that he brought to this most demanding and challenging of public offices.

John Nichols, former H.M. Ambassador to Berne
11 December 2010

Introduction

The title of this book comes from the very first visitor to the British Consulate at Zürich, who happened to be a dual-national friend from Argentina. There are certain distinctions in the English language which do not come easily to speakers of Latin languages: one is the difference between the words 'honorary' and 'honourable'. Needless to say, my friend got the wrong one, and the occasion was perpetuated by the then Pro-Consul, Alison Mothersill, who stuck the words HONOURABLE CONSUL on to my in-tray. I am grateful to her, and to her successor Yvonne Wespi, for their assistance and support in helping me fulfil my duties, as well as to Christine Kaczmarek of the passport section in Geneva, who was always ready to lend a hand, and share a joke.

What follows is a record of some of my experiences during 11 full years, from 1997 to 2008, as British Honorary Consul at Zürich, and on previous occasions when I worked with or for British Consulates elsewhere.

The book begins with a modest amount of autobiography, together with some travelogues, many of which reflect consular expertise when I was on the receiving end. Steam trains figure prominently. Other reminiscences are included to leaven the bread, together with - be warned! - a measure of propaganda, overt or hidden, for three of my favourite causes: microcredit, water and the Durrell Wildlife Conservation Trust (see below).

In the second part of the book, my view-point in retrospect is not that of a professional consular officer (retired), but, rather, that of someone who approached this experience from an oblique angle, at a late stage of his working life; someone who was at times amazed, at other times puzzled - on occasion, exasperated - at the way the British Foreign and Commonwealth Office

1

(FCO) functioned. While there is a droll aspect to many of the stories told here, there is usually a much more serious side to consular life. Because many consular experiences are, by convention, by law, or by the rules of common sense, confidential (notwithstanding the Freedom of Information Act), names have been changed where necessary.

'*Acte Finale*', at the end of the book, contains acknowledgements and literary references.

This is the story of many lives, not just one. It is dedicated to Angelika, wife and principal proof-reader, my four fine sons, and their multi-faceted families, who have been on much of this trip with me.

I

What Went Before

CAPTAIN COMPASS

One winter evening, Captain Compass was sitting by the fireside with his children beside him. 'Oh, papa,' said little Jack, 'do tell us a story about what you have seen in your voyages. As you have sailed round the world so often, you must have come across many strange things.' 'That I have, my son,' said Captain Compass, 'and, if it will interest you, I will tell you of some of the curious things I have seen.'

A dictation exercise of the author, age seven, at St George's School, after the family's return to Jersey when the German occupation had ended.

ROOTS

'Hello everybody!

For the last few months, I have been doing a genealogical study of our closest family, with a view to trying to put together a basic family tree.

I had no idea when I started this project what an 'infinite' exercise it would turn out to be. Some ancestors and their relations are fascinating characters in their own right; the cast includes military men who served in Russia and Switzerland, and latterly at the Battle of the Somme and on the North-West Frontier of India; one British Ambassador; sundry churchmen, two convicts who were transported to Australia, Tallulah Bankhead, politicians, master shoe-makers, waggoners, a Queen's College Librarian, a Viceroy of Ireland, an Earl of Essex, a Mayor of Plymouth who had sailed with Hawkins and was the first to record the words 'potatoes' and 'tobacco' in the English language; a famous sea-captain, and a Prussian aviation engineer who taught the 'Red Baron' how to fly.

The line to the left, based on a document which Grandfather Francis Alexander ('Pop') McCammon found in his loft in Ballycastle in 1948, should, I believe, be regarded with some reservation, in spite of the fact that I have confirmed most of the succession in independent sources. Those whose surnames had a 'Fitz' prefix were an unconventional lot. More work needs to be done on the McCammon line: if any of you feel like looking, there is a list of over 400 McCammons on one Mormon website. The more recent connections, such as the Meissners (my Brazilian/German in-laws), also need to be better explored.

> There is somewhere a 'McCammon bible', last known to have
> been with the late George Tisdall McCammon, Pop's brother.
> I remember from some correspondence I had with Lord Lyon
> King of Arms in Edinburgh in the 1970s that the Scottish
> McCammons are connected somehow to the Calmans.

The above is from a letter dated 8 February 2002 which I
addressed to various family members. The 'line to the left' (of my
paternal grandmother, née Bland) descended, through mixed
male and female issue, from Edward I and Eleanor of Castile.
Curiously, the Sparke family (maternal grandmother's side) also
claimed descent through marriage from Edward I. (These claims
seem more feasible in the light of the Most Recent Common
Ancestor theory.) Great-great-grandfather McCammon was
from Donaghadee, a favourite landing-place in Ireland of early
immigrants from Scotland.

Further research has shown that the McCammons are indeed
connected to the Calmans, the McCalmans, the McColmans and,
as the name appears in one Irish form, the Mac Calmáins. The
ancestor of this sept of the Scottish Buchanan clan was Anselan
Okyan (or O'Kyan) the first. The dramatic story of his early life,
during the times when the Danes were bullying the Irish, is taken
up by William Buchanan of Auchmar:

> Sueno, or Canutus, at this time [around AD1015] king of England,
> and Denmark, his birth day approaching, which all the Danish
> officers and souldiers resolved to solemnize with great joviality,
> Turgesius [Thorkil], the Danish general, sent orders to all the
> Danish officers in Ireland to repair to Limrick being their
> principal garrison, and his residence, to assist at the solemnity,
> fearing nothing that the Irish would or could do in such low
> circumstances. The general at the same time sent orders to the
> Irish nobility and gentry to send to Limrick against the king's
> birth-day a 1000, or as others say, 2000, of the most beautiful of
> their Daughters, to dally with the Danish officers at that festival.
> Of this the Irish king getting intelligence, resolved to send the
> desired number of the most clear complexionable youths that
> could be found, cloathed in womens habit with long Irish skiens
> or daggers below their cloaths, with orders that as soon as they
> went to bed with their several paramours, being generally drunk
> on such occasions, they should stab them with these concealed
> daggers, and afterwards seise upon their guard-house, where

their arms were laid by, and if matters succeeded, to give a signal
by kindling a large fire upon the town wall... These Irish viragoes
put their orders in execution to the utmost...

The Danish king of England sent a powerful army to Ireland to
avenge this massacre and only a few of the Irish perpetrators
escaped. Among these was the above-mentioned Anselan Okyan,
who would become the first Laird Buchanan. His great-great-
great-great-grandson, also Anselan - the third of that name
and seventh Laird Buchanan - had three sons: the third, called
Colman or Columan, was ancestor of the MacColmans.

If the above account is to be believed, then great-great-
grandfather McCammon from Donaghadee, mentioned above,
may have travelled *back* to the land of his ancestors.

The name Colman is said to be derived from *Colm*, a dove,
and the anglicised forms of McCalman and McCammon -
Dow(e) or Dove - are also known in Ireland. Might it be
stretching the bounds of possibility too far to suggest that St
Columba, who travelled from the Emerald Isle to Iona, not too
far north of Donaghadee, could have played a part - at least
etymologically - in this story?

GREAT-GRANDFATHER

We, George William Frederick, Earl of Clarendon, Baron Hyde
of Hindon, a Peer of the United Kingdom and Ireland, a Member
of Her Britannic Majesty's Most Honourable Privy Council,
Knight of the Most Noble Order of the Garter, and Knight Grand
Cross of the Most Honourable Order of the Bath, Her Majesty's
Principal Secretary of State for Foreign Affairs &c. &c. &c.

Request and require in the Name of Her Majesty all those
whom it may concern, to allow

The Reverend Francis McCammon, (British Subject), travelling
on the Continent with his Wife, to pass freely without let or
hindrance, and to afford him every assistance and protection...

Given at the Foreign Office, London, the 4th day of
August 1857

[signed] Clarendon

Transcription of the first page of the handsome, leather-bound passport of my paternal great-grandfather, where the titles of the issuer are manifestly more protracted than the description of the holder. The passport, found among the possessions of grandfather 'Pop' McCammon, contains visas from, among others, the Royal Austrian Mission and the Royal Prussian Consulate General in London, as well as the British Consulate General in Geneva ('*bon pour l'Allemagne et la France*').

The Reverend McCammon seems to have travelled for over two years around Central Europe, possibly (if underlinings in his *Black's General Atlas of the World*, 1873 edition, are to be believed) as far as St Petersburg and Montenegro, which I was to visit, with my wife Angelika, 150 years later. He had been Minister of the Non-Subscribing Presbyterian Church in Banbridge, Co. Down, for 18 years until his early retirement due to ill health. His trip seems now to have been an extravagant holiday for a retired minister of the Church to have taken. Possibly his second wife Minnie, the daughter of a noted Irish historian, paid the bill. In any event, an extended stay in Baden Baden and Switzerland may indicate that he successfully 'took the waters' as part of a cure for his illness. Whatever he did seems to have worked, as he died a full 28 years after returning home.

POP

Their's not to make reply,
Their's not to reason why,
Their's but to do and die...

...brutal words of Alfred, Lord Tennyson, alluding to one of the most absurd, bloody events in British military history.

If my grandfather, Pop McCammon, genuinely did not want his life in the trenches to be talked about - and he made no bones about this when he was alive - *why did he leave behind an envelope, pregnant with unborn fables of war?* Does this, in any event, fit into a book which is overridingly concerned with consular life? During war, after all, bilateral diplomacy is suspended.

There is a sub-theme in his story which has moved me, after all, to put something down for posterity; or could this sub-theme, in reality, be a vital, moral credo?

Among the documents in the said envelope, there were:

- A Certificate signed by the progressive theologian and scientist, Monsignor Gerald Molloy, Vice-Chancellor, showing that 'the Degrees of Bachelor of Medicine, Bachelor of Surgery, and Bachelor of Obstetrics were conferred on Frank Alexander McCammon at a Public Meeting of the Royal University held in Dublin on the Twelfth day of May 1905'.

- The original Royal Commission, countersigned by Edward R. & I., to Frank Alexander McCammon, Gentleman M.B., with his Appointment to be 'an Officer in Our Royal Army Medical Corps from the Thirtieth day of January 1906... in the Rank of Lieutenant in Our Land Forces, or in such higher Rank as We may from time to time hereafter be pleased to appoint you to... exercising authority according to the Rules and Discipline of War... over the Soldiers of Our Royal Army Medical Corps... and over all Patients in Military Hospitals...'

- A card signed Mary R. and George R.I., with twin pictures of King George V and Queen Mary, by the Royal photographers W. & E. Downey of Ebury Street, and the message: 'With our best wishes for Christmas 1914. May God protect you and bring you home safe.'

- A creased, dirty, hand-written memo dated 18 April 1915 from Lt.-Col. J. McKellar, RAMC To Capt. F.A. McCammon: 'In accordance with instructions..., you are being reported... as "wounded" on 1st January. A note will be added "wounded slightly, on duty." Do you know of any NCOs or men of the unit who were slightly wounded and returned to duty after being dressed?...'

- Two mimeographed letters of exhortation, folded and worn, signed for the General Officer Commanding the 4th Division, before and after the opening day of the Battle of the Somme, 1 July 1916, when the British Army suffered its worst one-day combat losses in its history, with nearly 60,000 casualties: '30th June 1916... The 4th Division has glorious traditions throughout this war from our first big fight throughout the retreat, on the AISNE and MARNE at PLOEGSTREERT and YPRES it has known how to stand heavy losses, to stick it, and to win through.

    We have now a long and glorious battle before us and with my old comrades of the 4th Division in the centre we are sure of winning.'

9

'July 3rd 1916...General Joffre has expressed his appreciation of the hard fighting carried out on the English Left. It is greatly due to the fact that the Germans were so strong and so well provided with guns in front of the VII and VIII Corps that the French, and the British troops in touch with them on the Right of the Fourth Army, were able to make their brilliant and successful advance.'

(It is a sobering thought that it was these 60,000 casualties in one day, the result of appalling inter-ministerial muddles in Whitehall, which led to the creation of the Cabinet Office.)

- Two Mentions in Despatches from Field Marshall Sir Douglas Haig, GCB, GCVO, KCIE, the first in the name of Capt. F.A. McCammon, MC, MB, RAMC of the Army Medical Service, dated 9th April 1917; the second in the name of Maj. (T./Lt.-Col.) F.A. McCammon MC, MB, Non Convalescent Depôt of the RAMC, dated 8th November 1918. Both citations were for 'gallant and distinguished services in the field' and were signed by Winston S. Churchill, Secretary of State for War.
- A Warrant of Appointment by George the Fifth, dated 1 January 1919, of 'Our trusty and well beloved Frank Alexander McCammon Esquire Bachelor of Medicine on whom has been conferred the Decoration of the Military Cross Major Temporary Lieutenant Colonel in Our Army...to be an Officer of the Military Division of Our said Most Excellent Order of the British Empire. [Signed] By the Sovereign's Command. Edward P. [Edward Prince of Wales, later the short-lived Edward VIII], Grand Master.'
- A Royal Commission, countersigned by George R.I., dated 1 April 1927 to Francis Alexander McCammon OBE, MC, MB, appointing him 'to be an Officer in our Land Forces...in the Rank of Major'.

The wheel had come full circle in 21 years, and he was a soldier again, albeit still an officer in the Royal Army Medical Corps. Curiously, the career of his son, my father, was to follow a similar pattern.

There was one other manuscript in the aforesaid envelope - a poem, entitled 'Balaclava':

Light Dragoons - Hussars and Lancers,
Dare ye tempt yon hostile plain?
Never would these noble prancers
Bear you to your ranks again!
Look! The pointed cannon, ready
To give forth the lightning flash -
Look, the bristling bayonets, steady
To receive your headlong dash!

'Comrades, cowards, wherefore mock us,
Rather than such wailing fear.
Now let Balaclava's echoes
Thunder out one British cheer.'
Grimly gazed the gallant riders
As in that dread charge they go,
And their war-steeds bear them prouder
While they near the Northern foe.

Hear we only armour ringing,
See we only sabres bright,
As into a canter springing
Furiously they seek the fight!
Ha! already some are reeling,
From the whistling bullet's stroke,
But to their brave steeds appealing,
They, too, sweep into the smoke.

Crash! The Cossacks fly before them –
Chaff before the whirling gale.
Now the thunder closes o'er them,
And the shot comes on like hail.
'Charge the guns in front!' No sooner
Said, than lo the feat is done –
There lies many a Russian gunner
Sabered, cleft, beside his gun!

(over)

These verses take us inexorably towards the same dreadful
end for which Tennyson provided the climax in his lines at the
beginning of this essay. In brackets, after the fourth verse, is the
word 'over'. Was there more to the poem on another sheet? Or was
the battle simply 'over'. We will never know.

If Pop McCammon did not go so far as to take these lines with
him into battle, they were certainly vital enough for him to have
given them pride of place in his simple filing system. But who
wrote them? The only clue is another short, adulatory poem, in
identical handwriting, found elsewhere among his possessions,
entitled 'To Frankie' and signed 'Grandpapa' above the date 9
July 1880. Pop McCammon would have been one year old. The
elegy begins

11

Pop in full dress uniform, 1937.

Oh cherub, here in human guise!
Is any fairer in the skies?
Do any soar the fields of light
With softer smiles, or eyes so bright -
Do voices reach the dazzling throne
More sweet or artless than thy own?

This - and 'Balaclava' - could only have been penned by Pop's maternal grandfather, the Reverend George Hill. He was a well-known author and longstanding Librarian of Queen's College Belfast, partial to such prize-winning poetic themes as *The Burning of Moscow*, and, according to his memorial, predisposed towards 'the sound of war and the clash of arms...'.

The ill-fated Charge of the Light Brigade happened during the Battle of Balaclava, which, in turn, was part of a campaign between the unlikely alliance of Britain, France, Turkey, the Kingdom of Sardinia, the Duchy of Nassau and the disintegrating Ottoman Empire, on the one side; and the Russian Empire, on the other. This was known as the Crimean or Russian War, and lasted from October 1853 to February 1856; it was essentially a contest for influence over the territories of the declining Ottoman Empire. The slaughter on both sides was horrendous.

In 1855, eight years before the foundation of the International Red Cross, a Medical Staff Corps was created; two years later an Army Hospital Corps came into being. From this embryonic body, over 40 years later, when Pop McCammon was 19 years old, the Royal Army Medical Corps was born. Was Pop attracted by the romance of his grandfather's poetry ('... Thunder out one British cheer')? Or was it altruism, and the wish to mitigate the effects of war, which moved him to join the RAMC? Or a bit of both?

At the outbreak of the Great War, there were some 4,800 officers and men of the RAMC serving a Regular Army of 247,000. On the Western Front alone (where Pop was posted), the Corps had to look after the medical needs of some *two million* sick or wounded soldiers of the British Expeditionary Force and such of its opponents as fell into British Hands. By the end of the war, 13,000 doctors (half of all UK civilian doctors) had been recruited, to the serious detriment of the civilian population.

Is it surprising that Pop did not want to be reminded of this? He had been in France with the Army of the Rhine for one month short of five years, according to his service record, 'without any break'. He had saved others in order to save us – and he simply did not want to talk about it. Intransigence is the prerogative of grandfathers.

We remember him now as a softly-spoken, warm-hearted Irishman, who drove a green Austin 12, with black mudguards, the engine racing at a constant speed of 30 m.p.h. – because he didn't know how to change gear – and with a tendency to park it across the line in the middle of the road, with the engine on, to the chagrin of the Royal Ulster Constabulary. Pop came to Paris with us right after the Second World War, and became quite upset when we loaded our car up with bottles of whisky to pay the hotel bills: whisky in France, he told us defiantly, was free. It turned out that he had last been to Paris on Armistice Day 1918, when every Frenchman opened his door and handed out tots of the stuff to the allied troops.

It was Pop McCammon who (when our mother Gwynneth was out of the room) assiduously taught my brother David and me how to belch. He never in his life went to a dentist, and I fondly remember him flinching when his teeth struck shot while he was crunching up the bones of a snipe. And he had whisky on his porridge. This took on a new dimension when, in the course of some quite separate correspondence, an old friend and colleague, Dr Nikolaus Voegeli, longstanding Honorary Consul General of the Kingdom of Morocco at Zürich, wrote that his grandfather, serving with the Red Cross on the Saloniki Front, had once told him how impressed he was at the insistence of British troops, only to mount an attack after having had a good breakfast, *ein sehr vernünftiger Grundsatz* ('a very sensible principle').

In his much thumbed and disintegrating shooting register, Pop carefully entered every game bird he shot (in addition to peacock, quail, sand grouse, black bear, bison, panther, stag and a tigress when he was in Kashmir from 1929 to 1931); and every fish he hooked, between 1898 and 1957. The last time he pulled the trigger of his Purdey 12-bore, as he recorded in the register on 29 January 1957: 'I got 2 snipe flying with one shot!' His last fish, which 'played very well', was a 2 lb 6 oz trout, which he caught at the Grands Vaux reservoir, just down the road from Le Ponterrin in Jersey. This contrasts vividly with the grand signatures on his citations for bravery.

He died during 'the troubles' in Omagh, with a loaded Colt revolver beside his bed.

GWYNNETH

Jersey in 1912: population about 51,000; largely farming, fishing, knitting. Early Oldsmobiles and Ford Motor Cars are cluttering up the island's lanes; women drivers are beginning to appear.

The UK in 1912: George V and Queen Mary are two years on the throne; the Queen Mum is 12 years old...

The *tango*, recently arrived from Argentina, has taken Europe by storm...

The world in 1912: Emperor Peter II of Brazil was dethroned 23 years ago; the country is now called the United States of Brazil; jolly good coffee comes from there. The last Queen of Hawaii was deposed 20 years ago. The Ch'ing dynasty of China collapsed earlier this year. The French colonialists have recently deposed Queen Ranavalona III of Madagascar. William II of Prussia is titular Head of the German Empire.

Italy has a King; Korea has an Emperor; Persia has a Shah; Turkey has a Sultan who considers Egypt a tributary state; we have just ousted him from the Sudan.

Tsar Nicholas rules the Empire of All the Russias; he has a vice-consulate in St Helier.

Four sections of velocipedists have just been introduced into the Swiss army.

It was in 1912 that Gwynneth was born in Sydney to Lewis ('Lew') and Linda ('Muzz') Sparke Davies, who were descended from the Davies's of Cardigan and the Sparkes of South Brent near Plymouth. Lew was the son of Lewis Davies, a sea-captain who plied the immigrant routes to North America and Australia. Lewis senior had been first mate/master mariner of various barques out of Liverpool between 1857 and 1870, and insisted upon 'bringing his wife, two daughters and three sons to sea with him'. He is known to have settled fights among members of his crew, with his own fists.

Gwynneth was a determined little thing who spent her childhood rowing out to the ships in Sydney harbour and chatting to the seamen. When she was ten, her father asked her how many funnels a certain ship had, and realised that she could not even see the ship. With the benefit of her new specs, she recalled seeing the leaves on the trees for the first time. She also remembered looking out of the windows of the Hyde Park Hotel in London at some red smudges which moved haphazardly across the foreground. Once she had her glasses, she realised that the red smudges were actually guardsmen in their red tunics.

Her father Lewis, together with his brother Arthur, had formed a small private finance company in Sydney, which was eventually incorporated as the Australian Guarantee Corporation (AGC). It was the threshold of the 'booming twenties', with the inherent demand for luxuries like the motor-car. The model T Ford was then retailing for £280, £20 less than the average cost of a motor-car. This amount of money then represented more than a year's income for most Australians, and it was here that the brothers Davies sensed a golden opportunity. They held the Australian franchise to import and distribute all new Ford vehicles. This was later extended to take in used cars, motor-cycles and even trucks. AGC became the largest finance company in Australia. Business flourished until the Great Depression. The group was later absorbed into the Bank of New South Wales/Westpac.

With her father and mother, Gwynneth voyaged all over the world: to the East Indies, to the West Indies, to North and South America. Travel was by ocean liner in those days, and it was on board the SS *Strathnaver,* in April 1934, when she was once passing through Bombay that she met her future husband, Lieutenant Francis Tisdall Archibald McCammon, of the Sixth Gurkha Rifles, who was stationed on the North-West Frontier.

The above is from a tribute I paid to my late mother Gwynneth McCammon, née Davies, later Huelin, on the occasion of her 90th birthday, over dinner at the Grand Hotel in Jersey. Dear Mama: she could be very anti-social. She enjoyed the evening in the end, but it had started badly, when she told me she was '*not* going into that room with all those people'.

She was an individualist. Here is a letter about her, relating to 'surfing'.

To the *Financial Times* (published 26 August 1997) in reply to an article about the difficulties experienced by senior citizens with PCs and the internet. The letter was entitled 'Surfing: age no barrier':

> I am proud to inform Louise Kehoe that my mother, in her mid-80s, has just taken delivery of her second computer. She has been taking lessons from her grandson. We're not certain what went wrong with the first model, but we suspect its memory was inadequate.

She was also adept at another sort of surfing (wave-riding) which she had enjoyed at 'The Watersplash' (St Ouens, Jersey) since before the war. In 1950, my brother and I brought two of the latest hard-rubber models back from Australia. Previously, we had shared with Gwynneth the use of her pre-war plywood boards. Her indomitable dachshund Pongeon could occasionally be seen perched on the front.

She always respected animals, and animals – always – respected her. She was 80 when we took her on safari with us to Malamala in South Africa. Plodding through the undergrowth one day, we walked straight into a fully-grown male white rhinoceros. I will never forget how this three-ton beast took one look at Gwynneth – as always clutching her large handbag full of keys – and made off at a gallop.

Gwynneth owned a small Chubb safe which sat for many years on the floor of the cloakroom at Le Ponterrin in Jersey. My father closed it for the last time a few days before he left the island, just before the war, in order to rejoin the British Army, and the code went with him. Miraculously the safe survived the German occupation. I only managed to open it again, with the help of a friendly safe-cracker, in September 2002, 63 years later. My mother watched from her wheel-chair, with a tear in her eye. Inside we found a Jersey Savings Bank deposit book, showing a balance of £512-11s-6d (original deposit of my father dated 19 November 1938). This balance was repaid to my mother, with statutory war-time interest at 4 per cent p.a. We also found her collection of coins from the many countries she had visited on her travels. On the sealed envelope which contained a few gold sovereigns and half sovereigns (the only items which my mother recalled having put in the safe) there was, in a child's handwriting,

'This money belongs to Gwynneth Davies.'

WILLIAM THE CONQUEROR

We,
Lieutenant-General
Sir Arthur Edward Grassett,
K.B.E., C.B., D.S.O., M.C.
His Excellency the Lieutenant Governor
of Jersey and its Dependencies.

Request and require in the name of His
Majesty all those whom it may concern to allow
the bearer to pass freely without let or hindrance
and to afford <u>him</u> every assistance and protection
of which <u>he</u> may stand in need.

Given at the Government House
Jersey by His Excellency's Command
<u>this Third day of August 1948</u>

[signed] R.M.H. Lewis
Secretary to the Government.

* * *

'Grandpa. What does it mean: "Jersey and its Dependencies"?'
  'Where do you see that?'
  'Here on the first page of your old passport.'
  'Ah yes.'
  'Surely it can't mean the Écréhous and the Minquiers – they're
only little specks in the ocean. What *does* it mean?'
  'What marks did you get in History this term?'
  'I was good in History.'
  'Have you heard of the Channel Island toast: *La Reine notre Duc*?'
  'I know what toast is. What's that got to do with it?'
  'Never mind. Let me ask you another question: have you heard
of the Norman Conquest?'
  'Don't be silly, Grandpa, of course I have! Everybody has.'
  'Do you know when it took place?'
  '1066, Grandpa.'
  'Do you know what else happened in that year?'
  'Nothing else happened in that year – just the Battle of Hastings.'

'Do you know what William was before he became King of England?'

'King of France?'

'No. William was duke of Normandy and count of Maine.'

'Smith Junior told me that William was a bastard – I told him to shut up.'

'William *was* a bastard.'

'Grandpa!'

'Do you know what the word means?'

'Not really.'

'It means that William was illegitimate – that his father was not married. But let me ask you again: what *else* happened in 1066?'

'I don't know, Grandpa.'

'If I told you that it was in 1066 that England became a dependency of Jersey, would you laugh?'

'Of course not, Grandpa.'

'You see, when William duke of Normandy, moved across the Channel and defeated Harold II, to become William I of England, Jersey was already part of his dukedom. With time, later English and British monarchs lost what they regarded as their possessions in Normandy, except for the Channel Islands.'

'Grandpa. Was Calais really written on Queen Mary's heart? I think that's disgusting.'

'What she actually said was: "When I am dead, you will find Calais lying on my heart." That's quite a different thing. After Gascony, Brittany and Aquitaine, Calais was the last French possession to be lost, and Queen Mary was very sad. That's what she meant.'

'But what happened to Jersey, Grandpa?'

'Nothing.'

'So it wasn't lost too?'

'That's the wrong question to ask. Do you remember me telling you that England became a dependency of Jersey? Do you understand what I said?'

'I think so, Grandpa.'

'Then, if you were to ask me: Did Jersey lose England? – that would be a better question.'

'And did Jersey lose England?'

19

'Why don't you read those words in my old passport again?'
'You mean: "Jersey and its Dependencies?"'
'Yes. That's what I mean.'
'Grandpa. You remember the other day when I told you
that you were not being serious, and your moustache began to
twitch...?'
'I remember.'
'Well, your moustache is twitching again...'

* * *

I have had similar, jocular discussions on this subject many times,
with adults *and* children, though – admittedly – the moustache is
an invention.

TONY

The intense but long-drawn-out courtship of my parents,
Francis Tisdall Archibald ('Tony') McCammon and Gwynneth
Linda Sparke Davies, is documented by hundreds of love
letters. When they met, two worlds came together: the finite,
pragmatic world of a professional soldier; and the blinkered
environment of a well-to-do, but shy and opinionated, middle-
class lass.

He was with the 2nd Battalion, 6th Gurkha Rifles in
Abbotabad, on the North-West Frontier of India, on an eight-
year army contract. He was the son of a surgeon and highly
decorated officer of the Royal Army Medical Corps ('Pop').
According to my mother, he missed the Sword of Honour at
Sandhurst only because of a practical joke played on him by
David Niven, already then a notorious prankster.

She was the daughter of an international businessman, self-
described 'merchant, general', whose own world was made up of
figures, negotiations, hotels and passenger ships.

They were eventually married by Commander Starling
of the SS *Strathnaver,* and then in St Thomas's Cathedral in
Bombay in June 1936. After a one-night honeymoon in the
Taj Hotel, they took the train up to Abbotabad (then in British

The 2nd/6th Gurkha Rifles, Abbotabad, 1936.

India, now in the Islamic Republic of Pakistan) where my father continued his military service. Fifty-three years later, while on business in Bombay, I went to the Cathedral and obtained a copy of the marriage certificate. Their first children, had they not miscarried, would have been born in the British Forces Hospital in Rawalpindi.

It was into this world, in Jersey, Channel Islands, after my parents had returned from India, a few months before the German occupation of the islands, that I was born. Headlines in *The [Jersey] Evening Post* dated Monday 18 September 1939, varied from RED ARMY SWEEPS INTO POLAND (an 'act of treachery', according to the *Daily Mail*), to BRITISH PAMPHLETS DROPPED IN GERMANY ('You Cannot Win This War'), and ISLANDERS' MESSAGE OF LOYALTY ('...an expression of "the assurance of our loyalty and devotion to the person of His Majesty the King Emperor..." from the Sultan of the Maldive Islands to the Governor of Ceylon').

My mother was a very private person and I got to know very little about my father beyond his early correspondence with her. He died from a coronary thrombosis at the age of 37.

Only on one bizarre occasion, in 1978, did I run across his memory. I was working for Lloyds Bank in Zürich at the time, and was given the difficult task of finding a businessman who had set up a company in the bank's books many years previously. There were no more funds to support the company, and only he could liquidate it. I traced him to the Balearic Islands and eventually managed to get him to Zürich and sit him down in my office. I explained the problem to him. He got up and said, 'I know what you want me to do, but I am not going to do it.' And he left. A few minutes later, he returned and asked,

'*What* did you say your name was?' I told him. He continued: 'Are you related to F.T.A. McCammon by any chance?'

'He was my father, Sir.'

'Was he at Campbell College Grammar School in Belfast?'

'I believe he was, Sir.'

'I see. Where would you like me to sign?'

And the problem was solved. But he wouldn't tell me why.

WRITING ON THE WALL

On behalf of the Istimurardars and Citizens of Ajmer Rao-Gopalsingh of Kharwa, Thakur Shimbhoo Singh of Barli, Rai Bahadur Seth Tikamchand Soni, Rai Bahadur Seth Birad Mul Lodha, Mr. Magan Lal Bar-at-Law, and Meer Nisar Ahmad request the pleasure of the Company of <u>Mr. F. T. A. Mc. Cammon</u>
to meet the Hon'ble Mr. L. W. Reynolds C. I. E., M. C., I.C.S., Agent to the Governor-General in Rajputana and Chief Commissioner Ajmer-Merwara and Mrs. Reynolds at a Garden party on 17th December 1927, at the Anasagger Bund at 4P.M.

R.S.V.P.
Magan Lal, *Barrister-at-Law*

The first evidence in family files of the existence of my father-to-be F.T.A. McCammon, who was to marry Gwynneth Davies.

* * *

I do not think the family will return to Sydney until late next year...

Last Wednesday I went over to Jersey (Channel Island) intending to remain until Monday, but as this operation [Gwynneth's appendectomy] had to take place yesterday, I had to return Saturday. I think the Isle of Jersey is charming and I shall have to try to go over there again, especially as I have two or three families that I know there...

I am, your affectionate father L.S.D.

Extract from a letter dated 21 August 1928 from my grandfather, Lewis Sparke Davies, in London to his son (by another marriage) Frank in Australia. This is the first indication of L.S.D.'s interest in Jersey, which led to this writer being born there 11 years later, and becoming the proud holder of a Jersey passport.

BOMBAY AT A GLANCE

It was a doubly secret mission. On the one hand he had to keep quiet about all banking business entertained in any fashion. On the other hand he could not betray to his employer the real reason for his trip. The name of the Bank, too, had to be kept strictly confidential; and he even had to be careful to whom he gave his visiting cards, with the characteristic backward-glancing black horse on a white and green background. Bank bards used to interpret this picture as 'looking back on the competition'. One smart Swiss banker had added, '...and riderless too!' The bards had not been amused. It was a fine-looking horse though, and the Bank had seen the emblem on tee-shirts coming from Italy. Nobody seemed to know where they had been manufactured. Legal Department was baffled. But that was somebody else's problem.

January is the best month in the year to visit Bombay, in between the real heat and the rainy season. There seemed to be more of humanity than ever on the streets, and it was only 7 o'clock in the morning. He had had a *chota hazari* in his room in the Taj Hotel, on Apollo Bunder, right by the Gateway of India, where his father and mother had spent one night half a century ago, before taking the train to Abbotabad. This phrase for a light breakfast had crept into family usage, with other essentials like *asti* ('slow'), *bas* ('stop'), and *Mumbai*, the Marathi word for Bombay itself.

Gwynneth and Tony on their wedding day, Bombay, 4 June 1936.

Notwithstanding his Airey & Wheeler light-weight suit, which he had to have on for the official part of the day, he was sweating copiously by the time he reached the Cathedral of St Thomas, on the south side of Church Gate Street. The high ecclesiastical tower stared defiantly at the Chamber of Commerce, across the *Hautatma Chowk*, as he slipped into the grounds, past the once-proud fountain which had been donated by Sir Cowasjee Jehangir, a local notable, and in through the west door. It was 7.05 a.m.

There was only one person there, sitting quietly in the gloom at the back of the Cathedral: man or woman, he couldn't tell. The incumbent was nowhere to be seen. The Cathedral seemed to be a mixture of Classical and Gothic in style, and the chancel looked like latter-day out-of-place-by-a-hemisphere Early English. But some people liked this architecture, and in one guide-book he had read that Bombay was 'the finest Gothic city in the world'. It was absurd, really. Like it or not, Bombay had come a long way since the mid-1600s, when Mumbadevi, the largest of seven swampy, malarial islands, had been acquired by the British as part of Catherine of Braganza's dowry, when she married Charles II. It was later leased, with the other islets, to the East India Company for £10 in gold per annum. That had been a bargain then.

For some reason he was relieved that the shadowy figure at the back could not know his fascination, as he read of the glorious military engagements: 'Mangalore defended against Tipu in 1784... served with Clive in Benghal... defence of Herat,' and so on... Life must have been so cheap in those distant days. And then there were the regiments: the 3rd Bombay Light Cavalry, the 27th Native Infantry, the Southern Mahratta Irregular Horse, the Kolapore Light Infantry, the Sikh Regiment of Ferozpore and countless others. He sat in a pew, and his head nodded in the cool.

He awoke with a start. There was a movement behind him. The shadowy figure slowly got up, made his way to the aisle, genuflected, and was held for a moment in a ray of sunlight shining through the tracery. It was a young man, *and he was wearing a tee-shirt with the distinctive black horse design on it.* Then, without a backward glance, the youth walked slowly out of the Cathedral.

As the figure disappeared into the shimmering brightness of Bombay, the priest-in-charge came out of the vestry, holding an envelope. It had taken some time to locate the records for 1936. The document was certified as a true extract of the Register kept at St Thomas Cathedral (Church of North India), 'Exempted from stamp duty under Section 7 (1) (b) of Act V: of 1906 of the Governor-General of India in Council'. It was 7.20 a.m.

As he left the Cathedral, clutching the copy of his parents' marriage certificate, he reflected what a short honeymoon Gwynneth and Tony had had, before heading back to the camp of the 6th Gurkha Rifles, to the piquets and the butchery of the North-West Frontier. So little time. And he had solved the mystery of the Taboo Tee-Shirts, simply by glancing over his shoulder, just as the black horse had done: it was being printed in a market nearby, and would be on *saris* soon. And the day had hardly started.

On a business trip to Bombay, I was once playing squash at the Willingdon Sports Club, when my ball was cut in two by a fan in the ceiling. The club was named after Lord Willingdon, Viceroy of India from 1931 to 1936. My father was for a short time on his staff, before being posted to Abbotabad. It occurs to me now that, for the many years that they lived apart from each other, my parents' own little world must have seemed to them like that bisected squash ball. I wrote the above true story in the third person, initially to allow it to fit in to a series of short articles which I penned for St Andrew's Church in Zürich. Two things are, in retrospect, not reflected in the tale: the bureaucratic difficulties involved; and the tension I felt as I waited to see, for the first time, my parents' marriage certificate.

KANALINSELN

H.M. Embassy, Moscow
To Lord Pembroke, The Foreign Office, London
6th April 1943

My Dear Reggie,

In these dark days man tends to look for little shafts of light that spill from Heaven. My days are probably darker than yours and I need, my God I do, all the light I can get. But I am a decent fellow, and I do not want to be mean and selfish about what little brightness is shed upon me from time to time. So I propose to share with you a tiny flash that has illuminated my sombre life and tell you that God has given me a new Turkish colleague whose card tells me that he is called Mustapha Kunt.

We all feel like that, Reggie, now and then, especially when Spring is upon us, but few of us would care to put it on our cards. It takes a Turk to do that.

(Signed) Sir Archibald Clark Kerr, H.M. Ambassador.

I make no apologies for including the above gem, a faded photocopy of which has been in my possession for years. These were dark days indeed, not just in Moscow.

My parents had no idea if we would ever see our farm in Jersey again, following the German occupation of the Channel Islands. We - my mother, grandmother and I - had been evacuated between 21 and 23 June 1940 . I have found a crisp diary entry dated 21 June, where my mother wrote, 'Left Le Ponterrin' but I do not know how long we spent down at the docks before departure. In any event, we were lucky: the last mailboat evacuation took place on 28 June via Guernsey when the *Isle of Sark* was bombed and strafed by the *Luftwaffe*, causing a number of deaths and injuries, before the ship escaped to Southampton. Jersey was bombed twice on the same day, and there was further loss of life.

I have found two letters with separate reflections of our predicament, a few days after we had arrived in England.

The first was from a man called Greenland, a poacher turned gamekeeper turned poacher again, who had ingratiated himself with my parents and was to spend the next five years in our house in Jersey, out of Interpol's ken (dated 24 June 1940):

Dear Captain,

We were so relieved to hear that you had all arrived quite safely.

You would have been more than shocked if you could have seen your home when I arrived there at 2.30 pm on Friday, I was greeted with an accordion playing and someone singing very lustily seated on the kitchen table with bottles of beer all around. Poor Maria and Cook were absolutely petrified...The object on the table was Le Monnier [farm-hand] drunk as an owl, he seemed quite surprised when I ordered him off the premises. It appears that earlier in the morning he and l'Homme [a larger farm-hand] opened up the larder and proceeded to drink whatever was there in the way of booze. L'Homme gave orders to Cook to prepare dinner for five, and to Maria to have your bedroom prepared for he and his wife, as they were taking possession...I will not stand for any funny business with your property.

The second letter was from Uncle Willy, married to my father's sister, in Ballycastle, Northern Ireland (dated 1 July 1940):

My dearest ones,

Thank god you are safe - It's been terrible not knowing where you were or what was happening to you... What a ghastly time you have had. How awful having to leave your lovely home and your dogs and everything...I wonder where you will go now...Your darling wee Anthony [!] must have been very tired on that awful journey but he evidently was a very good wee man...

According to a stamp in her passport, my mother first returned to Jersey in January 1946. She once told me that Greenland greeted her with, 'Why didn't you die like that damned husband of yours?' Years later (Gwynneth learned in a roundabout way), *he* predeceased *her.*

My father was a professional soldier, fresh from the North-West Frontier of India. He and my mother had written to each other almost every day, for 35 months, before and after their wedding, as, except for brief periods of leave, he was on active service up-country, while she remained as a *memsahib* in the military base at Abbotabad.

His letters to her from Waziristan - hotbed 75 years later of the Taliban - reflect a hotchpotch of boredom, suspense and drama, spiced with whisky, gin, beer, 'flickers' (what we now call moving pictures, movies), seamy jokes about Mae West, 'vangty-un', the occasional bath, understatement and *plus ça change.* According to his army contract, my father had to spend two years in every eight on the frontier. Some samples from 1935:

Bannu, 20 January: I was riding one afternoon on your mare down below Razmak by myself when a swine took a pot at me. He fired at a long range but the bullet hit the bank so close to me that the mare shied and the dogs fled in all directions! - I didn't wait to see who it was...

Razmak, 5 March: I've never felt so positively frightful in my life and actually all I had to drink the whole evening was eight whiskeys and four beers...

Roqan Raqza, 16 March: A perfectly bloody day...The rearguard lost a piquet and as we were being shot up at the time people were getting rather anxious one way and another - I twisted the old knee...

Razmak, 18 March: The papers seem a bit grim about Germany at the moment - I'm afraid there isn't much doubt about what they are up to and it looks as if it wont be long before we are at each others throats again. Serves us right and we have only ourselves to blame. [On 16 March Hitler had announced German rearmament in violation of the Versailles Treaty of 1919. This act enjoyed Britain's tacit approval.]

Razmak, 30 April, 12.30 a.m.: This is all so secret and confidential that I will have to lock up this letter until I send it. It looks as if the balloon may go up at any moment. The big man in these parts has been shot up and killed and we are all waiting and wondering what is going to happen. Old Bottle has been given the very hairy job of road patrol tomorrow with three armoured cars and the rest of us are standing by in case he catches it - I hope to heavens nothing blows up as it may give the old tribesmen just the chance they are waiting for. For heavens sake don't say anything about this 'cos as I have already said the whole business is so secret that one is hardly able to think about it!!

Razmak, 1 May, 7.30 p.m.: It appears that this man is not the only one who got bumped off yesterday. His two brothers - son daughter wife mother and father have also shared his fate. The people who bumped them off then barricaded themselves in a house with all their relations and were this morning mined and blown sky high. Meanwhile the rival tribes are mobilising as hard as they can...

Razmak, 7 May: The tribesmen were having a bit of a scrap this evening just the other side of the golf course - don't know what it was about - some private war or other I suppose!...Do you remember my telling you about the couple who got engaged in the ship coming out here - I was put in charge of her coming up in the train. They were married a couple of months ago - Both of them have been killed in the Quetta earthquake...a most frightful show [60,000 lost their lives].

Razmak, 21 September: Yesterday was an awful day and I am afraid we all hit it a frightful crack...On the way back we went into the Club for 'just one beer'. Started off well but were joined by a crowd of blokes and - well that was that!...The war which has been going on here for the last month or so seems to be over and I hear that the tribesmen want peace. Now it only remains to see what Italy is going to do...[an obscure reference to the Italo-Ethiopian War (1935-36), which was clearly creating disquiet among professional soldiers, even on the North-West Frontier of India.]

Razmak, 3 October: We have had a little more news in about that Peshawar show and I am afraid it is every bit as bad as the first reports painted it to be...The Brigade moved out about 2am led by the Guides and occupied a ridge. The Guides sent one coy (about 100 men) in front of them to take a scrubby bit of country. All done in the dark - morning came and the Guides found themselves completely cut off and up against about 1,800. All communications went the Brigade withdrew and the Guides had to cut their way out.

Razmak, 6 November:...A miserable mule took a toss down a *khudd*[cliff] of about 30 feet - they are extraordinary animals, it didn't seem to mind in the least and just got up and walked off.

Razmak, 25 December: I see that pal of mine who was killed up Peshawar way has got the V.C. I'm very glad indeed as it may be a wee bit of comfort to his miserable wife - he certainly deserved it as he put up a really good show.

My father took early retirement from the army, and he and my mother set up house in Jersey. He had intended to take up farming. Instead, because of the Nazi threat, he joined the Jersey Defence Volunteers, and, only days later, returned to England and enlisted with the Officers Emergency Reserve.

He was once again separated from my mother, and once again, this time for 23 months, they wrote to each other almost every day they were apart. Life, as he recorded it, seems to have been a hotchpotch of boredom and drama, with an admixture of more droll experiences. The dramatic bits - mainly air-raids - were always alluded to with understatement: 'catching it a bit', 'unpleasant show', 'frightfully noisy night - 1 sod down', 'bit of a party: batman hurt', 'C Coy caught it but nothing went off '.

A typical 'Dad's Army' episode was recorded in his letter of 19 August 1940:

We had an extraordinary incident in the mess tonight. An officer's revolver fell off the hook in the hall and went off. The bullet flattened itself on the ground between the padre's legs - a lucky escape if ever there was one, but it gave us a bit of a shock...

Another unspecified 'extraordinary experience' he had in Lydd, Kent ('reminds me of Razmak without the hills') may have referred to the time when a Messerschmidt Bf 109 crashed very near to his gun emplacement. From the wreckage, my father was able to recover a *Junghans* dashboard clock, used by the *Luftwaffe* for blind flying; he gave it a wooden mount and it worked perfectly for years after the war.

My father was attached to various regiments, mainly on anti-aircraft duties (first as plain Mr, then reinstated as Captain, then, for a short time, promoted to Major), and was transferred round the country, with us, so to speak, in hot pursuit. Tragically, he developed a serious heart problem, was invalided out of the army, and died, at the age of 37, in November 1944.

My own distant memories of these difficult times are punctuated by the wails of air-raid sirens, then the howls of the German V2 rockets, but very few actual detonations. After many changes of address, including residences at Sutton Courtenay, Trevor Place in Knightsbridge, Melton Court in Kensington, Crockham Hill near Edenbridge, Hitchin where my brother David was born, and some short, expensive stints at the Dorchester and Claridges, the final family refuge from this cacophony – I remember this very clearly – was the space under a large table in a windowless room of Pinemount Lodge, Camberley. My earliest friendship, dating from these times, was with John (later General Sir John) Wilsey GCB, CBE, DL, later to become General Officer Commanding Northern Ireland.

As the war went on, such treasures as Sir Archibald Clark Kerr's, letter, above, with its veiled praise for the Turk, were part of the key to survival.

*　*　*

Bannu is just to the north of what became the fiefdom of the Pakistani Taliban leader Baitullah Mahsud, who was killed in August 2009. The Mahsud clan were already a problem in my father's time. Razmak is, as the crow flies, 80 km south-west of Bannu, on the Afghan border in North Waziristan. I have not been able to locate the camp at Roqan Raqsa; a Raqsa or Raghza was a treacherous, bush-covered plain, fringing the foothills of most mountain areas, unsuitable for the permanent piquet, where the Mahsud, in those days, had the whip-hand.

QUO VADIS, HUMANITAS?

In July 1946, my mother returned with my brother David and me from England to Jersey.

It would be another 18 months before my wife-to-be, Angelika, with her parents and elder sister, Ingrid, would finally reach the safety of Brazil. My father-in-law Ernesto Meissner, born in São Paulo, had travelled to Germany from Brazil, age 18, with his violin. He was a musician, a linguist and a philosopher. His language skills were to save him from starvation during hostilities. Ironically, it was these same skills which were to confine him to Germany for the duration, as they were considered by the Nazis to be of strategic importance. His first job was with the *Deutsche-Südamerikanische Bank* in Hamburg. He had been told by his violin professor that his left hand would not take him to stardom. After being transferred to Berlin, he met and married Liselotte, the daughter of his landlady Marie Kadziora. He played the violin; she played the piano. It was Liselotte's father, Benno Kadziora (the name was also written Kendziorski or Kedzionski), who had taught the 'Red Baron' (Manfred von Richthofen) how to fly.

The name 'Kadziora', judging by an excerpt, in German, from a document registering the birth of Benno's father, Jan, seemed to come from a mysterious place called 'Shipy', which, German-speakers will know, is a very unlikely spelling in this purely phonetic language. After some research, the word turned out to be Słupy (pronounced 'schwhoopee'), a village 7 km south-west of Szubin in Poland. Evidently, the German official who typed this document in 1880, when this part of Poland belonged to the kingdom of Prussia, either misread the word, or had no 'ł' on his keyboard.

In 1938, Ernesto was with *Focke-Wulf*, whose endeavours to build up business in South America, however, foundered when Brazil felt itself threatened by nazified Argentina and became an ally of the UK and France. He was then made to work with the *Reichsrundfunk Berlin* (the Nazi radio organ) where he found himself translating for Lord Haw-Haw until allied bombing forced these broadcasts to be moved to Luxembourg. It was perhaps the virulent antisemitic nature of the programmes which moved Ernesto to begin to use his interpreting and translation skills to assist many disguised Jews, and other foreigners, to emigrate, first from the Nazi capital and later from the Russian-occupied zone of Berlin. He did this by simple misinterpretation of their documents to the authorities. He himself, by that time, was down to one copy of his Brazilian birth certificate, which, with his language skills, was to save his life.

One day, as the Russians were advancing on Berlin, he accompanied an Egyptian professor out of the city towards Halberstadt where his family had found lodgings at the time. The professor's family had also taken refuge south-east of the city. Anyone travelling against the refugee stream excited interest but, for some obscure reason, Ernesto decided to dress up in flowing white robes, like the Egyptian's, and bluff his way through the control-posts. No motor transport was available and the roads were almost impassable, so they resolved to go by bicycle, which he had to teach the Arab how to ride before they could leave. En route, they parked their bicycles and went off in different directions to look for food. When he got back, the bicycles had disappeared, as had the Egyptian.

Shortly afterwards, he stumbled into a Russian patrol, and was taken to a *Komendatur*, where he was thrown into a room with a number of other foreigners. As he was being pushed up against a wall, his birth certificate fell out of his robe. It was retrieved by a Russian storm-trooper who began to tear it up, but suddenly spotted the five-pointed star in the Brazilian coat-of-arms, and bellowed at him in Russian, '*Kommunist?*' Ernesto shouted back '*Kommunist!*' He was taken to the *Komendant* and was fêted all night with caviar and vodka.

All the other foreigners in the group were shot.

On another occasion, while the family was still in Berlin, a very heavy bombing raid took place. The family was in the cellar. Ernesto arrived from work some time later; he was covered in white dust and looked dazed. He had got home and raced up the stairs to their third-floor flat. As he opened the door, there was an enormous explosion which lifted him right out of the building and deposited him, quite unharmed and still clutching his briefcase, at ground level. It was not his moment. Angelika's grandmother, 'Omi Omi', used to boast that, for many months after this direct hit, which had removed the back wall of the apartment building, she was able to stir the soup while sitting on the loo. She may have been described as 'Prussian' in her passport, but her humour was that of a *Berlinerin.*

The exact date of their departure from Hamburg in the *Santarem* is illegible on the 'Certificate of Identity in Place of Passport', issued jointly by the Brazilian Military Mission and the Control Council of Germany on 9 December 1947. On 1 January 1948, Liselotte wrote to her mother that the ship was being searched for stowaways and that planned departure time was 16.00 hours. In any event, she, Ernesto and the two girls landed in Brazil on 2 February 1948, and began to pick up the pieces of their lives.

One member of their little family was missing. Wolfgang, Liselotte's older brother, had been posted to the Eastern Front as an infantryman with a tank regiment. He was killed at Konstantinovka on 19 August 1943, during the fourth and final battle for Khar'kov (Ukrainian: Kharkiv). He was buried with full military honours at the Heroes' Cemetery of Merefa. In November 1942, he had been awarded the Iron Cross, Second Class. Posthumously, he was awarded the Iron Cross, First Class. He was 27.

In August 1948, Gwynneth took David and me with her to Australia. I have never really understood why. I imagine she may have been trying to go back to her roots. Her long, frustrating courtship had been followed by her father's death, a bewildering wedding, and a miserable time in the barracks in Abbotabad, when she was often unwell while her new husband was away fighting what appeared to her as a pointless war. There was the blight of catty officers' wives, the miscarriages, more sickness, a worrying trip home to Jersey, another war, evacuation and, once again, her husband's protracted absence, this time on anti-aircraft duty, followed by his terminal illness. Perhaps there was a new suitor; perhaps she simply wanted to turn over a new leaf, in the security - or so she imagined - of the land where she had been born. Whatever she had in mind was not to be; and we were all back in Jersey within eight months. My mother took up farming and raised a prize-winning herd of Jerseys.

34

I suppose it was during this trip to Australia that I became conscious of what having a British passport really meant. King George VI had lost his title as Emperor of India the year before we travelled, but nothing seemed to have changed. From our carefully insulated world, we could view Egypt as we steamed sedately through the Suez Canal. We could enjoy the gully-gully man with his conjuring tricks and cards and corks and day-old chicks. We could watch as boys of my age, dressed in loin-cloths, dived from the top decks of the *Strathaird* for coins, off Aden. We could admire the Gateway to India in Bombay. We could drive up into the hills to visit old family friends who owned a tea plantation near Colombo.

We could gawp at the lights of Fremantle after seeing absolutely nothing for eight days – a very long time in the life of a nine-year-old. And we could continue to talk English and use our pounds, shillings and pence, after disembarking in Sydney. But we could do all of this, somehow preserved from the foreignness and the distances by our British passports. I remember thinking: we weren't superior; we were simply invincible. (Many years later, on the north bank of the St Lawrence river in Canada, I was able to test this theory.)

My future parents-in-law did not have an easy start in Brazil. Although Angelika's grandfather had been a successful businessman (refining and manufacturing oils and dyes and waxes), the family fortune disappeared, and Ernesto had to make his way as a carpenter, and later as an accountant, another new venture for him. He was a senior executive in the *Serviço Municipal de Transportes Coletivos* (*SMTC*, the Santos Municipal Collective Transport Company) when the 1964 Goulart Revolution broke out. Ernesto found himself once again in an unenviable position. A powerful local politician, close to the military, wanted to take over the *SMTC*, and discredited certain of the senior employees so that its stock market value would fall – opening the way for him to buy the company for a pittance. This is, in any event, my later interpretation of developments. (I had myself arrived in Brazil just after the Goulart Revolution – see below – and was dating Angelika at the time.)

Two plain-clothes policemen came round to Ernesto's flat one morning, and invited him to go with them. He happened to have seen a traffic accident that morning, and went, in the firm belief that he was needed as a witness. That was the last we saw or heard of him for ten days.

We later learned that he had been accused in closed court (he was not at the proceedings) of receiving illegal gifts from unnamed parties (Christmas hampers and a bottle of champagne). Ernesto was one of four to be charged: his other colleagues had fled the country. *In absentia,* he was sentenced to prison for 14 months under article 317 of the Penal Code which dealt with 'passive corruption'. He had spent the ten days in various jails, forced to stand with prostitutes and thieves in crowded cells, before being moved to army barracks. With the help of an old family friend, a retired policeman, we managed to arrange a midnight meeting with Ernesto in a lay-by on the main road to Santos, after the guards, suitably bribed, had agreed to let us have 15 minutes with him. It was a dramatic and frightening encounter.

He spent seven months in detention, and was perfunctorily released with a shallow apology, when the politician in question began to feel the legal pressure which, after several false starts (sabotaged by him), we were eventually able to exercise from our side. I remember, on one occasion, sending two crates of Black Label Scotch Whisky to our lawyer who, we later found out, was working for the other side. An application for compensation for wrongful arrest came to nothing. In retrospect, this was the time that unwanted political prisoners were being dropped from helicopters into Guanabara Bay (a 'forbidden' chapter of Brazilian history to this day), and Ernesto may have got off lightly.

He was a wonderful father-in-law, blessed, thank goodness, with enormous reserves of patience and bonhomie. Curiously, he had the same locked finger on his left hand (an accident from his carpentry days) as did my step-father. It stopped Ernesto from playing the violin; it stopped my step-father – whose name was also Ernest, and who was a wonderful step-father – from playing cricket.

And they had something else in common: during the German occupation of Jersey, Ernest had been jailed by the Nazis for some months and for just as spurious a reason.

They had strangely complementary senses of humour. Ernest (we all called him 'Pa') kept us children – and Gwynneth, for that matter – hooting with laughter at some childish ditty, for example the one we always sang as we drove down to see Mont Orgeuil Castle lit up during the long Jersey summer evenings:

High in the mountains,
Green grows the grass;
Down came a nanny-goat,
Sliding on its...overcoat!

Ernesto ('Vati') was usually more subtle: 'There was, for example, the story of the little man on the platform of the *U-Bahn*, trying desperately to wrestle his colossal double-bass on to the underground train, when a large *Berliner* went up to him, as if to help, and said, "*Wissen Sie, Mannequin, Flöte müssten Sie spielen, Flöte müssten Sie spielen!*" ("Little man, you should learn how to play the flute!")' Ernesto died in Brazil in March 1971; Ernest followed him in London, four days later.

The title of this essay comes from a Brazilian typescript of Ernesto, the only piece of his writing still extant. It is an obscurely philosophical piece of what he called cosmo-psychic import and 'thingness', drawing from Ortega y Gasset, Socrates, Goethe, Schiller and Garve; from Beethoven and beyond. Sadly, the work is incomplete.

Quo Vadis, Humanitas? Indeed!

DAME SYBIL

In the mid-1950s, while Admiral Sir Gresham Nicholson was Lieutenant-Governor of Jersey, I was quite often invited to Government House for dinner, in order to provide company for the Admiral's son, John, a school-friend of mine; we were both in our early teens. Boys, we had to understand, were to be seen and not heard at these gatherings, at which distinguished guests were often present.

For me, the most memorable occasion was a dinner invitation which had been extended to Sybil Hathaway, Dame of Sark.

37

Even if we had to remain silent unless addressed, John and I were thrilled to have the opportunity to meet this icon of the German occupation of the Channel Islands. Not only that: she was the great-great-granddaughter of John Allaire, a well-known privateer; and – most exciting of all – there were rumours that she had a wooden leg.

Conversation during dinner was animated. Dame Sybil acquitted herself with a force which was almost masculine. John and I were busy with a secret code which we had developed for the evening and took very little part. I do remember thinking, though, after the ladies had withdrawn, and the gentlemen had ranged themselves around the lawn to do what comes naturally, that it would have been almost appropriate to have found Dame Sybil outside with us men.

She walked with a stick and seemed to have a stiff leg; but we never found out if it, too, was made of wood.

It occurs to me now that this teenage contact with Government House in Jersey was my earliest exposure to affairs at Whitehall and the Foreign Office.

INVINCIBILITY

In the essay entitled *Quo Vadis, Humanitas?* (above), I recorded a feeling, when I was at a more tender age, that my British passport somehow made me invincible. On the north bank of the St Lawrence river, in early 1960, still only a 21-year-old, I was able to test this theory.

It was vacation-time. Students at McGill University, in those days, were expected to go off for four months or so, and look for a job to defray the costs of their education. My friends duly headed off west to find jobs on farms in Ontario or Manitoba or Saskatchewan or Alberta or even British Columbia. I went east. As far as I knew, the vast majority of students went west; a few went south and south-east; hardly anyone went east, for one simple reason: the snows would not have melted yet.

I went east because I speculated that, statistically, I would have a better chance of finding a job. I invested in a smart new Norwegian rucksack, a pair of stout, knee-high leather boots, some snow-shoes and a thick canvas jacket, and set off towards Sept Îles, hitchhiking. I made it quickly to Trois Rivières (one river, three mouths) and Quebec, which we drove straight through, as the driver wanted to make La Malbaie before nightfall (this was where, in 1608, Samuel de Champlain, founder of Quebec, tried to anchor but couldn't). The next morning, the same driver took me on to Baie Ste Catherine and across the Saguenay river by ferry to Tadoussac (which had been the first trading post in 'New France'). A friend of his, in a Land Rover, was leaving for Baie Comeau and Godbout after lunch the next day, and, in quick succession, we crossed the Rivière aux Outardes ('wild geese') and the Manicouagan, which he called 'le Manic', both times by ferry.

When we reached Baie Comeau, however, the road became impassable because of the flooding, and I had to take another ferry on to Godbout. Nobody seemed to be going in my direction - nobody was going in *any* direction - so I started to wade towards Pointe aux Anglais, a small town named after eight ships of a British fleet which ran aground and sank in 1711, with the loss of over 900 men. I wasn't aware of this historical snippet at the time - I didn't really know *where* I was - and it was perhaps just as well.

As I splashed along the road beside the St Lawrence, I saw that, although there was not much snow left, there were extensive lakes everywhere. The Land Rover was, in fact, the last *char* (French Canadian for 'car') which I was to see until I reached Sept Îles. A few enormous loggers' trucks went by, without stopping. One roared past, creating a bow wave in the flood, and water slopped over the top of my boots. It was getting dark and cold, and I became quite concerned.

Finally, a smaller truck did stop and the driver asked me where I was going. I told him: Pointe aux Anglais. There was one bar-cum-rooming-house in the village, and it was here that we 'landed'. We paddled from the truck, up the timber steps and in through the door. He was an enormous lumberjack with aquiline features and massive claws, straight out of a horror movie. He could not take his eyes off my rucksack. Then he left the room for a moment, and came back with two more ugly giants; threateningly, he held out a glass of beer. I had had nothing to eat all day and the last thing I wanted was a glass of beer, but I took it and thanked him. He stood there with his two cronies, staring at my rucksack. They said nothing. Then, abruptly, as if on cue, they began to close in.

At times like these, one's mind goes into overdrive.

My right hand held the glass of beer; and my left hand was clutching my passport, deep in my trouser-pocket. Neither of these items made very good weapons. The three behemoths were, by now, very close: they were looking bigger and bigger. Then instinct - and my classical education - took over. With a ringing voice, I intoned:

'Je vous offre une libation - ça, c'est pour les dieux.'

And I poured a liberal amount of beer over their boots. They all recoiled. I do not believe that, in all of classical history, there could have been such a dramatic sequel to the simple pouring of a libation to the gods.

Seconds later, with as much ceremony as I could muster, I extracted the faithful old blue passport from my pocket and flourished it under their noses. I cannot recall exactly what I exclaimed, but my passport - I swear it - had the same effect on those three monsters as that cross had on Dracula. They flinched. They cringed. They downed their drinks, and they left. My rucksack was safe. I *was* invincible, but I was shaking all over.

Absurdly, while trying to remember the sequence of this story, which I have never been able to explain, I recalled Robert Lambert (see below) bewitching his men by reciting passages from Homer's *Odyssey*, in Greek, after their landing in Sicily, not 20 years before I had 'landed' at Pointe aux Anglais.

The rest of the trip to Sept Îles went like clockwork.

LINESMAN, SECOND CLASS

Walsh Canadian's office in Sept Îles looked like a mobile home without the wheels. It was run by a tough French-Canadian, who, as I approached, was physically ejecting two Montagnais

(Algonquian) Indians. Montagnais were usually employed because they were not afraid of heights; these two, quite evidently, had had too much to drink.

'*Qu'est ce que vous voulez? Vous voulez dzu travail? Vous l'avez!*' ... and I was hired...for the price of two Indians, it seemed. It was 7 o'clock in the morning.

All I can recall from the inside of his office is that there was a large white bookcase, with one thick, grey-covered book in it: *The Linesman's Handbook.*

He noted my name (with some difficulty), and my address in Montreal. Then he handed me a badge (n° 453), a green fibre-glass safety helmet and a fly-net.

'*Un dzollar quarante-cinq par heure; ça c'est pour les simulies.*' Can$1.45 an hour! More than my wildest dreams, whatever *simulies* were.

'*Nonante-huit heures par semaine...*' 98 hours a week? But I kept silent. His accent was unmistakable; *huit* he pronounced 'wit'.

'*...Moins les impôts, moins accomodzatzion, plus V.P. Vous recevrez cent tzrois dzollars cinquante-quatre; les tzransports inclus.*' I didn't know what 'V.P.' was but I didn't care. I had no idea what I would be doing; my only clue was that book on his shelf. But I had already calculated that Can$1,400 (14 weeks at Can$100) would be more than enough to pay for the whole year at McGill.

'*Venez ici à 5 heures...*' He continued writing; then he looked up at me again,

'*...dzu matzin!...dzemain!*'

That afternoon, I explored Sept Îles (which the locals pronounced 'S-till') and came across All Saints Anglican Church. The door was open and I went in. Alex Stringer, the incumbent, invited me back to the Vicarage for a cup of tea. He and his wife Margaret were, I believe, quite pleased to see a new face, and whenever I could in the weeks that followed, I attended matins: there was, on occasion, a congregation of two (including me). Alex and I have corresponded at Christmas-time ever since.

Next morning, after a sleepless night at a hostel, I made my way back to Walsh Canadian, and got on to the back of a truck with some other very somnolent characters. We drove for over four hours, back to the early twentieth-century settlement

41

of Port Cartier, then northwards on a gravel road, strewn with boulders, along a railway line which was being laid, up to Gagnan. This was a community of the Quebec Cartier Mining Company, which had been incorporated in January 1960, only a few weeks before I arrived. It was the industrial relations officer at Quebec Cartier who had given me a list of the company's contractors and consulting engineers. Walsh Canadian was pencilled on to the bottom of the list. It had been my lucky day. Our base was at Camp 99 (i.e. 99 km north of Port Cartier).

My job, I then discovered, was trainee linesman. I had to dig holes for telegraph poles, which were being erected along the railway line as far as Lac Jeannine. The holes, wide enough for me to stand in and wield a shovel, had to go straight down for over two metres through snow, ice, earth and gravel. Whenever I reached solid rock, I had to call for Émile the foreman, who doubled as dynamite-man. His, I discovered, was an extremely skilled job. He needed enormous patience and knowledge of the various rock-forms and their brittleness. He usually got it right and I returned to my hole to clear out the debris. On one occasion, though, after we had retired to a safe place and he had detonated the blasting cap, we both saw a boulder, the size of a man's head, shoot out horizontally across the valley and take the middle out of a Red Pine tree, which hung in mid-air for a moment before crashing down to the ground vertically, and slowly toppling over. Émile went quite pale.

As time went on, I was promoted to 'linesman, second class', with the less strenuous job of drilling and dressing the poles, and helping to erect them. Later still, I was allowed to climb the poles with spikes ('gaffs') strapped to my ankles, and put the finishing touches to them. The wiring was somebody else's job.

On site, I was puzzled by the two-metre-high stumps surrounding me, until Émile told me that trees were felled in the winter because it was much easier to slide them on the deep snow down to the river. He was a fount of knowledge, and taught me about animal tracks and spores, local geology and the different types of snow and ice - so important to him when he was dynamite-man. One morning, I came back to my hole and found mature wolf-tracks nearby. On another occasion, I saw a mother skunk sauntering regally past with her young. I kept my distance: they are afraid of nothing.

Our day began very early. I had my 'elevenses' (in Switzerland: z'nüni) shortly after 7 a.m. The only way to eat it was to roll down one's sleeves, tuck one's trousers firmly into one's stockings, don the fly-net (over the helmet), put on gloves and walk briskly backwards and forwards along the newly creosoted sleepers of the railway track, puffing on a hand-rolled cigarette, just ahead of the swarms of blackfly (which got up for one hour at this time of day), quickly lifting the fly-veil and slipping a morsel into one's mouth. If a fly got in, one crunched him up, as fast as possible, with the sandwich. I had, in my first interview, been warned about *simulies.* I found out now what they were. They didn't sting: they devoured. These aggressive, hungry little beasts paraded up and down one's seams, looking for openings. Allegedly, they didn't like tobacco smoke; I am not so certain. Once I had to go to hospital in Sept Îles, after a truck, in which I was a passenger, had rolled off the road, and I met a Greek colleague there. He had tucked his trousers in, but not rolled down his sleeves: the flies had got into his shirt and tried to chew their way out of his trouser-legs.

This adventure was a kaleidoscope of experiences, and each of my colleagues had a story to tell. Jacques was a French crook on the run, on his way to Vegas, where, he told me, he would make big money. His speciality was stealing and pawning tools. Then there were several *Paras* who had deserted from the French Army in Algeria. The tales they told were not nice. There were two French *Légionnaires.* Bizarrely, they called each other 'Jean', while they told us that their names were, respectively, 'Boris' and 'Georges'. We never found out why they were there. *Légionnaires* are always shy about their past. I preferred Émile.

I had another good friend, Arnaud, who drove an enormous petrol tanker between Sept Îles and Gagnan. I hitched many a lift from him. He kept a .22 rifle in his cab to shoot wild turkey. On one occasion, he was winding his way along a track which was below the surface of a wide expanse of floodwater; he knew it by heart. We were making slow but steady progress, like an ocean liner, when, suddenly, the rearmost pair of wheels on the starboard side slipped off the edge. I wondered what he would do now.

Arnaud pulled on a pair of waders and went to have a look. He came back to the cab very quickly, grabbed his rifle, mumbled something – he was a man of few words – and disappeared for about half an hour, returning with a large turkey which he handed up to me without ceremony. Then he climbed back into the cab and started the engine, let it warm up, went into four-wheel drive and, very gently engaged, then immediately took his foot off the accelerator. He repeated the process – on, off, on, off – each time with a little more pressure on the pedal. Then I realised what he was doing. Steadily the momentum of his 9,000 gallon load took over. Backwards and forwards, backwards and forwards it surged, with ever increasing thrust, until he jabbed his foot down, full throttle, and we were, miraculously, back on the road.

On one trip with him to Sept Îles, I visited the Hudson Bay stores and purchased a beautiful soapstone statue of an Eskimo (Inuit) carrying a seal. It cost Can $20. I sent it, sea freight, as a birthday present to my grandmother, but apparently put the wrong postage on it. This was only spotted after it had crossed the Atlantic, and was returned to Alex and Margaret's home. By that time I had departed, and Alex held it for me, thinking that I would return to Sept Îles. He eventually re-dispatched it. This time round, someone misread 'Jersey' for ' New Jersey' and poor Alex received it back *again,* 'undeliverable'.

By then, I had left Montreal for all stations west, so he sent it for the third time. This well-travelled ornament had crossed the Atlantic five times before it finally arrived in Jersey.

It was left to me in Muzz's will, and now resides, proudly, on our dresser, together with the King of Afghanistan's butter dish (see below).

* * *

Gagnan is now a ghost town.

COD

Feeling a little despondent, after saying goodbye to my friends in Walsh Canadian, I decided to relive a little bit of that period of Jersey history when the island's cod-fishermen were making their money from a three-cornered trade: salted or dried fish from Newfoundland and Gaspé to England; wool from England to Jersey; woollen waistcoats ('jerseys') and stockings from Jersey to France. Gaspé was said to be full of Channel Island names. Privateering was big business too.

I set off on the Ungava Transports ferry from Sept Îles across the St Lawrence to Gaspé, landing, after a six-hour trip, at Sainte-Anne-des-Monts. Months on the pole-line had left me very fit, and I resolved to walk as far as possible around the peninsula. After all, Charles Robin (see below), born in St Brelades, Jersey, had once (back in 1787) walked all the way from Gaspé to Quebec.

I passed Rivière à Claude ('Claude's River'), Mont Louis, Gros Morne ('Big Hill'), with the Shickshock Mountains to the south, and plodded on through Rivière Madeleine and Petite Vallée before reaching my first objective: St Hélier (written with an accent, unlike its namesake in Jersey). Not much to see there, so on to L'Échouerie ('place where ships go aground'), Rivière-au-Renard (settled by Irish and French Canadians in the 1790s, the 'capital of fish', was to be virtually destroyed by floods in 2007) and l'Anse-aux-Griffons (toponymists are not unanimous: *anse* meant a 'shallow bay'; the *Griffon* was a seventeenth-century sailing boat which paid regular visits; however, the first fishermen reported having sighted some geese which resembled griffins). More interesting was the fact that this little town had been founded by a Jerseyman, John LeBoutillier (also spelt with an h: LeBouthillier), in the early nineteenth century. He built warehouses there for salt, flour and salted cod, some of which can still be seen.

My sightseeing was making me run seriously behind schedule and I began, intermittently, to catch buses: north to Gaspé itself; down again to Barachois (from the Basque *barratxoa*, meaning a 'coastal lagoon'; it was Basque fishermen who had started the salted cod industry). I went through Malbaie and past the Perce Rock (an over-rated mirror-image of the elephantine Falaise of Étretat in Normandy, and Ponta da Piedade, near Lagos in the Algarve).

I hitch-hiked through Grande Rivière, Chandler and Newport, and arrived at a town with the extraordinary name of Paspébiac (the *Paspé* in the name may have an etymological connection to Gaspé). It had been founded by a Jerseyman,

Charles Robin, in 1767, who set up his own company, trading in codfish and furs, shortly after the Hudson Bay Company had been established. It was here that I learned why Jerseymen came to the Gaspé peninsula: this was very simply because cod used to be plentiful between one and three miles off-shore, and the gravel beaches were ideal for the drying process.

Time was running out, and I hurried along the north shore of the Baie des Chaleurs, past Maria, St Omer and Restigouche (said to be from the M'Kmaq Indian word for 'five fingers'; the Restigouche watershed is the traditional home of the M'Kmaq nation). So much still to see and do.

As I dozed in my *chambrette*, after leaving Matapedia (from a M'Kmaq Indian word meaning 'meeting of the waters') by train for Montreal, I wondered what title I would give to an article about this trip – should I ever decide to write one.

* * *

There is a postscript to this travelogue, which, to an extent, 'joins up the dots'. I have since discovered that one William LeBoutillier Fauvel was from a family of Jersey merchants engaged in the cod trade. William's mother may have been the sister of the John LeBoutillier (one word) who founded l'Anse-aux-Griffons. William's father, John Fauvel, had been manager of the Perce (Paspébiac) operation of Charles Robin, having married the daughter of Charles's nephew; later, he started his own firm at Malbaie. This was all very typical of the complex business and family relationships of Jersey people in Canada.

Jersey's nineteenth-century banking history is very complex. The decline of the Gaspé fishing industry and Jersey's three-cornered trade was just as much due to the collapse of the island's banks as it was to increased competition, growing interest in agriculture and tourism, and declining stocks. William Fauvel himself became involved as proxy for the creditors of Le Boutillier Brothers, which was being liquidated as a result of an association with the Jersey Banking Company. Robin Frères appear as the rescuers of the Jersey Commercial Bank in the list I later compiled for *Currencies of the Anglo-Norman Isles.*

Last but not least, William LeBoutillier, who became increasingly involved in public life, was appointed vice-consul of Portugal at Paspébiac. There cannot have been any other vice-consuls *anywhere*, who would have occupied themselves so exclusively with the business of cod.

ACROSS CANADA

The original idea had come to me during a students' gathering in Mount Royal cemetery. After two indifferent years at McGill University, my friends were canvassed for support and company for the trip - to no avail. The idea of making my way westwards from Montreal back to Europe, however, persisted, and one morning in March 1961, I travelled by train to visit the Embassy of the USSR at Ottawa, to see if I could begin to assess the feasibility of travelling through the Soviet Union from east to west.

I was received by a Mr Leonid N. Bobkhov, Second Secretary and Consul. At first Comrade B., it seemed, thought he was having his leg pulled, and the conversation descended into an exchange of ideologies which I found difficult to sustain. However, at a later stage of the conversation, provoked by some caustic remark about capitalism, I asked him if capitalists would be charged double for passage on the Trans-Siberian railway. Curiously, Comrade B.'s tone immediately changed, and he asked for details of my passport. Would I please make contact again in a fortnight?

I rang him up again at the appointed time. No, he did not know yet; would I please call him again in another two weeks? One week, OK? OK. After one week had elapsed, an answer came: there was absolutely not the slightest chance of my landing anywhere on the Siberian coast. However, if the Chinese would let me in, I could join up with the Trans-Siberian railway at Chita or Ulan-Ude, and Comrade B. would ensure that a visa would be issued for the rest of the trip. Yes, the Chinese authorities should be contacted first. I had never heard of these places.

The nearest Chinese representative was the Chinese Chargé d'Affaires in London and I immediately wrote to him, special delivery, telling him of my abortive contacts with Mr Bobkhov.

The rather facile letter continued:

> As confirmation [that it was impossible to enter Siberia] has only just been received, this has been my first opportunity to apply for a Chinese Visa.
>
> In brief, I wish to work my passage across the Pacific Ocean, arriving in Peking, and to leave Peking on June 20th, travelling on the Trans-Siberian Railway via Moscow to Europe, and returning to England.
>
> I should be very grateful if you would issue me with a visa for my visit to China.

I had done some homework on current affairs, which I felt might cement my case:

> With respect to my passage from Canada to China, I would have great difficulty in finding a route from Japan or Korea to China, if I was to travel first to one of these countries. However, I understand that the first shipment of grain, according to the terms of the recent Sino-Canadian 'agreement of intent', will leave Canada for China about June 1st. If this is the case, I should be grateful if you would arrange a passage for me with this first shipment of grain, which would, I assume, land me directly in China. I hope you will appreciate the difficulties that I would encounter in working my way across the Pacific Ocean.

The final paragraph of this letter takes the prize for misguided audacity, particularly in the light of the knowledge I have since acquired of Chinese Consular procedures:

> Once again, I apologise that this request comes to you at such very short notice; as you will understand, the circumstances have been beyond my control. I need not point out to you that there remains very little time, and I should very much appreciate a speedy acknowledgement of this letter in order that I may effect a comprehensive schedule.

A speedy reply did indeed arrive from the Chinese Chargé in London. It was dated 10 May 1961, and was signed with a large red consular stamp, which said it all. The answer was no.

I immediately phoned Comrade B. in Ottawa and told him of this latest rebuff. The Chinese refusal to help seemed to unlock a door. Yes, he remembered who I was. No, he had no news as yet. But wait; perhaps he *had* had a reply from Intourist. Long pause. I could possibly enter the USSR through the recently opened port

48

of Nakhodka, near Vladivostok. As soon as an Intourist voucher was to hand, with its inherent authority for my entry into the USSR, Comrade B. would issue the necessary visa. No time was lost in visiting Thomas Cook in Montreal, who were asked to cable Intourist in Moscow, requesting a single ticket by train, hard class, from Nakhodka to Moscow. I then confirmed this request to Comrade B., and sent him an impatient follow-up letter, a few days later:

> The Soviet authorities seem to be having some difficulties in reaching a decision and Thomas Cook have still had no reply [to their last letter].
>
> I am sure that you appreciate the difficulties in the planning and timing of this trip. Before I can go ahead with my plans to work my way across Canada and the Pacific, I must know if I shall be allowed to travel on the Trans-Siberian Railway.
>
> I should be very grateful if you could possibly find out what decision Intourist has made, because there is not much time for me to make plans for an alternative route back to England.

The USSR had just put the first man into space; plans were in hand to detonate the 'Tsar-bomb', the AN602 hydrogen device – the largest, most powerful nuclear weapon ever detonated; the U2 had recently been shot down and the pilot, Gary Powers, carrying his lethal modified silver dollar, had been captured, tried and incarcerated in Moscow. The U2 incident had led to the collapse of the Four Power Paris Summit between Dwight Eisenhower, Nikita Khrushchev, Harold Macmillan and Charles de Gaulle. Sino-Soviet tensions were beginning along the Ussuri river on my intended route.

But the self-effacing, industrious, unpretentious Comrade B., in the midst of all these world-shaking events, managed, somehow, to come up trumps. It would be a close thing. However, even if I obtained a visa, I would still have to get to Nakhodka. And to get to Siberia, I still had to, somehow, get to Japan. And to get to Japan, the Pacific had to be crossed. And to begin that trip, I still had to get myself the 4,900km across Canada to – presumably – Vancouver, from my little room in Mrs Morris's B-and-B in Suter Street, Montreal, where most of the machinating for this mad wheeze had taken place.

There was no time like the present. I went to see a French-Canadian car-dealer I had met casually, and signed a contract binding me to drive a Chevrolet Impala from Montreal to Calgary where there was an enormous demand for automobiles. I should pay the fuel costs. There was a time frame: I had 120 hours to complete the trip and to deliver the vehicle, plus one day at the front end for preparation. I could take a co-driver as long as he had a valid Canadian driving licence; and, of course, I had to deliver the car in the state in which I had taken possession of it. Valid driving licence?

It was the quickest driving test I had ever taken – my first experience in an 'automatic' (the car I had contracted to deliver in Calgary) – and when my foot touched the accelerator (I could scarcely hear the engine), the vehicle leapt forward and nudged the car parked in front, luckily doing no damage. I then had to ask the young French-Canadian who was doing the test to please show me how an automatic gear-change functioned. Evidently, this was not the first time he had had such a customer, and he willingly obliged. After once round the block – this time without hitting anything – I was granted a *permis de conduire… pour une période d'une semaine à compter de la date d'émission de ce reçu.* It had cost me Can$5.50 for the driving test and the licence.

Later the same day, a cable arrived at Thomas Cook from Intourist, Moscow. It read:

OCCAMMON RESERVATION CONFIRM FARE NAKHODKA
MOSCOW HARD 88 ROUBLES

Twelve hours later, I (and a friend, John Scott, who had elected to come for part of the trip, and help with the driving) set out in the Chevrolet for Calgary. Things were beginning to roll. But I still had no voucher or ticket for the train, and no visa for Siberia. Somewhat optimistically, in a last telephone call to Comrade B., I left a message for him to please make sure that the visa would be waiting for me in Tokyo.

This stage of the trip is, in more senses than one, a blur. I had set myself two ancillary targets, which were, to visit the Russian Embassy in Ottawa, to try to obtain a visa from them; and, if possible, to pay a fleeting visit to the provincial legislatures on our itinerary; this excluded Edmonton and Toronto, which were not on the route. We managed both Winnipeg and Regina (where there was a young girl playing a flute high up in the rotunda roof).

While we were in Winnipeg, I also managed to spend a useful hour with James ('Jasper') Cross, British Trade Commissioner. (Nine years later, when he was in Montreal, Jasper got into the news when he was abducted by a cell of the *Front de Libération du Québec* (*FLQ*), and released two months later in exchange for safe passage for his kidnappers to Cuba.)

My laconic diary mirrors our haste:

29 May 1961: Car via Ste Anne-de-Bellevue & puncture to Ottawa. Russian Embassy. Visa refused. Parking tkt. UK High Commission. Rang Finnish Embassy.

30 May: Pd parking ticket. Left Ottawa. Hamburger in Pembroke. North Bay. Snack. Sudbury. Algoma. Sault-Ste-Marie. Ferry to USA. Gas at place near cafe. Kept on driving...

31 May: Gas at Bruce Crossing. John started driving Ashland. On to Duluth. Breakfast at McIntosh. Warren. Back to Canada. & Winnipeg. Cooks for Moscow Finland ticket. Cinema. Spent night in [RCAF] transient officers' mess chez Robin Oulton [another university friend].

1 June: Set sail into Prairies proper from Winnipeg after gas, oil, steering fill-up. Breakfast near inspection station. Lunch & gas at Oak Lake. Into Saskatchewan. Spent one hour in Regina. Gas at Ernfold. Supper at Swift Current on via Medicine Hat to Calgary.

The car, except for a vibrating bonnet, performed well, and we delivered it, not a dent to be seen, with the agent. He was so pleased with it that he let us keep it for two more days. According to a rough travelogue made at the time, we had hurtled the 3,500 km from Montreal to Calgary in 41 hours and 45 minutes at an average running speed of 83.8 kph.

I stayed with an old school friend in Calgary, Anthony Gray. He had a very odd job, plodding around a golf driving range, in a modern suit of armour, picking up golf-balls. Anthony had a multifarious group of acquaintances, one of whom was the editor of the *North Hill News* of Calgary: Roy Farran generously agreed to sponsor me for membership of the Calgary Press Club. With a Press card in my wallet, I would be able to travel free on the Canadian Pacific Railway over the Rockies and down to Vancouver. 'However, you will need to *look* like a member of the Press,' Roy added. 'You must, at least, have a camera. Go down to this drug-store (he wrote down an address) and ask to look around in their basement.'

I did so, and, for the princely sum of Can$20, acquired a venerable box camera in a leather case; a flash-gun, which didn't fit the camera; a lot of flash-bulbs, which didn't fit the flash-gun; and a professional-looking camera-bag; these items will play a part later in the story. When I got back to Anthony Gray's digs, I opened the camera case and found a splendid, much-used Zeiss Ikon Ikoflex. It took magnificent pictures during the rest of the trip (and a later expedition I made to Iran and Afghanistan), although the slides were inconveniently large.

The railway scenery after Banff and Lake Louise, all the way to Vancouver, was made up of spectacular mountain peaks; the extraordinary engineering feat at Field where two spiral tunnels have been built above the Kicking Horse river, so that, if you are lucky, you can see the tail of your train disappearing above you as you emerge below; and some curious station-names: Leanchoil, Twin Butte, Solsqua, Shuswap, Kamloops, Spatsum, Chaumox, Spuzzum, Hatzic and Whonock. I was so tired after the break-neck trip to Calgary that I slept in my luxurious couchette through most of the journey. A mud-slide and a substantial wash-out, leaving the tracks high and dry, delayed the train for some hours, but meant nothing more to me than some extra shut-eye.

On arrival in Vancouver, I set up camp at the YMCA, and went for a long walk around the docks and Chinatown, trying to plan the next stage of my odyssey. All research was to be done in the municipal library, which had ample facilities.

Oddly, my incidental knowledge of the Sino-Canadian 'agreement of intent' not only provided a focus for my search for vessels to take me across the Pacific, but it also gave me a theme for the article which Roy Farran of the *North Hill News* in Calgary had been promised, in exchange for the Press Pass he had arranged for me. In fact I sent him a 'scoop'. While walking around the docks on 4 June, I picked up rumours that the newly commencing sales of Canadian grain to Communist China had hit serious problems as two British tankers had taken on board American-made suction unloading equipment. The US authorities had subsequently embargoed this procedure. These were very important sales for Canada, and China was, at the time, ravaged by famine. Having wired the story to Roy, I felt that I had completed my side of the bargain. The news broke the following day. On 9 June, the USA lifted the ban.

Good contacts were made in sundry Vancouver travel companies, including Ingrid Haedrich of Universal Travel Services. I visited over 20 ships in the dock complex, including one, the Greek SS *Despina*, which was bound for Nakhodka; but it was to no avail. On 8 June I went on board the SS *Yamahime Maru*, which would have taken eight passengers to Yokohama, but all cabins were booked. The following day, however, Ingrid phoned to say that there had been two cancellations at US$300 a head; was I interested in one of the berths? I immediately said yes, left a deposit and arranged for a transfer of the balance. This was not in my budget, but there seemed to be no alternative.

The *Yamahime Maru* was to leave for Japan on 17 June from the port of Bellingham in Washington State. I had in the meantime received from Thomas Cook the train ticket and voucher for the Trans-Siberian. But I still had no visa; and I did not yet know how it was possible to get from Yokohama to Nakhodka. Time was spent on housekeeping and inoculations.

I had had an introduction to David Brower at the British High Commissioner's office in Vancouver, and David proved to be a kind-hearted and useful contact, as well as an enthusiastic supporter of my initiative. He even brought some sea-sickness pills round to the YMCA one evening. He it was who introduced me to Jan Solecki, in case I made it to Siberia.

Jan gave me some unique insights into the contemporary Soviet Union as well as some useful tips about travelling on the Trans-Siberian. He was born in Inner Mongolia to a Polish father and a Russian mother. His father was one of the 10,000 Poles the Russians had sent to Manchuria to construct a railway. He boarded at a Polish high school in Heilongjiang, and later won a scholarship to study in Hong Kong; this, however, came to nothing when Germany invaded Poland. In 1941, Japan attacked Hong Kong. Jan joined the Hong Kong Volunteers and fought on the front lines for 17 days, when he was captured. For four years he was in Japanese prison camps with Canadian POWs, during which time his fascination for Canada was born. Jan was fluent in Russian, Polish and English and spoke and wrote good Mandarin.

On June 14, he found time for me at the University of British Columbia, where he worked. He gave me a studied and concise run-down on the situation in the Soviet Union, and a mini-course on how to negotiate with the more senior Soviet functionaries, who, he said, would almost certainly be Communist Party members (the more junior ones might still be members of the Young Communist League). Then he turned to the Trans-Siberian railway.

He described the port at Nakhodka and - most importantly - he spoke of a nondescript shed which lay diagonally across the port facilities from where the *Alexandr Mozhaisky* (the only ship then plying the Yokohama-Nakhodka route) would dock. If a Russian visa materialised, I would certainly be met by someone, and I should, if at all possible, avoid contact with this person until I had reached the shed and bought a ticket, hard class, to Moscow. These 'guides' only ever travelled soft class, and I would be pressed to purchase a soft class passage all the way...and have this man round my neck for the following ten days. Jan told me to run to this shed ('don't be embarrassed; everybody who really needs something has to run') and avoid conversation with anybody on the way. Among the utilities which he advised me to take on the train were:

> Paper tissues and toilet paper
> Cups and a thermos
> Soap
> Coffee, if possible Nescafe
> Pens

Tobacco in any form (even if I did not smoke) and
Concise dictionaries (English/Russian and English/Japanese)
(No tea or sugar necessary)

It was my last night at the YMCA in Vancouver. Joni James was singing her remake of 'Little Things Mean a Lot' on a portable gramophone in the dormitory.

Jan's list of mundane necessities suddenly became important.

ONE OLD MAN

On 16 June 1961, I got my things together at the YMCA, and boarded a Greyhound bus to Bellingham, about two hours to the south, across the US border. I located the *Yamahime Maru*, which was still loading, made my number with the captain, and went for a very long walk, in preparation for the Pacific crossing. That night I slept soundly at a 'Y' nearby. The following day (from my diary):

> 17 June: Brunch. Packed up and taxi to *Yamahime Maru*. Walk. Back for supper 5. First chopstick meal. Met Jack and Prof Honda. Sailed for Japan.

It took two weeks to cross the Pacific, including one day when we went over the International Date Line ('Did not exist' reads my diary entry for 24 June). After we had dropped the pilot at Port Angeles, we were soon to sight an albatross, then two, then a whole flight. By way of contrast, we later saw some puffins, a seal and a school of whales, some flying fish and a lone sea-gull. The weather was changeable. I washed my clothes. We all had to go to our cabins while the Captain swatted a golf-ball, attached to a long piece of elastic, from the bridge; the lethal little missile donged around the ship until it got caught in some corner and had to be loosed by a member of the crew, and eventually settled back on the bridge. The Captain's hobby belied his manners: he was a slovenly, bossy man, a marked contrast to his immaculate crew.

This was my first exposure to the Japanese way of life. I had never been particularly interested in food, but the choice on board this ship was remarkable. According to my notes, there was a wide selection of fish: raw bream, clam, cod, crayfish, cuttlefish, eel, flounder, giant sardines, herring, mussels, oysters, pilchard, salmon, swordfish, tuna, whale and, oddly, kippers. Passengers were offered (from the items which I could recognise) asparagus, bamboo, cold spinach, crisp lettuce, cucumber, egg-plant, ginger, onions, parsley, sea-weed, shredded cabbage, shredded horse-radish, shredded radish, sweet beans, sweet-potato, water-melon, yams and, oddly, baked beans.

There was always *sake* at supper and a cordial atmosphere. The fantastic service of the Head Chef, with his beautiful arrangements of sundry spices, and apples, sculpted tastefully into the shapes of rabbits, contrasted with the revolting manners of the other Japanese guests. But the Captain, with his scratching and belching and seamy talk, outdid them all.

Anglo-American differences were discussed. I made some money giving English lessons to the radio operator. We passed close to Amlia, Atka, Little Tanaga, Kagalaska, Adak and Amatignak Islands, all in the Andreanof Group of the Aleutian Islands. I did not know it at the time, but my trip across the Pacific followed almost exactly the same route as my mother did, when she sailed - west to east - from Yokohama to Victoria, Vancouver Island, with the RMS *Empress of Japan*, on the ship's maiden voyage in August 1930. From the *Yamahime Maru*, we sighted one small boat, and a couple of ships on radar. I had a hair-cut. We just missed the full force of a typhoon. 'Cheered to hear it was only a little one [reads my diary] - just over 50 dead.' As it was, our cargo of timber shifted and we limped into Yokohama with an acute list, on 30 June.

My two companions on the crossing were 'Jack', a very large Japanese, with whom I played drafts; he was going home after two years absence in the USA (I never found out what Jack did for a living); and Professor Heihachiro Honda, returning to Osaka University for Foreign Studies (*Osaka Gaidai*) from Harvard and the University of Washington, after an earlier period at St Andrew's in Scotland, where he taught Japanese poetry in English translation. With the four other Japanese passengers I had no contact at all. At meal times, their joviality was somehow insulated from the rest of us in a very oriental way. With Jack, who was, on the surface, bluff and hearty, one could only have a very shallow conversation. I found out more about his interests after our arrival in Yokohama.

In contrast, Professor Honda was a fascinating and intellectually generous travel companion.

I sat with him for hours, learning all I could pick up from him. He explained his fascination for *Haiku* and the challenges of teaching it in a foreign language. For a whole morning he spoke of the reasons why he felt that *Haiku*, in translation, should not be rhymed. What patience he had! On other mornings, he spoke about the poet Bashō and about Harold G. Henderson, the authority on *Haiku*; about its origins in the *Tanka*; about the *Renga* (composed by two persons), and the separation of the first verse or *Hokku* of 17 syllables. I was in the land of dreams. The Professor told of his particular fondness of a *Senryu* of Takuboku on a traditional theme:

> More loathsome than the ugly leech
> That takes delight in man's blood is
> A lovely maiden whom no speech
> Will cause to offer me a kiss.

He also wrote down for me a sonnet which he had composed in English – with a difference: it has only one word in each line. It is the story of a little girl, sobbing because of her father's anger at rising prices. It is entitled: 'Japanese Girl's Lament'.

> 'Why
> Do
> You
> Cry?
> Pie
> Grew
> Too
> High,
> Beer
> So
> Dear,
> Lo,
> Mad
> Dad!'

On June 29, the day before we anchored in Yokohama, I borrowed the Captain's typewriter to copy out the following allegorical poem which I had drafted overnight for Professor Honda, in inadequate appreciation of the days which had gone before. How dated it now seems – but then this did all take place over 50 years ago:

One Old Man

An old man sits in an old arm-chair:
His hands are clasped and his feet are bare.
His thoughts are those of the albatross,
Who glides alone o'er the wake, across
The same dark sea, to his fate resigned.
Then three young birds flutter through his mind:
Two bright-beaked puffins and one white gull.
The sea is calm but the wind is full.
The albatross with the old man's eyes
Now takes a look through the birds' disguise.
The sea-gull (well does he know by sight)
Will soar high up then on sea alight
At one choice spot, gobble up his meal,
Again rise high, naturally feel
Secure, his technique infallible;
To him, puffins are not feasible:
Down there they splash in their clumsy fun;
Have they no plans? method? – They have none.
Yet, 'muddle on' is their life-long game.
Of each the albatross knows the name.
Sea is calm and wind begins to die.
Three young birds...One old man breathes a sigh.

TRANS-SIBERIAN

After disembarking in Yokohama, I arrived in Tokyo on a Saturday, booked in at the *Toganeya Ryokan* near Ueno Station and became a tourist for a few days. Jack from the *Yamahime Maru* took me in hand. We went up the Tokyo Tower for a panoramic view of the city. We took in temple after temple, travelling everywhere on the Metro. We visited the Golden Pavilion in Kyoto, staying at the *Izuyasu Ryokan*, and the *Todai-ji* complex in Nara. And, when evenings approached, Jack took me to night-clubs; the first time was fine; the second time was alright. On the third occasion, I carefully asked Jack if he shouldn't be spending more time with his wife and child. Jack replied (after a three-year absence in the USA) that he hadn't been home yet: 'family rife can wait' (or words to that effect). After that I made my own programmes.

I also had more serious business to attend to: I still had no visa for Siberia.

I presented myself at the Embassy of the USSR in Tokyo as soon as I could, *and* on the following day *and* the day after that. Had they heard from Comrade B. in Ottawa? I also visited the Japanese Travel Bureau to discuss the Yokohama-Nakhodka section. I was kindly received at the British Embassy by Sir Herbert de Vere Redman, Counsellor, another contact of David Brower in Vancouver. During my third visit to the Russians, a consular officer told me to return that afternoon as my file had been located. I had a distinct impression that Sir Herbert may have somehow oiled the machinery. Suddenly, I had my visa, and not a moment too soon. A few days later, the SS *Alexandr Mozhaisky*, of the USSR Far-Eastern State Steamship Line, sailed for Siberia: and I was on board! As I embarked, I was handed a leaflet which told me I was in Class 3, cabin n° 316, table 52, meal sitting n° 1.

One of the first people I met on board was Miss Ogai Olga, the librarian, who told me something of the fascinating history of her ship. Originally named the *Patria*, she had been launched in 1916 from a Dutch shipyard in Vlissingen, and, for 16 years from 1919, she plied the routes from Holland to the Dutch East Indies. In 1935, she was sold to the USSR, and became the naval training ship *Svir*, which was sunk in the Baltic in the early war years. Subsequently raised from the seabed, repaired and reconditioned in Wismar, she was given a new lease of life, renamed *Alexandr Mozhaisky*, on the Vladivostok-to-Petropavlovsk/Kamchatka, and Nakhodka-to-Nagajewo routes. In 1961 the ship was transferred to the new Nakhodka-to-Yokohama route, and I was one of her very first passengers. Olga could not tell me why the good ship had GLASGOW on her wheel. Alexandr Mozhaisky was the name of a Russian naval officer turned aviation pioneer (1825–90), who was said to have got some of his earliest ideas for heavier-than-air craft, from watching albatrosses in flight.

I began to see all Comrade B.'s efforts on my behalf in a new light...

Most of my fellow passengers were on their way to a World Youth Forum in Moscow which was to start later in July. The others included sundry Russians, returning home to various parts of Siberia; Duncan Thomson, an Australian, who had also discovered a cheap new way back to Europe (the trip from Nakhodka to Moscow cost me US$99): we have remained close friends ever since; and Chiyoko Sasaki. Chiyo had had a complicated history. Her foster parents in Moscow had given her a Russian name: Marina. Her speciality was Slavonic languages and she was travelling this time at the invitation of the government of Czechoslovakia. I was to see her again under very unusual circumstances.

As we approached the port of Nakhodka, the loudspeaker announced in Russian, Japanese and English, that lunch would be served at the normal time. However, a dozen or so Russian soldiers were seen boarding the ship from a launch which had obviously been recommissioned for official use. Lunch was an hour and a half late, and there wasn't much left for us passengers.

After we had docked, all my attention was on Jan Solecki's little shed, which I had spotted about 200 metres away. After nominal immigration procedures I was the first passenger ashore and the first to run through the door of the shed. Several others – Jan had been quite correct – sprinted after me. I had roubles and vouchers ready and soon held the hard class ticket in my hand. As I left the shed, a woman in her 40s came up and said, in one breath:

'Hello are you English I am an English teacher what a coincidence I am going to Moscow too...' It was exactly as Jan Solecki had predicted.

Then she saw what I was holding and became quite angry. Only later did Svetlana introduce herself, saying that she was travelling to the Ukraine to meet her husband.

A bus took us to the station and, mid-afternoon on July 15, the first train drew out of Nakhodka and was soon circling the approaches to Vladivostok (then closed to foreigners), and heading north-east along the Ussuri river (the Chinese call it the *Wusuli*). We stopped – but could not disembark – at Artem, Ussuriysk, Spassk Dal'niy and Bikin, arriving the following morning at Khabarovsk. Here, Nikolai, a schoolmaster, took over from Svetlana for the day. Nikolai insisted that I leave my rucksack in a hotel while he took me for a hike around the city. We saw the frugal sights of a Far Eastern Soviet city, dropped two postcards into a postbox (as I had been asked to do by the British Embassy in Tokyo; one to them and one to their colleagues in Moscow), and had an ice-cream in a people's park.

I had been taking pictures with my venerable Zeiss camera, and was in the habit of re-wrapping the exposed film in the silver paper provided, and labelling the boxes. When I got back to the hotel to shower and pick up my luggage, I found that someone had rifled my belongings and removed all the films from their boxes, unwrapped them, and stuffed them back into the boxes without re-wrapping them – except for one film taken in Japan: this had

Chiyo Sasaki with the Wrestler, Moscow, 1961.

disappeared. Nikolai was not a good actor - and I remembered his awkward insistence that I leave my rucksack behind in the hotel room; he quite clearly knew that the rucksack was to be searched.

Later, I boarded the Trans-Siberian proper, drawn by a steam engine which (judging by a fading slide-image) was a war-time model manufactured by Baldwin of Pennsylvania. I again contacted Svetlana, who was still glum, and made the acquaintance of the chief train guard (which Jan had advised me to do - and a very good piece of advice this turned out to be). Svetlana and I travelled the whole way back to Moscow together: I was at the back of the train; she was up at the front, next to the massive, coal-burning locomotive. I learned, as time went on, that hard class was actually more comfortable than soft class, quite apart from the fact that dear Svetlana could not crowd me. I was furnished with a straw palliasse which was clean, comfortable and stable; in soft class, one tended to bounce and sway. The steam and soot, in any event, made classes immaterial; and we were all, very soon, very dirty.

The train set off punctually at 12.40 p.m. A timetable gave the times of arrival and departure at the 70 railway stations on the route across the USSR. The train duly arrived and departed exactly on time at all the stations - with one exception. We were in Birobidzan for five minutes; Arkhara for 12 minutes; Magdagachi for ten minutes...

At every stop, there were two stone busts - Lenin and Stalin - as well as a large clock with Moscow time, and a kiosk where one could buy a *pirozhok* (pie) or a boiled egg. There was a large samovar in every carriage, from where one could draw tea at any time, though plain boiling water was difficult. I added my Nescafé to the tea and was soon doing a brisk business with my new comrades (thanks, again, to Jan!). I was able to dispose of the flash-gun (which didn't fit the Zeiss), and the flash-bulbs (which didn't fit the flash-gun) quite lucratively. I sold the tobacco and cigarettes during my first hour on the train.

We were in Mogocha for 15 minutes; Chita for 18 minutes. Ulan-Ude (where we saw the railway-line coming up from Peking and Outer Mongolia) 15 minutes. Then we travelled along the southern shore of Lake Baikal and the driver stopped the train so that we could all paddle - for hygiene as much as for pleasure, we suspected (the only period of ten minutes which was not in the timetable); then on round the south-western tip of the lake to Irkutsk (15 minutes).

The exception was Krasnoyarsk, which should have been a full 20 minutes. It was 7.15 in the morning. I waited for Svetlana to catch up (by then she knew *I* knew what she was really up to!) and we hurried down the hill and into the town to buy some postage stamps. We found the post office quite quickly, but, to this day, I do not know what happened then. We returned to the station in very good time, but the train wasn't there. First we thought we had gone to the wrong platform; but this was not the case. Svetlana burst into tears. And then we heard the squealing of brakes being applied quite a distance away, and guessed that it was our train stopping.

The chief train guard, Oleg, with whom I had enjoyed generous slugs of vodka for the last four nights, noticing I wasn't in my carriage, had run down the length of the train to see if I was with Svetlana. Seeing that she wasn't there either, he pulled the emergency cord. The train was about a kilometre away, and Svetlana and I stumbled along the sleepers until we reached it and clambered on board. Nobody said a thing. That evening, Oleg was there as usual; it was he who volunteered, with a grin on his face, how far we had run down the tracks. Poor Svetlana, who obviously thought she had really blotted her copybook, never came down the train again and refused all further invitations to join me for the post office excursions.

My precious Russian transit visa was valid for 12 days; I would have been nine days on the Trans-Siberian; the next train was only due in three days time and I still needed at least 48 hours to leave the Soviet Union. I had been very lucky indeed not to have been left behind. Actually, the postcard exercise worked remarkably well: my mother Gwynneth received four, postmarked Nakhodka, Khabarovsk, Tyumen and Kirov.

Then it was Novosibirsk and Omsk. At Sverdlovsk (18 minutes), we began to cross the Urals into European Russia. We took the north-west line to Perm, Kirov, where I had a full 27 minutes to get to the post office, and Büy, before turning south for Yaroslav and Moscow. As soon as we reached Yaroslavsky station in Moscow (at 10.25 a.m.), Svetlana found a phone box and I heard her say, 'OK, he is here. What shall I do now?' The answer was obviously 'Nothing,' as she nodded and walked briskly out of my life, handing me the receiver as she went past. I phoned the British Embassy to tell them that I had arrived and was heading for Finland, where no visas were necessary. The person I talked to was not greatly interested. I felt, after the incident at Krasnoyarsk, that I should keep going, and immediately headed on foot to the central office of Intourist, to buy train tickets to Helsinki.

As I left Intourist, I walked slap into Chiyo Sasaki, whom I had met on the trip to Nakhodka. She was with an enormous Russian. Chiyo had flown direct from Khabarovsk. She seemed to be as surprised as I was. But was it really a chance meeting? Greetings were strangely muted, until I realised how dirty I must have appeared. After nine days on a steam train and only a cat-lick in Lake Baikal, I was revoltingly begrimed.

The large Russian, who turned out to be a heavyweight wrestling champion (he was looking after Chiyo, after she had hosted him in Japan at an international sports meeting the previous year) said one word : ' *Vannaya*' which, I knew full well, meant 'bathroom' – and I wasn't going to argue with him; so we all trooped off to the municipal baths, where a formidable woman ordered me to undress and take a shower. After a quick swim and feeling much more presentable, I donned my last change of clothing, rejoined Chiyo and her king-sized friend, and spent a most enjoyable (and now more convivial) day with them, before heading to Leningradsky station for the departure to Helsinki. My diary records that the train left at 22.20, and arrived the following day at 18.35. In Helsinki, I headed for the YMCA for a few hours solitude and some real sleep.

Those nine days on the Trans-Siberian had been worth a guinea a minute, and I had met some very special people. Particular events stand out. The debate I had one evening with Konstantin, a student/soldier/member of the Young Communist League. There were copious amounts of vodka and Georgian cognac on hand and a number of the other passengers in our carriage crowded into my compartment to join in the fun. We rather ambitiously agreed to address the differences between capitalism and communism. '*Ya Kommunist*' began

Konstantin (I am a Communist). 'I accept that,' said I; '*Ya Kapitalist* (I am a capitalist). 'Oh no you are not,' retorted Konstantin, and that was as far as we got. He simply could not imagine that he was sitting together with a stereotypical 'capitalist hyena'. Everyone started talking at once, and we all stayed around that makeshift table, chatting, and drinking to 'Peace and Friendship' until there was not a drop left in any of the bottles.

A game of chess with Alye, a beautiful blonde with a trim figure, who always wore trousers. I could not understand why not one of my fellow passengers seemed interested in her – until the train guard took me to one side and confided that 'Russians are apt to lose the thin ones in bed.' Neither of us was very good at chess, and, on one occasion, played down to three pieces on the board: my king and queen, and her king. I chased her around the board for a bit, and then (playing the gentleman) said, 'Shall we call it a draw?' Later that evening, I overheard Alye telling someone that she had won that game, and reminded her that it had been a draw. She countered with, 'You wanted to stop!'

And an occasion when I was trying to take a picture with my Zeiss. I was actually holding it out of the window as the panes of glass were opaque with smut, when someone came up behind and tried to dislodge it from my grasp. Once again, Oleg the guard came to my rescue, told the man (whom I had never seen before) to back off, and advised me, in the man's presence, to be more careful when I was using my camera. 'You were trying to photograph the bridge,' accused the man. 'I didn't see a bridge,' said I. 'We were going over it,' retorted the man. My friend shook his head knowingly as if this sort of thing happened all the time.

BACK TO THE HIVE

Yes, it had been quite an adventure. I had crossed Canada, the Pacific Ocean, the vastness of the USSR, and reached Helsinki: I was back in the 'Free World'. But Helsinki was still a long way from Jersey.

The next morning, I checked in at the British Embassy. I had taken stock of my financial state, which was considerably alleviated by my discovery of a 5,000 Yen banknote in my rucksack. But flying home was out of the question. Later in the day, I went back to the Embassy as it was difficult to find anybody who spoke English. I still wasn't certain how to get home. Someone in the commercial section gave me a lesson in lateral thinking: hiking was out of the question (between 2,500 and 3,500 km, depending on the route); bicycling too; I did not have enough money to buy a second-hand car, nor even a second-hand motorcycle; so, what about looking for a second-hand moped? The helpful Attaché gave me a list of businesses where I might find one.

I did indeed find exactly what I wanted – or so it appeared at the time. My diary continues:

26 July: To motor bike dealer after Finnish Licensing Bureau. Eventually bought machine [cost: 1545.- Finnmarks]. Magneto trouble.

27 July: Walked to collect machine from garage. Bought ferry ticket.

28 July: Packed up. Just caught [Helsinki to Stockholm] ferry at 2. Violently ill between Helsinki and Turku. Slept on luggage rack.

29 July: Arrived about 9. Set off. Lots of trouble with plug, etc. Eventually reached Norrköping. Dance Hall. Birgitta. Slept on floor chez Jeremy Wells. [This referred to a bizarre evening spent with Jeremy, whom I met at the railway station. He lent me a pair of trousers to go with him to a dance at a *Folkets Park*. He was quite small and his trousers were very short on me. Birgitta was the drummer's girlfriend.]

30 July: Left 11 a.m. Machine conked completely (magneto) between Linköping and Mjölby. Night at hotel.

And I had hardly started. It wasn't going well – and it got worse. In between short periods when it functioned, I pushed and pedalled the wretched machine; I heaved it on to goods wagons and trucks and ferries (from Helsingfors to Elsinore and Gedser to Grossenbrode). And somehow we made it to Copenhagen. The moped seemed to like Copenhagen, and I did too. I found a students' hostel – a large friendly house, covered in Virginia Creeper, where I met Irja, who had located a hole in the fence at the Tivoli Gardens, obviating the entrance fee. We went there for two nights and had a lot of (cheap) fun. There was only one problem: on the first night, I got on to the last tram, but it was going the wrong way, and by the time I had walked back to the hostel, the doors were locked; and, by the time I got in, there was someone else in my bed. I should have gone by moped! Taking its revenge, it seemed, the machine started to play up again, the moment I left Copenhagen.

Having changed my 5,000 Yen in Hamburg and my last Can$10 in Maalbroeck, I somehow coaxed the moped down to Normandy, where it finally gave up the ghost. Luckily I was only a few miles from some old friends, the Comte and Comtesse de la Boutresse at St Romain de Colbosc (she was a cousin of Antoine de St Exupéry). They let me stay for a few days and do some work on their estate, for which I was generously recompensed. My companion gardener was a large Norman who sank a tumbler of Calvados every breakfast. It was from Grosmesnil that I first phoned my mother in Jersey. She wasn't too pleased, but, very sweetly, took the ferry to St Malo to pick me up. The hospitality at Grosmesnil had made me feel like a *Petit Prince*.

It was good to get home; but travel had somehow become a way of life. I recalled one of the *Haiku* stanzas which Professor Honda had taught me, and which I had inscribed in many a visitors' book while I was in Japan. It is by Bashō, on the occasion of his leaving the home of Toyo, one of his pupils, near Nagoya.

Japanese: *Botan-shibe|fukaku| wake-izuru| hachi-no| nagori| kana*

Literally: Peony-pistil | deeply | part-and-go-out | bee's | reluctance | *kana*

Translated by Henderson, with his characteristic rhyming of the first and third lines, which Professor Honda frowned upon:

Out comes the bee
from deep among peony pistils –
oh, so reluctantly!

ORIENT EXPRESS

In May 1962, I had returned from a Spanish course in Málaga and spent some months living with an old friend in a flat in Southampton Row.

Penton Lewis and I enjoyed having cocktail parties and got into the habit of inviting the Cultural Attachés of sundry embassies in London to add spice to the proceedings. We didn't continue this for long as we began to sense that certain Eastern European representatives were taking an undue interest in us. The Cold War was, so to speak, heating up; 1962 was the year of the Cuban missile crisis. We did, however, meet some fascinating diplomats from other countries, including Minou Hamidi, who worked for the Cultural Attaché at the Iranian Embassy; she was full of fascinating snippets of information about the Persian empire. Her family was from Shiraz, 'city of poets, wine and flowers', birthplace of the two famous Persian poets, Hafez and Sa'di, and famous for its inlaid handicrafts.

Minou's enthusiasm was infectious and, with my interest in Iran growing, I resolved to take some time, if possible, to get to know her country. I had two enormous strokes of luck: I had managed to land a job as an overseas trainee at the Bank of London & South America (BOLSA); and there was sufficient time between my resignation from the Chartered Bank and my commencement with BOLSA to pay a visit to Iran. Not only that: I also found an unpaid position at the British Institute of Persian Studies in Teheran for the duration.

The day of my departure dawned, and I flew to Paris and caught the Simplon-Orient Express to Istanbul, with a bunk in a second class sleeping-car through Switzerland as far as Milan, where there was a change of train. I travelled across northern Italy and into Yugoslavia, stretching my legs at Milan, Trieste and Belgrade. As the train was approaching the Bulgarian border, there were two terrible earthquakes in Skopje (three minutes apart: 6.1 and 8.5 on the Richter Scale). Nobody on the train knew anything about them.

Skopje is down the branch line at Nis, towards Thessalonika, and we were in no danger. Nevertheless, the quakes killed over

1,000 people, seriously injured over 3,000 and made three-quarters of the local population homeless. There were also rumours that a train-load of passengers was missing: in fact, some empty carriages had been buried in the destruction of the city's main station. This caused some consternation at home until I wrote my mother a hurried note from Nusaybin, on the Syrian border, reassuring her.

My only real problem was at Plovdiv in Bulgaria. I had left the train and crossed a square outside the station to buy some *pirozhkis*, boiled eggs, chocolate and a bottle of beer from a kiosk, negotiating in my rusty Russian. Suddenly I heard the departure whistle of the train and ran for it, catching my moccasins in some tram tracks, wrenching both ankles, and flinging the precious shopping all over the road, but, miraculously, smashing only the chocolate bar. How I got back on to that train I will never know.

Excitement increased as we crossed the Turkish border at Uzunköprü...

...Every gal in Constantinople
Lives in Istanbul, not Constantinople...

TAURUS EXPRESS

I had travelled on the Orient Express from Paris to the Bosphorus. Fixing up the next stage of the trip down to Baghdad was not easy and there was no time to see the sights of Istanbul; but I slept well at the *Büyük Emperyal Oteli*. Having taken a ferry across the Straits to the extraordinary, German-built, neo-classical station of Hydarpasa, I could not at first find anyone there who spoke English or French or Spanish. My Turkish was non-existent. I tried out some phrases from Hawker's *Written and Spoken Persian* which I had with me, but it was no use. Then I had a stroke of luck. I met a young Iraqi of Turkish stock who was returning to Kirkuk to try to recover some of his family's assets, confiscated during political upheavals. Ziya was reluctant to associate with other Iraqis as

69

he did not want to be recognised. He was very happy to have a companion for the trip, and he spoke French. Courtesy of the *Kompani Enternasyonal de Vagonli*, we travelled together in a double compartment all the way to the Syrian-Iraqi border at Tel Kotchek.

The Taurus Express bumped along – often at not much more than walking pace – east along the north shore of the Bay of Izmit to Sapanca before turning south and then east again, around the site of Gordium (where Midas ruled and Alexander cut the Gordian Knot), then sadly reduced to featureless ruins, and on to Ankara. There was no time to leave the train before we were off again east and south, traversing the Cappadocian uplands, and descending through the 'Cilician Gates'. Strictly speaking, we did not go through this narrow 'Corridor of History', which the German railway engineers had been unable to negotiate in the early 1900s: what they constructed instead was a series of spectacular tunnels and viaducts which led us down to Adana (mentioned by name in the *Epic of Gilgamesh* and identified with the birthplace of St Paul).

We dipped in and out of Syria at Muslimiya (not quite to Aleppo), through the scrawny desert, along the northern border of Syria to Nusaybin and across its north-east corner to Tel Kotchek. A rickety bus then carried us across the Tigris and down to Kirkuk in Southern Kurdistan. As we drove into the city, Ziya became very nervous; this was, after all, his home turf, and there were armed soldiers everywhere. The bustle, however, was such that nobody recognised him and we transferred back into a train, drawn by a steam locomotive, for our final push to Sharaban (written in the timetable as Qaraghan), across the Diyala (a tributary of the Tigris), and into Baghdad.

It had been a gruelling journey and I was extremely happy to have a travelling companion. We took a room together in the two-star Middle East Hotel, not unlike – I have always imagined – Agatha Christie's 'Tio Hotel' in *They Came to Baghdad.*

Things were not good. One could tell that conversation was stilted even if one understood not a word. One of the first things I saw was a body hanging from a lamp-post. In a letter to my mother dated 1 August 1963, I noted:

70

...this is the most uncertain, unhappy, chaotic place that I have ever seen. Nobody smiles and nobody is polite or trusts anyone... Tanks and machine guns are guarding strategic points and there are soldiers everywhere with Russian-made sten-guns. All the army transports are also Russian. Headlines in the Arabic newspapers proclaimed today that another 21 people were executed yesterday. Nobody really knows why and most are past caring... The danger still lies in the trigger-happy young members of the Army and National Guard who (for the time being anyway) support Arif... At the moment a swing to the West is under way – Communists (and nobody really knows what a Communist is) are... being shot by Russian guns.

Only five years before, the King of Iraq had been overthrown and executed by the Free Officers movement, led by Brigadier General Abd al-Karim Qasim, who soon had himself made Prime Minister and Minister of Defence. After the King had gone, Communism flourished. Qasim's position was weakened when Kurdish separatists chose to wage war against the central authority; it was at this time that Ziya's family's property in Kirkuk was confiscated. Qasim lost further stature when he laid claim to Kuwait, but had to stand down when the British came to its rescue. (Things were so uncomplicated in those days!) In February 1963 (five months before my arrival in Baghdad) the Ba'ath Party under the above-mentioned General Arif, with the hidden involvement of the CIA, unseated and executed Qasim, and it was at this time that Saddam Hussein returned from exile in Egypt and became head of the country's secret service. Executions of opponents continued for months.

Ziya only wanted to go out at night as he was very wary of being recognised, and the daytime heat was oppressive. We spent our time at roadside stalls by the Tigris, eating delicious lamb kebabs, or beef with dried fruit to be followed by *mamounia* (wheat pudding); drinking pomegranate, date or lemon juice, visiting his relations and going to cinemas. Government offices were not functioning.

After about a week of unnerving anarchy, Ziya helped me buy a bus ticket to Teheran, a trip which was to take 36 hours. He had to return to Kirkuk. We said a heartfelt goodbye. The crowded vehicle left Kadimain (a northern suburb of Baghdad) at 4.45 a.m., 45 minutes late, as many of the passengers did not realise they were going abroad and had to go and get their passports; a surprising number, I felt, *had* passports. I missed Ziya's company and found that, even after crossing the Iranian border, just past Khanaqin, my *Written and Spoken Persian* still didn't get me very far.

I have two particular memories of that trip. One was the cold: I had not been prepared for the Zagros mountains of Iranian Kordestan - the road went up to 2,650 m at a place called Avaj. The other was Abdul.

From a letter to my mother, posted from Teheran 11 August 1963:

> There was a man sitting in the wide back-seat complete with family (large numbers of children and women who might easily have been his wives or his daughters or his aunts or his grandmothers under their cover-all black shrouds) and this man's name was Abdul. On several occasions the whole of the bus's hindquarter dissolved into tears when Abdul was left behind, and my memories of Abdul, tearing frantically after the departing bus in his flowing robes and cap (which never stayed on) are hilarious. I cannot remember a stop where nobody was left behind, but Abdul, who was quite happy where he was - wherever he was - was the worst offender...

I arrived in Teheran on August 6, 14 and a half days after leaving Paris. The price of the bus ticket was the best £3 I ever spent. And the road had been spectacular. My first few days in the city were spent with some new Arab friends, some of whom I had met on the bus. I was hampered by three public holidays ('Republic Day? Mahommed's Birthday and one for luck') and could not check in at the British Institute of Persian Studies. Instead, I found out what young Arab bachelors did when they were on vacation. According to the same letter, 'we led a reasonably abandoned life'.

After I had moved into the Institute, I worked classifying and cataloguing the books in the Institute's library, a dream job; I paid just over £1 a day for accommodation, three meals, laundry (bliss!), scintillating company and a camp bed on the roof of the building. I encountered arcane cross-references among the books and learned journals. For example, the simple tomb of Cyrus the Great at Persepolis, according to Plutarch, once bore the following inscription:

O Man, Whoever Thou Art, and Wheresoever Thou Cometh; for I
Know Thou Wilt Come, I am Cyrus, Who Founded the Empire of
the Persians. Grudge me not, Therefore, This Little Earth that
Covers my Body...

I was invited to accompany Brian Spooner, the director, on
expeditions to survey archaeological remains prior to their
being flooded as a result of the construction of new dams. We
visited and toured Samiran (already partly submerged by waters
above a new dam at Manjil, just past Qasvin); and Karadj, 96 km
from Teheran, where the completed dam, officially opened by
the Shahanshah nine months previously, was smaller but more
spectacular. We were royally entertained on both occasions
by the construction staff. Our host at Karadj had been the
author of a thesis at Utah State University, on the economic and
sociological aspects of the High Dam; he had, however – at least
on this occasion – completely overlooked archaeology, and it was
Brian's job, under considerable time pressures, to put this right.

AFGHANISTAN

I was sad to take leave of my friends at the British Institute
of Persian Studies, in Teheran, but a new ambition was taking
shape: to reach Bokhara in Turkmenistan and still get home
in time for my new job in London. It was one of the silliest
decisions of my life to set off on such a trip with no preparation,
but I would not have missed it for all the pomegranate juice
in Asia!

Still feeling sore (stiffness and sunburn) from climbing Mount
Demavend with two engineer friends, I set off by train to Mashhad,
926 km to the east of Teheran, known as the holiest city in the
country, and site of the Shrine of the Imam Reza, as well as a
modern memorial to the poet Ferdowsi. En route, I met a charming
man who was travelling home with his family. Mehdi Behravanfar
invited me to tour his spare-parts shop, and took me to a farewell
party for someone. Communication was not easy, but I was treated so
hospitably that, in an idle moment, and in view of the journey I
was starting out on, I felt rather lightheadedly that the gathering

73

might have been for me. Mehdi also provided a bed, insisting that there were no hotels suitable for foreigners in Mashhad.

At 6 o'clock the following morning I hitched a lift in a 1950s Kenworth oil-tanker which was heading down to Kandahar. Driver Ali had picked me up from Mehdi's house at 04.30 in his jeep. He had shaved since the night before, when we had first met at the benzine station, and was, at first, difficult to recognise. We drove to a shop in the suburbs to pick up provisions. Noticing that Ali had purchased nothing, I left the place with two bars of chocolate, a tin of sardines and two rather doubtful lamb sandwiches. Half an hour and one lamb sandwich later, after Ali had collected an old coat and said goodbye to his wife, we found ourselves back at the benzine station.

I checked that my rucksack was strapped securely inside the spare tyre on top of the tanker, and climbed into the cab between Ali and his co-driver who was, I am convinced, deranged. They were both small, stocky, dark and moustachioed. Driver Ali had an open, kindly expression, in contrast to the shifty, underhand and treacherous attitude struck by the Afghan, who carried a large knife and flourished it constantly. I never found out the man's name.

Ali's ready smile and tuneless, cheerful singing was a fortunate counter to the co-driver's ready temper and tuneless, cheerless snoring: we were both happiest when he was asleep.

I had agreed to split the incidental travelling costs and, after I had paid the nominal 30 *tooman* semi-official bribe to a superintendent at the benzine station, driver Ali started the engine, ground through a very intricate and fierce sequence of gears, and off we bumped.

It was midday, the sun was high, and we were shuddering and surging along the corrugated dirt road towards Afghanistan. The rough features of this plain, bounded by distant hills, gave the impression that we were proceeding down the centre of a vast valley, hot and dusty and still, punctuated by little conical whirlwinds and the occasional dromedary. A vulture sat sadly by a white mound of bones; and little, squirrel-like marmots, which – though I wasn't to know this yet – would become much more plentiful on the return journey, scurried to their holes as we drove past. One could almost sense the forlorn heaps of sedimentary rock being fragmented and scattered by the heat.

We spent one night at the frontier as the customs post was not manned when we first approached the barrier. Next morning, after the frontier guards were awake, we crossed the border and banged and rattled along the desert track for three days and two nights, stopping quite frequently to replace burst tyres. There seemed to be an inexhaustible supply of inner tubes, and my rucksack stayed where it was inside the spare wheel.

I lay down on the beaten sand beside the truck, whenever my companions stopped for a snack or a prayer. Although they shut their eyes for an hour or two after sun-down, I was only able to relax when the Afghan started to snore. Feeling thoroughly unwell and unslept, I was not unhappy to say goodbye to them, and climb on to the Ariana Afghan Airlines flight from Kandahar to Kabul on 6 September. I sat next to a large woman in a *chador*, with a trussed-up goat in her arms.

The only accommodation available was in an appalling hotel in the centre of the city near the souk. The latrine was a hole in the floor outside my room. It was hard to believe that there could be any worse smell than that of my neighbour in the airplane. I very quickly learned that Great Britain was not a popular phrase in Afghanistan and, soon after leaving my hotel room for some air, and to pick up my mail from the British Embassy, discovered that the border with the Soviet Union had just been closed: my Bokhara adventure was not to be.

The next six days have since dissolved into a push-me pull-you of conflicting memories. Kabul was obviously a fascinating place to be. Life was totally different to anything I could imagine. In such a short time though, there seemed to be no way that a foreigner, not speaking Arabic, might derive any benefit at all from such an experience. It was a bridge too far... Money and time were running out, as was the film for my trusty Zeiss. I made friends with a Frenchman, Alain, who had been waiting three weeks for a part for his Harley-Davidson so that he could continue his trip to the Far East. We got to know this chaotic city like the back of our hands. We visited the Kabul Museum which housed, among many extraordinary antiquities, haphazardly displayed, some magnificent coins; on show were choice examples of the silver coins of the Khisht-Tepe or Kunduz hoard of 1946.

We were also given a tour of the *Hochtief* plant on the outskirts of Kabul which, as a sideline, used to cut and shape white aragonite-onyx. The King of Afghanistan had ordered a set of butter dishes to be made from this brittle semi-precious stone; one extra had been made in case of mishaps. I persuaded the factory to sell it to me and took it home for my grandmother. She later left it to me in her will (together with a splendid soap-stone carving which I had sent her from Sept Îles in Canada, two years previously).

For those six days I looked for ways to get back to Teheran to pick up the rest of my belongings, before returning to London. Turkmenistan was shut. For some reason there were no flights or buses to Kandahar, and hitch-hiking was not an option. I had wanted to visit Bamiyan and the Khyber Pass, but they were (as I then thought) in the wrong direction. I left little bits of paper stuck on notice-boards and trees all round Kabul: YOUNG MAN, ALL-ROUNDER, SEEKS TO WORK PASSAGE BACK TO UK or words to that effect. And I made a nuisance of myself at the British Embassy.

Bob Allstone, Second Secretary at the Embassy, it turned out, was to be my salvation.

At midday on September 11, I returned to my abominable hotel room to find a note pinned to the door. It was headed OXFORD UNIVERSITY EXPEDITION TO AFGHANISTAN EXETER COLLEGE, OXFORD, ENGLAND:

Dear Mr Mac Maine,

Allstone told me you might like to come with us back to England.
    We want to leave Kabul after supper tonight and I wondered if you have any more preparations to make so that if you should want to come there will not be any delay.
    We will pick you up at 7.00 on the way to supper with Allstone!

(signed) Philip Empedocles

The next seven hours were the longest of my life. But Philip duly arrived at the hotel, and his letter remains a treasured possession.

My job, I found out over a delicious dinner at the Embassy, was to help drive a converted 1944 Austin K2/Y ex-Army Heavy Ambulance (nicknamed 'Katie'), which housed the expedition members, back to England. This was exciting enough. But, I later learned, the expedition had obtained a special permit to travel with a government guide over the northern, desert route and down to Herat before setting course for the UK.

We first drove up to the Khyber Pass to drop off one of the expedition members, Peter Andersen, a medical student, who wanted to travel further east before resuming his studies. It was his change of plan which led to my being employed as driver. Peter simply got out of the vehicle, bid us goodbye and started walking the 65km or so towards Peshawar. His nonchalance – even in those days – was phenomenal.

I could then tick off one of my two unfulfilled ambitions (forgetting about Bokhara). This was to get as close as possible to the mountainous border, on the Afghan side of the military divide, opposite Waziristan, where my father had fought with the 6th Gurkha Rifles in the 1930s. Although we were still some 250km to the north-east, to get as far as the Khyber Pass frontier post was a real bonus.

We then headed back west to a village called Pusht-i Mazar, which lay a few miles east of the Unai Pass. Here we picked up Bob Woodd-Walker, medical officer in charge of collecting and transporting blood specimens, and Habibullah Pazyra, another medical student, together with their equipment, and set off (wonder of wonders!) towards my only remaining unfulfilled ambition: the great Buddhas of Bamiyan, which were to be destroyed by the Taliban in March 2001. How impressive they were! But we could only admire them for 20 minutes.

It took us three days to drive from Bamiyan to Mazar-i-Sharif, and another day to reach Balkh where the other members of the team sang 'Happy Birthday' as we all sat on a carpeted *takht* under the watchful if perplexed eye of the headman of the district. We then needed another five days' continuous driving through the desert of the southern Hazhdanahr to Andkhui and Maimana, around Bala Murghab, to reach Herat and the Iranian border on 23 September.

This part of the trip alone was the experience of a lifetime. Memories include: views of the great White Mountains to the west of the Khyber, rising almost vertically for thousands of metres, somehow contriving to shut out the sunlight above us. This was where Osama bin Laden was to build the *al-Qaeda* ('the base') headquarters at Tora Bora; the vignette of another westerner serenely sketching the statues at Bamiyan from the viewing platform: he did not even look up as we arrived; digging Katie out of the desert sand with the help of two specially made aluminium panels which Philip had prudently added to the provisions; riding on top of Katie with the camera while taking a break from driving; getting hit on the back of the head by a stone from a distant goat-herd's catapult; and waiting for tea with the headman at a village near Andkhui, after we had driven all day

Bamiyan: the Greater Buddha, Afghanistan, 1963.

without seeing a soul, until he asked gently if we would like to take a cup to our sick friend still inside Katie; how could he possibly have known that there was still someone inside the ambulance, and that he was sick? But then, in a land where there was no means of communication whatsoever, he had greeted us with 'Ah. You have arrived,' as if he had known we were coming all along.

After crossing the Iranian border, it was a rush towards home: Teheran, to pick up my things and say farewell to friends at the Institute; Tabriz, Mount Ararat (with a camel grazing decoratively in the foreground - years later I turned this scene into a Christmas card); Erzurum, where we caught a glimpse of the Great Mosque (which was to collapse one year later); and Ankara - where we all had a shower, a haircut and a shave; Istanbul, Xanthi (to avoid Bulgaria as we were driving in what looked like a military vehicle); Belgrade and Trieste - where we paddled in the Adriatic for 20 minutes; and over the St Gotthard (where Katie's brakes failed and I had to drive her on her gears), to Calais and London.

My colleagues' timing was tighter than mine (I still had a good two weeks before I was to start work with BOLSA), so I dropped them off one by one and drove triumphantly down to Bromley, where my two landladies (Miss Brooke and Miss Martin - known collectively as the 'Lesser Spotted Brooke-Martin') soon had a cup of tea ready. Frustratingly, they did not once question the presence of the outlandish and begrimed vehicle which was parked outside 105A Widmore Road.

This journey took place as a result of the infectious enthusiasm of Minou Hamidi, of the Cultural Department at the Royal Iranian Embassy in London, to whom I am extremely grateful.

*   *   *

Both Philip Empedocles and Bob Woodd-Walker went back to Academe. Not long afterwards, Philip was killed in a tragic family altercation. In 1967, Bob, with two colleagues, published 'The Blood Groups of the Timuri and Related Tribes in Afghanistan', which, to my knowledge, is the only other record of this expedition. In 1980, Clare Goff, whom I accompanied to a number of archaeological sites around Teheran, had set herself the task to 'try to crack the mystery of the Luristan bronzes'. She subsequently described her experiences in *An Archaeologist in the Making.*

A VISA FOR PARAGUAY

I went into a shed, set back on dry ground above the Paraná river.

'One return ticket to Paraguay, please.'

'My boat only goes to Paraguay.' No trace of irony.

'Do I need a visa?'

'Just give me your passport.'

He scribbled something on a scrap of newspaper, handed it to me, and pocketed my passport. José was the boatman and self-appointed immigration officer. In spite of the heat, he was wrapped up, incongruously, in a duffle-coat, several sizes too big for him.

'Why are you keeping my passport?'

'Let me put it this way. I am responsible for your security as we cross the river. Your passport will be safer with me. I do not charge you for the trip, because I am not allowed to ferry passengers across the river. So I charge you one dollar for the visa.' He pointed at the scrap of paper in my hand. 'My passengers do not usually have passports, and I do not have a rubber stamp. If someone stops you when we get across, and I have your passport, you will not be troubled to pay a bribe. You will be less tempted to jump out of the boat while I have your passport: people jumping out of my boat only bring me trouble. You will get your passport back when we return this evening. Take it or leave it. One dollar please.'

His Spanish was slow and his logic unassailable, so I gave him a $1 bill. He took it, then, after a pause, looked at me and nodded up at the enormous structure 80 m above us.

'Why aren't you going across the bridge?'

'I was told it is not yet open.'

'It isn't but you can cross it. Only costs a dollar.'

The climb all the way up, through the thick, sub-tropical undergrowth, would not have been worth it, and I opted to go with José. The *Ponte da Amizade* across the Paraná river was to be officially opened by the presidents of Brazil, Argentina and Paraguay three months later.

In a heavy rain-storm, I left the shelter of the shed, sloshed through ankle-deep mud down to the small motor-boat, and clambered in. There were already some 20 passengers with baggage on board, with seating for 12 at a pinch. José joined us, started the outboard motor, and we were off. We were very low in the water and the helmsman told us not to dangle our hands, as they might get bitten. I was unaware, until then, that *piranha* ventured so far south.

It was Christmas 1964. I had arrived in Brazil six months previously, just after the revolution which unseated the left-leaning president Jango Goulart. One of the stories still doing the rounds - my favourite - was that of two Brazilian armies, one from the northern military region and one from the south, which, in the aftermath of this upheaval, found themselves marching towards each other in an aggressive manner, the respective commanders having adopted slightly different political views vis-à-vis the incumbent government. Just before they collided (so the story went), the said commanders ordered a halt and contacted each other by field telephone. The two armies were then ordered to take a course which would ensure that they would continue to march more or less in the same direction, but, at a decent distance, *past* each other.

This story - almost certainly apocryphal - nevertheless illustrates the Brazilian knack for compromise. In fact, it had been a very Latin American sort of revolution. (We had learned all about revolutions in our trainee course.) Some dissident marines and sailors had protested the arrest of the president of their Association and occupied a trade union building. Called upon to surrender, they at first refused; but, when confronted by troops, they immediately did so and were pardoned forthwith. It was when President Goulart refused to reverse this amnesty that military leaders first registered their objections. There were at the time four military regions, each with its own commander. The First Army (in Guanabara, seat of the old capital) supported Goulart; the Second Army (in São Paulo) was against him; and the leanings of the Third Army (in the south) were initially unknown. It was the commander of the Fourth Army in the north-east – in spite of varying opinions among other senior men, (two of which were based firmly in superstition) – who began the march southwards. It was, however, only when Goulart learned that the United States Caribbean Fleet, led by the aircraft carrier *Forrestal*, had its guns trained on Rio de Janeiro, that he faltered; and it was when he received a communiqué that the new government to be set up in Brasilia was already recognised by the USA, that he fled to Uruguay.

Although the immediate effects of the revolution had abated, I felt that my own future in Brazil was still uncertain. It seemed a good time to get to know the country while I still could. Hence this visit to Iguaçu and Paraguay, which was known as a smugglers' paradise. A colleague in the Bank had asked me to bring back a sack full of steel cigarette lighters; and another friend, who knew this part of Brazil well, wanted two bottles of Benedictine.

The trip, so far, had been trouble-free. Our Varig flight had landed four times on its way from São Paulo to Iguaçu, and I had spent one night in the Cataratas Hotel and seen the sights. I remember, particularly, the thunder of the *Garganta do Diabo* ('Devil's Throat') with the myriad butterflies challenging the falls; lizards everywhere, running along with their little bottoms raised; and loitering *coatis*.

The boat was eventually safely beached in a clearing, surrounded by dense Paraguayan jungle. There were a dozen small wooden huts, piled up with every imaginable type of merchandise. One trafficker had dozens – if not hundreds – of bottles of Benedictine on his shelves. I located the man-with-the-cigarette-lighters quite easily. Then I was stuck: nowhere to go, nothing to eat, and nothing to drink – except Benedictine. José had disappeared. I thought of the Christmas pudding I was missing.

Hours later, José reappeared. Still sopping wet from the morning shower, I collected my purchases and made my way wearily down to the boat. The trip back to the Brazilian side started well. It had stopped raining and we were only six passengers. I wondered where the others had gone. Half-way across the river, the boat suddenly started to rock dangerously. At first I didn't see what was going on. Then it became clear that one of the passengers was having an epileptic fit. We all jumped on him and held him in the bottom of the boat. Several bags, including my sack of lighters, went overboard. One could almost sense the snapping of teeth in the opaque waters below. The Benedictine somehow survived.

I very nearly – but not quite – became a consular case myself.

'Next time,' said José sadly, as he handed me back my passport, 'You will be able to take the bridge.'

BANKING

Banking was my profession for 37 years.

Actually, I never was a banker, and never wanted to be one. I was, however, very happy being a bank *employee* and, for many years was fascinated by commercial lending (which spread money around and made things grow) and, in particular, by what are still called documentary letters of credit and the uniform customs and practice for these commercial instruments. I was less taken by asset management.

Banking took me to worlds which I never dreamed existed. Some of them are mentioned in this book. I like to think that travel broadened my mind and – who knows? – helped to groom me for my time as Honorary Consul.

Largely as a result of some very sound advice I received from Wilfred Thesiger, the famous explorer, to whom I had been introduced by my Uncle Ken, a barrister at the Inns of Court, I found a job in the City of London. My first job at the Chartered Bank was escorting the 'clearing' – a bag containing thousands of cheques presented during the day – to the Bank of England, for overnight sorting. Each time, I drew a whistle and a cosh, and, with the cosh tucked up my sleeve and the whistle held ready for blowing, I would be part of a twosome or threesome (depending on the volume of the cheques) which would make its way solemnly along the City pavements and through the portals of the 'Old Lady of Threadneedle Street'.

Simultaneously I was getting acquainted with the Far East and taking Institute of Bankers exams in preparation for a transfer to Burma. This was not to be: in February 1963, the Chartered Bank's Burmese branches were nationalised and collectively became 'People's Bank n° 2'.

At about the same time I began to hear about Sir George Bolton, who had been adviser to the British delegation at the Bretton Woods Conference of 1944, and was becoming known as the creator of the so-called eurodollar market. He had been chairman of the Bank of London & South America (BOLSA) since 1957. Although I had only been with the Chartered Bank for a year, I felt like a change. BOLSA generously agreed to take me on as an overseas trainee. Here, my first job (this is something my computer-savvy sons might not know) was to help with the programming of a 'KDP 10', a version of the RCA 501, which was one of the earliest computers intended for commercial data processing applications. It was manufactured by English Electric and was one of about ten machines sold. The whole contraption occupied an area of about half a tennis-court.

For me, I suppose, romance really began when I boarded the aeroplane for São Paulo in June 1964. It was to be a very long trip, with a stopover in Dakar, Senegal. Twelve trainees had survived the course, which had been given by a retired chief manager from the Bank's Argentinian circuit. Mr Smithson was an old fox who knew all the tricks, and he was a very good instructor. He taught us about banking morals, common-sense lending procedures, and basic guidelines on personal security. He told us of the dangers of drugs, women and venereal disease, religion, politics, police states and what he called the science of bribability. He shared secrets with us about double-entry accounting, letters of credit, the hazards of foreign exchange deals done on the radio telephone, and 'How to be a Millionaire' (in other words, 'inflation banking').

Finally we learned that there were two distinct lessons to be learned about liquidity: one concerned the economics and momentum of money; the other, the drinkability of water. Both these lessons have been of enormous importance to me, though on one occasion, I admit, I did not heed his advice on the latter, and had to live through a serious bout of amoebic dysentery as a result. It was not fun.

Bill Cole, on the travel desk, fixed our tickets, working visas and accommodation. The work-permit question was not as straightforward as it used to be, as countries like Brazil were beginning to erect barriers against foreigners who were seen to be occupying jobs which would otherwise have gone to natives. In fact, I only received my *Carteira 19* (identity card for foreigners) 15 months after I had arrived in Brazil. Bill was famous for asking each trainee one particular question: he would surreptitiously slide open a drawer and take out a box of bullets: 'Would you find space in your suitcase to take these out to so-and-so in Brazil/Argentina/Ecuador (choose a country)?' Rumour had it that this was a trick question: anyone who answered yes would fail the course.

My 11 companions were going out to various countries in Latin America. We had to be able to speak adequate Spanish or Portuguese before we left.

Patrick and I were going to Brazil; Keith, John, Richard and the others were going to Spanish-speaking destinations. We were all elated by our prospects. Our excitement was well founded: some weeks after arrival, I heard that Keith (with whom I had shared a house in Bromley) had been arrested in Comodoro Rivadavia in Southern Argentina, for having ridden a horse up the steps of the local police station. As there was no room in the cells, they detained him in the basement, where he turned all the taps on, shouted FLOODS! and walked out in the chaos which ensued. Keith, who had transferred across from the Chartered Bank, as I had, was always a bit of an anarchist.

John returned to his flat after a night out in Buenos Aires shortly after arriving. He opened the door of his apartment and saw someone going through his belongings. He pluckily charged at the man, and was shot in the back by a second robber who was standing behind the door. The bullet went right through him, somehow missing all his vital organs, and lodged in his wallet. He was back at work within three weeks.

Richard soon left BOLSA and the last I heard of him was when he was living and working in Tegucigalpa. I have never forgotten a story he once told me about his father, Edgar James Joint, who had been H.M. Ambassador to Colombia in the late 1950s: he was once reprimanded by the Foreign Office for speaking Spanish *too well.*

My own adventure, on arrival in Brazil, was more commonplace. We landed at the airport in what I thought was São Paulo, and I made for the nearest telephone kiosk, wanting to try out my new language. I dialled the number of Peter Oates, staff manager in São Paulo, and a seductive female voice said, 'Yes, dear, how can I help you?' I stuttered on with my elementary Portuguese. The voice then said, 'Come on, dear, don't be shy.' Then Patrick came up and said, 'Didn't you know? This is Rio.' By dialling the São Paulo number from the airport in Rio de Janeiro, I had somehow got through to a local brothel.

The first piece of mail I received at my new address in Santos was from John Hope, my other former flat-mate in Bromley, who stayed with the Chartered Bank and was posted to North Borneo during the so-called *Konfrontasi* between Indonesia and Malaysia: he sent me a postcard 'from under a taxi in Jesselton'. These were exciting times.

It was during my first week in Santos that I had a strange premonition of consular life. Paul Hawkins, a new friend, took me down to the dock area to show me 'the pub with the two bullet holes in the ceiling'. This was where a drunken German seaman had felled a policeman, who, while still lying on the floor, took out his gun and fired two shots into the ceiling. Two of his colleagues arrived and, without hesitation, 'extinguished' the culprit. I remember thinking: What happens now? Though I didn't know it at the time, Angelika and her sister, Ingrid, both used to work in the West German Consulate in Santos.

Just as I had wished, for much of my life in banking I became involved in international trade and commerce. There was coffee in Santos; dyes, nuts, jute, rubber, skins, woods and all sorts of other tropical products in Amazonas; cotton in Bahia; every conceivable finished product in São Paulo. Then came a short stint as Sir George Bolton's PA, and a few months in Spain.

From the BOLSA representative office, during our first posting to Zürich, I kept a track of reciprocity, worldwide, with banks and industrial companies in Switzerland, Germany, Austria and The Netherlands. There were building products, heavy equipment, snow-ploughs, textile machinery and watches from Switzerland to Latin America, Eastern Europe and the Middle East; lamb from New Zealand to Iran. Then came Portugal with its jewellery, Port Wine, textiles and shoes, as well as the special circumstances of the Carnation Revolution (see below). Finally we were transferred back to Zürich with Lloyds Bank (which had, by then, taken over BOLSA).

Lloyds Bank Zürich was a founder member of the Association of Forfaiting Institutes in Switzerland, which was behind the trade in 'without recourse paper' - a fascinating and very successful trading device, creating liquidity for exporters, until some traders got careless, and the USSR and its satellites began to abuse the system.

Essentially, a bank connects people who *have* credit, with people who *need* credit. Traditionally, deposits offset loans, with capital and reserves being held in the background for a rainy day. Following the messy bankruptcy of a large German bank in 1974, a set of minimal capital requirements was eventually set up by the Basel Committee on Banking Supervision in 1988, with a view to the protection of creditors. These requirements, known as 'Basel 1', were expanded, after subsequent banking scandals, into new guidelines called 'Basel 2' and, most recently, 'Basel 2.5'. Basel 3 is due in 2019. Sadly, common sense has become a concept of the past, and minimum capital requirements have now become mandatory.

Lloyds Bank in Switzerland had its own problems. In August 1974, shortly after I had been transferred to Portugal, a £32 million foreign exchange fraud was uncovered at the Lugano branch of the Bank. This was followed by another large internal fraud, this time in the Far East. The Bank very wisely instituted a new post of 'conformity' (later, 'compliance') officer at larger branches to combat further fraud attempts or, better still, to endeavour to nip them in the bud. I held that post in Zürich. I took the job very seriously and found that I was becoming rather unpopular: lending officers were being told to expand credit operations; it was my responsibility to rein them in. It was my job, too, to set limits for foreign exchange dealing; the dealers didn't like it at all.

In a later cycle, active lending business diminished, and the Bank moved towards portfolio management. It was then thought

- wrongly, in retrospect - that there was less and less need for a 'policeman', and I eventually took early retirement in 1991. This was followed by a further nine-year stint as accredited representative of Cater Allen Bank, an old-established City Discount House, until its merger with Abbey National and Santander.

Since my early days at BOLSA, when I had worked on the KDP 10, I have always been cautious about computers. As word-processors, they have been of enormous value to me; and the amount of available and accessible information on the Web - even pre-'Wikileaks' - is (for me) hardly conceivable. To use them, however, as instruments of control, as in bank lending, still leaves me uncomfortable, particularly when I know that the infernal machine is running at 100 or 1,000 or 1 million times the maximum speed of (my) human brain. Add to this such things as the theorem of momentum or velocity of money (one sum of money, as opposed to several sums, performing diverse functions simultaneously) - I had become very aware of this since the excellent trainee course - and the factors besetting credit control become labyrinthine. Such basic guidelines as the measurement of reciprocity had gone out of the window.

Volume, in this context, invites generalisations and the cutting of corners. Compound this financial felony by the juxtaposition of two very different organisations: a bank, with no knowledge of computer science, wishing to acquire a computer; and a computer company, with no knowledge of banking, wishing to install it, and the whole process becomes a witches' brew.

While still with Lloyds Bank, I had turned down postings to Monaco (Somerset Maugham's 'sunny place for shady people') and New York. Monte Carlo was easy to refuse: after one visit, I felt I would simply not fit in. New York was more complex. Since the time I worked with Sir George Bolton, I had not been impressed by American attitudes towards credit: the unlimited issue of cash by branches of the Federal Reserve, though not directly related to commercial credit, seemed to be setting a bad example. Fanny Mae and Freddy Mac, as seen from my 'compliance' view-point, seemed to be getting away with murder, and, rightly or wrongly, I did not like the idea of diving into the maelstrom of Wall Street with my preconceptions. I could also see problems of schooling for my four growing sons, particularly in Monaco. But my biggest consideration was that I very much liked living and working in Zürich.

My refusals came at a cost: perks for me as an internationally transferable executive, quite understandably, lapsed. No matter. Had I been anywhere else, such memoirs as these would probably have been still-born.

'Errs on the side of caution' was in one of my Lloyds Bank staff appraisals. I took this as a compliment.

> The early bird may get the worm; but it's the second mouse that gets the cheese.

MANAUS

My earliest experience with consular affairs was in 1965 in Manaus, capital of the State of Amazonas, Brazil, where I was training with the then Manager of the Bank of London & South America (BOLSA), who doubled as British Honorary Consul. In those days of rampant inflation the consular honorarium was six crates of inflation-proof Johnny Walker Black Label Scotch Whisky; this was deemed to be enough for the Consul to keep an eye on the affairs of the United Kingdom, the British Commonwealth and, *de facto*, most Western European members of the EEC and EFTA – a challengingly wide remit for someone who was responsible for such a massive area of the host country: the state of Amazonas alone is more than ten times the size of England and Wales. My Manager, the Consul, was a dour but charming Scot.

A long list of events spring to mind, many of which did not directly concern the Consulate. Most of the incidents were in some way related to the vastness of the land-mass which surrounded us. There was the Brazilian Army cadet who fell off a rope bridge during exercises not far from Manaus. He was swallowed head-first by a giant *piraiba* catfish; both the cadet and the fish were suffocated.

There was the time when Zuleide, my trusty maid, constructed (with my modest financial assistance) a tiny wooden house, and let out half of it to a lady who soon stopped paying the rent. When Zuleide asked me what she should do, I told her she should go round with her large cousin, give her tenant one month's notice, and, if she still didn't pay, she should evict her. What Zuleide did not tell me was that the lady was the girl-friend of the local *Delegado de Policia* (Police Commissioner), and was seven months pregnant.

While having dinner one evening at the only decent restaurant in town, I was approached by a scruffy, bare-foot individual who told me that Zuleide was on the run from the police, and would I please come with him and help her. One of my two dinner companions claimed to know the *Delegado*, and the other went to fetch his gun. The three of us then set off in 'Boadicea', my vintage Land Rover, found Zuleide (who was fast asleep in a hammock in the jungle), and set off for the *Delegado's* house. There, to my horror and embarrassment, my two large friends roused the man, pulled him from his bed and shook him, telling him in no uncertain terms to lay off Zuleide, who subsequently went home and had no more trouble. It was, indeed, the law of the jungle!

'Boadicea' was sold to an American who had been contracted (illegally as it turned out) to trap some Amazonian *cicadas* for an American zoo. The trapper gave me a small deposit and a series of promissory notes in payment. The following week, he was arrested and deported, and I bid goodbye to my money. Some months later, Sergio Gadelha, another brawny friend, raced into my steamy office, and told me he had just seen my Land Rover driving past the Bank. We gave chase in Sergio's Volkswagen, cornered the poor unsuspecting driver, and I witnessed my second Amazonian 'shakedown'. I got my money back, albeit from the wrong man.

These were the early days of the Free Port of Manaus and although much consular business was concerned with notarising documents under the Merchant Shipping Acts, so-called 'protection' work was unavoidable. To illustrate the vast range of consular responsibilities at such a post, three cases are described in the second part of this book, below ('Two Dutchmen', 'A Knifing' and 'Needles in a Haystack'). Seldom was tragedy or comedy very far away. The fact that Brazil was not yet a democracy added its own complications. As an *amuse-bouche*, three personal experiences are recounted here.

MEGASOMA ACTAEON

The *Megasoma Actaeon*, or rhinoceros beetle, is believed to be the heaviest insect on earth. One specimen in captivity has been known to consume almost an entire avocado in one day. Measured with its horn, the male insect can reach 120 mm in length.

At dusk, one balmy Manaus evening in March 1965, the hottest time of the year, I was sitting with a friend on a bench in the Praça São Sebastião, not far from the famous *Teatro Amazonas*. A fossil of the times when the rubber industry in Manaus was at its apogee, this theatre had been built in the 1890s with marble and frescoes brought in from Italy, wrought-iron bannisters from England, and tiles and crystal chandeliers from France.

We were watching the girls promenading by, when I became conscious of a shiny black object, in the middle of the *avenida*, the size of half a cricket ball, which seemed to be moving about on its own. I walked across to have a look and picked up an enormous rhinoceros beetle. It was disoriented, probably because it had collided with something and lost its horn. I resolved to take it to the Salesian nuns' *Museu do Indio*, which in those days had a small but fine exhibition of insects.

With difficulty – I could just get my hand around its upper shell, but the back legs were so strong that they were able to push my fingers away – I took it back to my flat and put it in a cardboard box in the refrigerator; I had no killing jar and could not think how else it could be put out of its misery. The next morning I was walking towards the museum when there was a scratching noise from inside the box, and I like to think that it was telling me it had had the most comfortable night of its life in the cool of the freeze-box. The nuns were very pleased with it and for many years it was by far the largest specimen of the family of *Scarabaeidae* in their collection.

Shortly after making my prize entomological catch, I was detailed to look after the wife of a visiting director of the Bank, who had been a senior diplomat at the British Embassy in Rio de Janeiro. It will become obvious why this good lady must remain nameless. I was a contributing member of the *Atlético Rio Negro Clube* just outside Manaus. *Atlético* implied that there were two scruffy tennis courts; *Rio Negro* referred to a small black tributary of the real thing, which had been dammed and turned into a makeshift swimming pool; and the *Clube* was a single shed, divided into two rooms (for Men and Women) with showers and duckboards, under which a venomous coral snake was prone to take refuge. This was no place for Her Ladyship. In fact, the only suitable place I could think of taking her, in the time we had available, was the nuns' museum, which we duly visited. My charge was, to say the least, very outspoken, but simultaneously she also managed to project extreme boredom. She was embarrassing to be with: the worst possible type of diplomat's wife, who liberally dispensed foul language and other indiscretions on her inferiors. But there was no escape.

My distinguished guest reached the acme of her indelicacy as we entered the area of the Amazonas Indian pottery exhibits, which included some crudely-made human figures in earthenware, exclaiming at the top of her hyperaesthetic voice, 'So, I suppose this is the "64 different positions room..."'

Later, when I proudly pointed out to her my beetle in the insect display-cabinet, she looked at it, and then at me, with an expression of disdain and moved on. I thanked my lucky stars that I had not taken the wretched woman out in a small boat to view the *Encontro das Aguas* ('meeting of the waters') where the black Rio Negro comes together with the brown Solimões: one of us might not have returned.

While speaking Portuguese to the Mother Superior who was hosting our tour, it suddenly occurred to me that she was using her native tongue so as to save me the embarrassment of being reminded that *she also* spoke fluent English, and could understand every word disgorged by my foul-mouthed nemesis. It was a memorable instance of ecclesiastical diplomacy.

That evening, during a cocktail party at the 'Super-Luxo' Hotel Amazonas, the only respectable hotel in town (as was later reported by the social columnist of the local *Jornal do Comercio*), '*muito uisque e da bôa marca*' ('much good whisky') was consumed. In another instance of – this time – Press diplomacy, the name of the person who had consumed most of the good whisky was not mentioned.

RORAIMA

I had intended to spend *Carnaval* 1966 in the Territory of Roraima, at the top of Brazil. In Boa Vista, at the time, there was only one hotel: the Hotel Boa Vista. Lights went out when the generator stopped, shortly after sundown. *Carnaval* was out of sight.

I had met a tough-as-nails but charming cattleman from Tennessee on the flight from Manaus, who had successfully brought 1,000 head of his tropics-hardened Zebu cattle to the savanna of northern Brazil. I knew about the savanna because an old friend, Robert Goodland, had written an article about it – at least about the Rupununi Savanna on the other side of the Guianese border. There were already indications that the spread of cattle-farming southwards marked the beginning of the destruction of the Amazonian Rainforest. My new American buddy drove me up to the border with British Guiana and showed me around. *Carnaval* was out of mind.

All too soon, it was time to go back to work, and I boarded the *Cruzeiro do Sul* DC3 flight for Manaus. We were following the course of the Rio Branco southwards when, about half-way home, the port engine stopped. The pilot turned around and landed back in Boa Vista. Luckily (or so we thought), another DC3, this time of *Riograndense*, had landed, on its way back to Manaus. Most of the passengers re-embarked.

We later learned that we were at almost the identical bearings where the first plane had lost an engine, when the port engine on the *second* plane caught fire. The pilot was able to feather it quite quickly and the fire seemed to go out. However, the starboard engine then began to splutter and, unbeknown to us, the authorities sent out the first plane, its port engine provisionally fixed, to see where we would crash-land. This reach of the river was the territory of some particularly inhospitable Indians; I cannot remember if they were from the Yanomami or Wai-wai tribes. In the event, we made it back to Boa Vista, and to our rooms at the only hotel in town.

Next morning we were taken to the airport. The FAB (Brazilian Air Force) engineers had worked all night to overhaul both planes, which were now parked side-by-side on the apron.

We were delicately asked which plane we would like to travel in. By now about half the passengers had elected not to go at all. In the end the planes flew back to Manaus wing-tip to wing-tip, and I was relieved to get back to my hot, stuffy, uncomfortable office at the Bank. I felt there was a good reason for my being a day late. All smugness dissipated, however, when I was informed, in no uncertain terms, that contrary to bank *and* consulate rules, I had forgotten to tell anybody where I was going for *Carnaval.*

THE RUBBER-TAPPER

At the end of my stint in Manaus, I made a marketing and information trip through some of the more remote areas for which the British Honorary Consul in Manaus was responsible. I travelled by air via Manicoré, Porto Velho and Guajará Mirim to Rio Branco, and then back for a few days to Porto Velho in the Federal Territory of Rondônia, before continuing to Vilhena, Cuiabá, Campo Grande and São Paulo. The police in Manaus had insisted that I take a gun with me on this trip, and I had purchased a small *Castelo* revolver with 50 rounds of .22-calibre ammunition, which I kept in its box at the bottom of my rucksack.

The Amazonian drought of 1963 was still very much in evidence. The water level of the Madeira river at Manicoré had dropped so far - nearly 20 metres - that the town, usually connected to the north-west by ferry, was completely isolated. There were even rumours that a massive geological fault had swallowed part of the river upstream.

Porto Velho, where tin had just been discovered, was now reachable by dirt road from São Paulo. The charming but tough *Dona* Nilce Guimarães, licencee of the Porto Velho Hotel, was married to the local *Delegado de Policia* (police commissioner), whose responsibilities, with the growing importance of the town, were increasing by leaps and bounds.

It had been a sultry day in mid-January 1966, and a very busy one, with visits to agents for the traditional nuts, skins, dyes, gums and rubber, but also discussions with executives of newly-registered tin-mining organisations. According to a letter I later wrote to the consul in Manaus, I had researched the activities of 'Luiz, a little man from Guajará Mirim, who smuggles vast amounts of gasoline to Bolivia and with the proceeds buys some beautiful Bolivian jewellery which he smuggles back and sells at very reasonable prices.'

The gasoline which Luiz ran came from a fuel terminal (also visited). The fuel, which was shipped in cans from Manaus on the deep and fast Madeira river ('22 days up as against 5–6 days going down') served to provide electricity to Rondônia as well as large adjacent areas of Mato Grosso and Amazonas. But the hand-filled generator was still turned off in Porto Velho at 8 p.m.

On this particular evening, the lights had just gone out, and I had lit my candle and my *Boa Noite* smoke-stick to discourage the ferocious mosquitoes, when there were some appalling crashes outside the hotel, which I recognised, as they got closer, as gunshots. There was a bang which I guessed (rightly) was the front door being smashed in, and then further bangs and crashes as the intruder broke down guest-room doors and fired again and again. My revolver was still in its box at the bottom of my rucksack, as was the ammunition. Not very James-Bondish at all. Then I blew out the candle, which was daft.

I found my way to the door and wedged a chair under the handle; then, realising that I had no chair to sit on, perched on the edge of the bed and, with my hands shaking, and sweating like a pig, managed, in the pitch darkness, to get the gun out of the box, get the ammunition out of *its* box, and load up. All the time the shots were getting closer. Suddenly, just as I got the gun pointing towards the door, there was a scuffling sound and some shouts, then dead silence. To this day, I do not know how long I sat there.

At breakfast the next morning, after a sleepless night, I learned from Nilce that a *seringueiro* (rubber-tapper), whom the *Delegado* had put into jail for killing Indians (a not uncommon occurrence), had been let out, had bought himself a semi-automatic rifle, and had come to 'get' the *Delegado*. The latter, however, knew the geography of the hotel better than the *seringueiro*, and 'got' him (with a knife) in the passage outside my room. Nilce told me it was by no means the first time that such a thing had happened. The *Delegado* did not want to talk about the incident but, when he confirmed later that crime figures in the town were right down, the word 'down' took on a whole new meaning.

SAINTS ALIVE...

'God is a Trinidadian', concluded the editor of a Port of Spain newspaper, the morning after Hurricane Bret swept up the channel between Trinidad and Tobago in August 1993, missing both islands by a meteorological hair's breadth. And no-one felt deprived...

Saints' names have always been fashionable. Early explorers religiously took their list of Saints' days with them on their travels. All they had to do was turn to the right page when they sighted a speck on the horizon and bingo! - St Helena was reborn, as were St Kitts, St Lucia and St Vincent; St Pierre, St Petrus, San Pietro; Sant' Anna and Santana; São Tomé and Santo Niño. There were Sta Marias everywhere. Centuries before the latitude became a term of observational astronomy, charts were peppered with sanctitudes.

Barbados, it is said, got its name from the Bearded Fig (*Ficus citrifolia*), and it is easy to be impressed by this odd-looking tree, with its fibrous, hanging air-roots. Or was it perhaps the hairiness of the primitive Carib inhabitants which inspired early Portuguese explorers to use the word *barbados* ('bearded')? Whatever the origin of this pagan appellation, the statutory list of Saints' days was not to hand when the liana-bedecked paradise hove, for the first time, into view.

Early settlers, however, quickly corrected this state of affairs, and ten of the eleven Barbadian parishes were subsequently named after Saints. The eleventh, Christchurch, appears now on local car registration plates as an X. G is for St George, L is for St Lucy, and so on. Poor old St James came off worst with an S, having been beaten to the draw by, respectively, St John (J), St Andrew (A), St Michael (M), and St Peter (E); St Philip had already bagged the P. St George and St Thomas got a G and a T, and St Joseph lost to St John and was awarded an O.

'You've got your shirt on inside-out,' said a lady in a shop in Dover (Barbados), offering me a room at the back in case I wanted to adjust it. I declined, hoping that I wasn't, in some way, offending against local superstition.

'You've got your shirt on inside-out,' called another passer-by from behind me, just after I had left the shop.

'You Barbadians are very observant,' I said, and told him of the lady who had made the same comment not two minutes previously.

'Just nosey I guess,' he retorted inconsequentially, and ambled off.

If you ever go to Barbados, try collecting churches. It is just as much fun as collecting car registration plates. In addition to the more conventional places of worship, you'll run across names like Abundant Life Assembly, Doyle Jippy Evangelistic Association, Ebenezer Revival Centre, Emmanuel Tabernacle, Moravian Church, and Worldwide Church of God. And don't be surprised if someone at a bus-stop asks you which church you attend, as if he were enquiring which horse you are placing a bet on. Barbadians are indeed very observant...

It was a lively event, Morning Prayer at St Lawrence Anglican Church, south-east of Bridgetown. The Minister took some good-natured swipes at everything in sight: local politicians, the crime rate, the IMF, the wealth of Queen Elizabeth II (Herod had made an appearance in the second Lesson). The ladies in the congregation sported mantillas in their hair and everyone sang lustily. The choir knew the Order of Service, the psalms and the hymns by heart. The word SLAVERY seemed to be peering out of the shadows, behind the altar. But, on closer examination, it was only a faded, puckered banner of ST LAWRENCE playing tricks on us.

The Thanksgiving Service at St Bartholomew's Anglican Church in Mayara, Trinidad, just after Hurricane Bret, was very different. It was a do-it-yourself affair, the incumbent having been stranded in the floods somewhere. The sexton lit the candles, flicking the matches pensively out of the window, and we were away. It didn't matter that there was not even a piano in the place, let alone a choir.

The pace was set by a lady of Indian extraction who didn't seem to mind much about the Order of Service. We got through several hymns, two Jubilates, two sermons (one from the sexton and another from an elderly gentleman who had arrived just as the Indian lady was beginning to run out of wind), and a Trinity of Lord's Prayers. The island was living up to its name.

It was extempore. But we felt just as good as we had at St Lawrence in Barbados, steeped - or so it seemed - in saintliness. For, with Bibleway Tabernacle, Church of the Foursquare Gospel, and Mafeking Pentecostal Delivery Centre in hot pursuit, we knew that St Bart's had run a good race in the Trinidadian Sabbath steeplechase.

* * *

This little travelogue is repeated here with a thought for the hundreds of West Indians who visited me in later years at the British Consulate. Although many brought me serious problems, most of them somehow sought to leave sunshine behind them.

DAVID

'God gave us our relatives; thank God we can choose our friends.'

My very first school was Elmhurst, Camberley (Headmistress: Mrs Mortimer; two guineas per term). I was three. These were the war years and money was scarce. The only thing I learned there was how to dance the polka. I wondered, in my little world, whether this was Blighty's way of digging Mr Hitler in the eye: 'You can bomb us to billy-o but we will continue to learn the polka.' Yes, he was always referred to as 'Mr Hitler', but I suppose, in retrospect it might have been heavy irony. After all, Winston Churchill once wrote (albeit referring to the declaration of war against Japan): 'Even if you have to kill a man it costs nothing to be polite.'

In the 1940s, my parents were regular subscribers to the *Daily Mirror*, the *Daily Sketch*, *Camberley News*, the *Sunday Express*, the *Sunday Pictorial* and *Radio Times*. I have found the invoices from W.H. Smith. My own literary fare consisted of *Tiny Tots* and *Chicks' Own*.

Just after the war, when we had returned to Jersey, I went to St George's Preparatory School, then in Rouge Bouillon, St Helier. All I can recall from that experience was the name of my schoolmistress: Miss Holmes. Then came Australia, and a tutor for the duration. Unfortunately, what with kangaroos, Captain Marvel Comics, bush fires, what seemed like dozens of great-aunts (in fact we only met six or seven), rabbits, roast lamb for breakfast, sharks, people talking funny, and Studebakers, the poor man did not stand a chance.

On our return to Jersey, David and I had a marvellous time mucking about on the farm. The war years had been a sombre period when everything seemed to be forbidden. Suddenly, everything was allowed – within reason: my mother kept a short thick stick which she flourished when she felt that a bit of discipline was necessary. I will never forget the 'Where's my stick?' she bellowed, whenever David or I hid it. On one occasion, we were playing with a chaff-cutter and I accidentally cut off the top of David's thumb; my mother jammed it back on (once we had found it) and, after a week or two, it was, if scarred, as good as new.

The stick was brandished, too, when David and I (mainly I) were caught stealing apples from the farmer, across the road from Oaklands, where our grandmother ('Muzz') lived; and when I went in the trap (having been forbidden to go) with Leslie Hill, our farm foreman, who was trying out a new pony. In the event, a piece of paper fluttered across the road while we were crossing Five Oaks, and the pony panicked and smashed the frail vehicle to pieces with its hind legs, which also caught my thigh, leaving a massive bruise, but thankfully nothing worse. That Mama had been right once again hurt more than the bruise.

Then we were sent away to school: I went first, desperately trying to be brave, with my trunk and tuck-box in tow; David followed. We were lucky: the original plan had been to send us away at the age of five and a half. Horris Hill was (still is) a preparatory boarding school, housed in a large, spooky, mock-Tudor building near Newbury. It was run by the Stow family. Monty Stow and Mr Liddell were the joint headmasters when I was there. Mr Liddell regaled us with stories about his times in Kenya when the Mau Mau were abroad, and how he slept with a loaded revolver under his pillow. It was all very 'Boy's Own' and I was enthralled. He drove up to London once, took a train back and phoned the police to say his car had been stolen; as the years have gone by, that story, hilarious the first time round, has become less and less funny.

We were visited by all sorts of interesting people: a musician and a diver and a comedian ('If your baby cries while drinking its milk, try boiling it') and Sir Edmund Hillary who had just climbed the highest peak: ALL THIS AND EVEREST TOO read a newspaper headline when Elizabeth was crowned. We were there, sitting in a grandstand: I am not certain if I saw the Royal carriage;

but I do remember the diminutive Emperor of Ethiopia, the Shah of Persia with his beautiful Empress Soraya, and the gargantuan Queen Salote of Tonga.

On the common beside the school, there was a Roman settlement, which we were allowed to excavate. I once found three-quarters of a 2,000-year-old grindstone, which might have been the beginning of a life-long interest in archaeology.

As a Really Funny Prank, we sent a sample of the water from the school swimming pool to a local laboratory; they sent back an analysis which read, 'This horse will be fit for work in three weeks.' It was without an exclamation mark: I was beginning to learn about English Humour.

I somehow got past the finishing line of college entrance, sustained only by my mother's keenness that I stay at school. I didn't really enjoy being away from home, from my cat and from the farm, where much more exciting things seemed to be happening. I recall the satisfaction in helping with the combine harvester on a hot summer's day; tying up tomatoes; parading our Jersey cows at shows where Gwynneth, who had become an accomplished cattle breeder, won lots of prizes; planting, banking and digging potatoes, and then driving them to the Weighbridge for export to the UK. Then came the broccoli and the gladioli. There was Jane the pig who only stopped being a house-pet when we could no longer take her in the car: she was too large; and Gussie the goose who was reared on the Aga-cooker; and the Blitz-rats by the pond, which were so big that they were almost – but not quite – a match for Pongeon the miniature dachshund.

I remember, too, the feeling of disappointment when I discovered that, with all my efforts to learn Latin, *nobody still talked it.* I didn't know *then* that my father-to-be had confided, in a letter of May 1934 to my mother-to-be in Jersey, when he was on army leave in Ballycastle:

> Ran into an old master [from Campbell College Grammar School, Belfast] today who used to try to teach me Latin and we had a long buck about old times during which he admitted that he had seldom met with less success in his efforts at imparting learning than he had encountered with me!! How I regret not

having tried harder and I must say that I have no doubt that an intimate knowledge of the finer points in the Latin tongue would have helped me no end to have become a shining light as a soldier?

The incongruous question mark at the end is telling: no wonder my mother, Gwynneth, kept her correspondence under lock and key until the end. In 1935, one year after he wrote his letter, there was an unsuccessful Irish Republican raid on the school in an attempt to secure the weapons of the College Officers' Training Corps, where my father had begun his military career.

David, I believe, enjoyed our schooling better than I did. While I tended to look for other things to do, he became a brilliant sportsman. Among other achievements, he played hockey for Oxford University and Wiltshire. We met during a rugby match once, tackling the same player from opposite directions, and I still have a loose chip of bone over my eyebrow to prove it.

We both left Horris Hill for Marlborough College, where I honed my interest in archaeology; there was once an Egyptian mummy for sale in the College Museum, which I was sorely tempted to buy. Common sense prevailed. Archaeology began to include history. Fired by my new friendship with Peter Heaton of the Birmingham Mint family, and encouraged by my step-father Ernest Huelin, history was then 'miniaturised' into numismatics, which has stayed with me, as a hobby, ever since. I have often wondered if my interest in travel was in any way fostered by another new friendship with a shy 15-year-old who was to metamorphose into the novelist, Bruce Chatwin. Recreation stretched to films and lantern lectures.

'Won't set the Thames on fire' appeared in one of my early school reports. Were these words meant to be read as heartlessly defeatist, or as constructively provocative? I like to think it was the latter.

Highlight of the - for me - humdrum existence at both Horris Hill and Marlborough was leave to go out with Aunt Dorothy (Gwynneth's elder sister) and Uncle Ken Mackinnon, who frequently came down to visit us. We usually had picnics in Savernake Forest, served from 'Rollie', a vintage Rolls-Royce Phantom II Tourer (LYT 40) with its very own cocktail cabinet. Grandfather Davies's last self-indulgence had spent the German

The Lord Chamberlain is
commanded by Their Majesties to summon
Mrs Lewis Davies
& Miss Gwynneth Davies
to a Court at Buckingham Palace
on Wednesday the 20th May, 1931 at 9.30 o'clock p.m.

Ladies: Court Dress with feathers and trains.
Gentlemen: Full Court Dress.

Invitations from the Lord Chamberlain to Muzz and Gwynneth,
1931 and, below, to Antony, Angelika and their son Charles, 2000.

E&R

The Lord Chamberlain is
commanded by Her Majesty to invite

Mr. and Mrs. Anthony McCammon
and Mr. Charles McCammon

to a Garden Party
at Buckingham Palace
on Tuesday, 25th July 2000 from 4 to 6 pm

This card does not admit

occupation years under a pile of straw in the garage, without being discovered. Stories that it 'started first time' were, I suspect, the product of a schoolboy fantasy, but the envious looks on our friends' faces, as we drove away, made it all worthwhile.

Marlborough was clearly a desirable place. I got my Certificate A parts 1 and 2 in the College Cadet Corps. This meant that I could reassemble a Bren gun: piston, barrel, butt, body, bipod. There was also a body-locking-pin (snigger!). This Light Machine Gun, which had been Czech-designed and modified at the small arms factory at Enfield (*Brno-En*field), had quite a kick when it was fired – which wasn't often, as the bullets were in short supply.

I recall one camp at the military training area of Buckenham Tofts, where, during one night exercise, we dashed across the plain in pitch darkness, pursued by 'the enemy'. That none of us ran into or fell into anything was a miracle. In the early hours, I was sentry, with the CO asleep in the cab of a military truck just across a clearing. A school-mate of mine came out of the bushes, a finger to his lips, with two handfuls of magnesium powder (which he had removed from some flares) and an old biscuit-tin. He up-ended the tin, poured the magnesium on to its base and set fire to it. The whole countryside lit up. 'What was that?' said the CO, waking up with a start. 'What was what?' said the sentry, and was promptly demoted to Lance-Corporal. I thought of David Niven.

In its favour, Marlborough was the first public school to introduce 'Civil Defence' for those (like me, in spite of my family's military background) who had no strong inclination to become soldiers. We learned about building walls and water-courses, and landscape gardening and wildlife. This last interest metamorphosed, years later, into life membership of the Durrell Wildlife Conservation Trust in Jersey, and the 'adoption' (courtesy of my four sons) of a Sumatran Orangutan by the name of Jaya. A longstanding friendship with Jeremy ('Pongo') Mallinson, for many years Director of the Trust, has led to many fascinating wildlife experiences.

I scraped up a meagre bounty of five 'O-levels' and one 'A' (Ancient Greek, which I managed to make use of once, many years later, on a visit to the monks' republic of Athos). I wonder what my father would have said. While making up my mind about What To Do Next, I decided to polish up my French by visiting a course for foreigners at the Université de Paris, and came away with an imposing diploma, covered in signatures.

While my A-level score was not enough to take me into any British universities, it was, at the time, sufficient for Trinity College Dublin or McGill in Montreal. I chose McGill. This was partly because I liked the sound of Something Really New; partly because I thought (erroneously as it turned out) that they spoke French there; and partly because of an inverted snobbery towards what my family and friends seemed to regard as important at the time. The Queen's presence at Court during the ceremony of the debutantes' 'coming out' had ceased one year before. My mother Gwynneth, in another era, had been presented at Buckingham Palace to George V and Queen Mary. We still have a photograph of the occasion: she looked very beautiful. Yes, the war was over and rationing was long gone, and this might have been a reason for celebration. But what filled the void was a studied empty-headedness (elegantly described in *Past Imperfect*, the novel by Julian Fellowes). At the tender age of 20, I found this offensive and longed for another world. McGill seemed to fill the bill.

Half a century later, I myself was the guest of Her Majesty, when she graciously entertained all Honorary Consuls from around the world to a tea party at Buckingham Palace. It was a memorable occasion and I wondered if my attitude in 1959 had not been a trifle misplaced.

McGill was indeed exciting; but the New World - at least the northern expanse of it - did not appeal to me. I was naïvely shocked by the number of students I met who admitted that they had absolutely no interest in the courses they were taking: they were there purely for the degree, which, in turn, would make it easier for them to find a job. In open revolt, I neglected the course for which I was inscribed ('Commerce', which I found as dull as ditch-water), and threw myself into ancillary activities: Psychology 111, Geology and Russian. I was shocked again when I came to take the first-year multiple-choice Psychology exam, for which I had worked like a Trojan: I discovered that one wasn't meant to use one's own brain: all the correct answers were direct quotations from Professor Hebb's book.

I became President of the McGill Cosmopolitan Club, which held all sorts of international meetings. On one occasion, we sponsored a series of concerts by a visiting musical percussion group made up of deaf-mute students from Korea.

Adolescent adventures included: registering, and being runner-up, for a job at McGill's Arctic Research Station at Axel Heiberg Island; going down a magnesite mine in Ontario; making friends in Indian Reservations and in the French-Canadian community in Montreal East; living with a diminutive Irish woman, Mrs Morris, and her family, in Suter Street; rescuing her washing after it had been stolen by a sneak-thief at 3 a.m. one warm summer morning; not knowing what to do with him after I had out-run and caught him (he told me his mother had sent him out to steal it, and I shook hands with him in sympathy).

Other off-beat experiences: idealistically spending all one night trying to talk an alcoholic fireman out of his habits ('I know what you're trying to do, Tony, but I am just not going to do it' was my reward); being arrested on Mount Royal for being in possession of an unwrapped bottle of Canadian Club rye whisky; driving down to New York, and getting lost in Harlem, with Sir Adrian Blennerhassett, Bart. (still a close friend) on our way to staying with the Count and Countess Wolf von Westarp, German-speaking aristocrats and expatriate members of the *Sozialistiche Reichspartei*; snowshoeing into a mountain hut in the Laurentians after getting lost in a blizzard at about 9 p.m. one evening, only to be upstaged, two hours later, by Fiona Guinness, a colleague, who breezed in on skis. And I was making friends from all over the world.

This essay, however, started off in a completely different direction, with a quotation of Ethel Watte Mumford about relatives and friends.

David and I were inseparable during our earliest times together. During our early schooling, we were close. As time went on, and we began to live our separate lives, we saw less and less of each other. This made no difference. As I write, we are both in our early 70s. We have romped and loitered and walked and discussed and argued together; we have played squash and rugby football, and soccer and cricket; we have boxed and surfed; we have even (David, with great patience!) knocked a golf-ball around together. We have had completely separate professional careers. We have profited and learned from the thrift and hard work of others; we have, I believe, stayed on the straight and narrow, and we have tried to base our lives on trust. And we both have wonderful wives and families. We have been very lucky together.

I cannot quarrel with what Ethel Mumford wrote 100 years ago. Nonetheless, if it were not my privilege to have David as a brother, he would be the first I would choose as a friend.

ANOTHER NEW WORLD

Pistol:
...the world's mine oyster,
Which I with sword will open.

It is a romantic notion: prising open oyster shells with one's sword to get to the pearl within. But Shakespeare's Pistol was a braggart and there lies the danger of too much reminiscing.

From a very early age, I have never really understood war: why anybody should wish to drop bombs on his neighbour. 'Jerry', for me, was a foreigner, yes, but why was he against us? What drove him to build flying bomb launchers all over Normandy, aimed at Britain? What were we actually cheering for when we gathered in front of Buckingham Palace on VE Day in 1945...thousands and thousands of us? Of course I was too young to know that people were celebrating (or so they believed) the end of war-time hardship. I was too young to appreciate that my mother, just widowed, had cycled nearly 20 miles to find a single strawberry cream chocolate, which I had said I wanted for my birthday. Rationing of food and clothing and fuel was, in fact, to continue for a period which would be longer than the war itself.

Those outlandish stories of Hitler and Mussolini and Stalin and the Emperor of Japan: how did they all fit together? And all those dreadful graves from *another* war?

I wasn't a good student: I didn't want to waste time studying. I wanted to go and see for myself. My father had fought on the North-West Frontier of India. What was it like? It was too late to ask him. My father's father had been *there,* in the trenches at the Somme, but, frustratingly, he got angry when I asked him to tell me what had happened; ordered me never to ask him again. All we have are his medals and some fading citations. My father's father's father was a churchman. A churchman? And why on earth did he travel to Montenegro? I was puzzled that everyone, everywhere seemed to invoke God in order to condone earthly actions: God Save the King; God Bless America; *Gott mit Uns.*

My elder siblings: what might they have been like, if they had not miscarried in Rawalpindi? What would have been our fate if the bomb which had destroyed the house across the road when we were living in Crockham Hill, had landed on us?

Why did our mother take my brother and me to Australia in the late 1940s? Why did my Uncle Ken Mackinnon, who later introduced me to Wilfred Thesiger the explorer, *not* want me to take the Foreign Office exams in the late 1950s?

Which direction might my life have taken if I had been accepted on to the McGill University expedition to its Arctic Research Station on Axel Heiberg Island in 1960? Or if I had taken up the Canadian Government offer to immigrate? Or completely missed the train in Krasnoyarsk? Or missed the ambulance in Kabul? What if I had stayed at my post as a computer programmer, or gone to Burma with the Chartered Bank and not Brazil with the Bank of London & South America (BOLSA)?

How close had I been to oblivion when my DC3 sputtered back to Boa Vista with one engine on fire and the other faltering badly or when the little ferry-boat nearly capsized as I was crossing the Paraná river? And what might have happened if the enraged rubber-tapper had reached my hotel room in Porto Velho before the police commissioner reached *him*? What if I had agreed to be transferred by Lloyds Bank to New York or Monaco, and not stayed in Zürich?

How close are 'missed opportunities' to 'lucky breaks'?

When I was still in my early teens, I once saw the actor James Robertson Justice coming out of a building off Piccadilly. I went up to him, hoping to get his autograph, and said,

'Excuse me Sir: are you James Robertson Justice?'

In his inimitable voice, he roared back: 'No, I am not!'

And I didn't get his autograph.

On another occasion in the late 1970s, I walked round a corner of a building in Zürich rather briskly, and collided head-on with Rudolf Nureyev; it winded him for a moment; then, with a smile, he carried on towards the Opera House.

In 1964, somewhere between these two events, I spotted my future wife, Angelika, at a tram-stop in Santos. We sort of collided; I don't know about *her*, but it took the wind out of *me*. She didn't say no; and I, so to speak, *did* get her autograph. The 'pearl' was mine.

SPEAKING IN RIDDLES

'Have you had your passport stamped?'

The question came to me through the clouds of tobacco smoke to my left and I thought: surely that question is not aimed at me. Then it came again:

'Ahem! Have you had your passport stamped?'

It was 1973, my first Wednesday in Oporto. We had arrived the previous weekend and were staying at the stately Oporto Cricket and Lawn Tennis Club. We had immersed ourselves in this new culture with gusto, and here I was, the new, green bank manager of the *Banco Inglês*, a guest of Alistair Robertson, managing director of Taylor, Fladgate & Yeatman, lunching at Factory House. There had been the choice of a White Port or a *Fino* to start, followed by a three-course *déjeuner*, accompanied by copious amounts of white and red table wines; cigars had been lit and a decanter of vintage Port was being followed around the table by the tawny. The vintage had been decanted six hours before the meal, and was disappearing fast. Conversation was lively.

Before we took our places on the solid mahogany green-leather chairs, I had been introduced to Ian, Michael, James and Peter Symington of the Warre Group, Gwyn Jennings of Sandeman,

John, Michael and Richard Delaforce, Reg Cobb and Antonio Felipe of Cockburn, Robin Reid of Croft, Alfredo Holzer of Cálem and many others. It was a treasure-trove of illustrious – many eponymous – Port Wine shippers. One could see, though, that it was a business lunch, and my table companions frequently left to attend to the exigencies of the moment. To all of these charming gentlemen – *very* belatedly – I would like to extend my thanks for accepting me, so readily and so warmly, into their company.

Various British Consuls, principally one John Whitehead, had played their parts in the early history of Factory House, right down to, and beyond, 1785, when construction of this handsome building eventually commenced: it was to be the headquarters of the British merchants – or 'factors' – of Oporto, some of whom were later to constitute the British Association of Port Wine Shippers. Consul Whitehead, an able architect and mathematician from Lancashire, had drafted the plans for the project. He almost certainly owed his appointment to the fact that his sister had married one of the most influential members of the British community: William Warre. Whitehead was British Consul for 46 years until his death in 1802. His nephew, another William Warre, also of the family which had established the oldest British Port Wine shipping firm, was himself, according to Foreign Office records, British Consul in Oporto from 1805 to 1812. At time of writing, the tradition of a Warre Group connection with the FCO has been re-established, following the recent appointment of Johnny Symington as British Honorary Consul.

Half-way up the august flight of stairs towards the dining room, one was greeted by an imposing portrait of the first William Warre's grandson: the distinguished Lieutenant-General Sir William Warre who, tradition has it, was dismissed from the firm at an early age, 'for fastening the pigtail of one of the Portuguese staff to his desk with sealing wax, when he was having an after-lunch nap'.

The life-blood of the Factory House at Oporto is still that peculiar reinforced wine which we call Port. It is a formidable essence, and not for the weak-hearted. I only got to know one shipper, James Taylor-Sinclair, manager of Gonzalez Byass – a classical scholar and a fascinating man to be with – who could sink a bottle of Port every day, without losing one syllable of his lucidity. He told me that he had met Manolo Gonzalez Dias in a trench in the Spanish Civil War. Story-telling reached its apex in the Port Wine community.

I once had the honour of being invited to address the Association at the annual Treasurer's Dinner, 150 years after General Sir Thomas Stubbs, who was at the time Commander of the British Forces in Oporto, was a guest. He later wrote:

> Our dinner was superb and we adjourned from the table to another room, en suite with the first, where such a dessert and such wines were served up, as quite to astonish our northern experience.

While I can readily associate myself with Sir Thomas's sentiments, the adjournment to an identical second room took me completely by surprise - in fact I thought that, for some reason, the meal had been curtailed and that I was no longer required. The place settings in the dessert room were identical to those in the dining room, and it was not only the wine that left me feeling rather dazed, as I took my place again in the centre of the long table which stretched off into the distance, to my left and to my right. Had it not been for the finger bowls, I would not have known how to start. In the event the old chestnut about Queen Victoria, the young Abd al-Aziz ibn Saud and the French Ambassador saved the day, and the address was politely received.

'Excuse me - yes, you there!' - the voice was much louder now - 'May I ask you again: Have you had your PASSPORT stamped? PASS PORT. PASS the PORT.'

Only then did the penny drop: I realised that both Port decanters had piled up to my right. I should have poured a drop from one of them and handed them on to my left: I felt as if I had committed a cardinal sin. After I had at last obliged, the elderly gentleman who had addressed me, Ron Symington, passed both decanters to *his* left without comment.

The following day, I had a terrible hangover and went for a walk to try to clear my head. I spotted Ron on the other side of the street and went across to compliment him. He looked at me blankly, and said:

'Who are you?'

Some weeks later, I learned that Ron had an identical twin brother. I had either approached the wrong one, or Ron, too, was nursing a thick head. It remained a mystery.

REVOLUÇÃO DOS CRAVOS

ATTENTION PLEASE:

THE WORKERS OF THESE FIRM, HAVE, UNFORTUNATLY, THE DUTY TO INFORM ALL CLIENTS, THAT, CONSIDERING THE REACHTION OF THE PATRONAGE ASSOCIATIONS, TO OUR WORK CONTRACT, MUST USE WORK PARALYSATIONS TO FORCE THEM TO KEEP THE WORD. W

SO WE WILL PARALYSE AS FOLLOING:

1.- MONDAY 5th . MAY BETWEEN 11 A.M. til 3 p.m.
2. TWESDAY 6th . MAY BETWEEN 6 p.m. TIL 10. p.m.
3. WEDNESDAY 7 ALL THE DAY (BEGGINNIG AT MIDNIGHT OF 6 TH MAY)

In retrospect, it had been a bizarre revolution, somehow encapsulated in the communiqué to guests (reproduced verbatim above), which I had torn down from a non-functioning lift in the Hotel Dom Henrique, in Oporto, on 1 May 1975. It had been eventful too, but, almost always, polite; similar, in ways, to the Goulart Revolution of 1964 in Brazil, when, to avoid unnecessary conflict, generals had remained on holiday and armies had marched past each other: that had merely delayed my departure for a few weeks. It had been very different from the de Gaulle Revolution of 1958, when one was lucky if one didn't become a victim of the head-cracking *Garde nationale.* And totally different from the Iraq Revolution, which I had stumbled into in 1962.

This was the Portuguese 'Carnation Revolution', harbinger of political developments in Spain, Greece, Latin America, Africa... and the USSR.

These days, people do not seem to comprehend the importance of it. Hopefully, when the definitive history of this period comes to be written, both 25 April 1974, when Russian communism began its ultimate campaign to outflank NATO, and 25 November 1975, the day of the Portuguese counter-revolution, will be seen as momentous dates in world history.

The reason, very simply put, is that, after the suppression by the USSR of the Hungarian Revolution in 1956, the construction of the Berlin Wall in 1961, and the rape of the 'Prague Spring' in 1968, Portugal (1974) *didn't work.*

Afterwards, the Communist myth began to crumble.

My own part in it began melodramatically.

The first indication I had that anything was afoot was a phone call from Hector Timistit, my Chief Manager, at the Bank of London & South America (BOLSA) in Lisbon, in which he managed to tell me, before the line went down, that there were tanks and soldiers armed with G3s all over the *Baixa* district. I should do what I could to protect the staff and secure the branch. I sent everyone home, closed the doors and left with the accountant by a side entrance. At that moment, there was the sound of firing and glass breaking from across the *Avenida dos Aliados.* We took to our heels and turned the corner towards where I had parked the Bank car. We both jumped in, I started the engine and the vehicle burst into flames.

This *évènement,* it turned out, had nothing whatsoever to do with the Revolution: a short circuit had been the culprit, and I was quickly able to get the blaze under control. The firing, we later learned, came from the occupants of a police car who had found themselves hemmed in by a crowd of people; the near-side passenger opened his window and fired in the air, shattering all the first-floor panes above him. No one was hurt. In fact, only four people were killed on the first day, said to have been shot by agents of *PIDE* (the Portuguese secret police) from their headquarters in Lisbon, before they handed over their arms to the army captains who were leading the coup.

Marcelo Caetano, Salazar's successor as President, surrendered to General Spinola, and was exiled to Madeira; later, Brazil was to give him asylum.

This was the Age of the Rumour.

One of the first stories, at least among the foreign contingent, was that a warship was on its way to Portugal to evacuate British citizens. To my knowledge, this was simply not true, although I do recollect that, towards the end of April, a Canadian warship had somehow become detached from NATO exercises (which were to include the Portuguese navy), and lay at anchor for a few days in Lisbon. Who knows if this was not the origin of this rumour?

Another canard was the story that Carlos Marighella, Brazilian arch-revolutionary, had arrived in Portugal and was planning to become active in Lisbon. In fact he had died five years previously.

The Communist Party of Portugal (*PCP*), under Álvaro Cunhal, was extraordinarily well prepared and, following traditional Marxist teaching, first made certain that every medium of communication was secured or effectively impeded. These included radio, television, roads, airports and immigration. At the frontiers, the *PCP* somehow managed to implement a dastardly simple strategy which saw to it that all customs officers were withdrawn from their posts for an indefinite period 'for consultations'. Angelika and I had direct experience of this when the very left-wing son of an old friend in Switzerland appeared at our house in Oporto out of the blue, looking for a bed, having walked across the border from Spain. He had come, he told us brazenly over dinner, to teach 'the people' how to make hand-grenades. 'The Party' had arranged everything for him. We were unimpressed and invited him to leave the house after breakfast the next morning.

Radio and television programmes began to fill up with virulent attacks on anything which did not fit in with the *PCP*'s plans and concepts. It must have been a challenging time for the army captains who felt that they had got things going in good faith.

Walls were very quickly covered in *graffiti*; some slogans were not unfunny:

Portugal estava à beira de um abismo; agora, deu um grande passo em frente...
(Portugal was on the edge of an abyss; now it has taken a great step forward...)

113

As putas ao poder; que os filhos já lá estão!
(Prostitutes to power; their sons are already there!)
Pedimos desculpa por esta democracia. A ditadura segue dentro de momentos.
(Please excuse us for this democracy. Dictatorship will be resumed within moments.)

May Day 1974 was quite a party; the communists were ready for it; nobody else was. Eugène Pottier's *Internationale* was being sung in Portuguese from loudspeakers *ad nauseam* on every street corner:

Arise ye workers from your slumbers
Arise ye criminals of want
For reason in revolt now thunders
And at last ends the age of cant...

As I returned home that evening, a neighbour's maid brought a bag of rubbish out for the refuse collection the following morning. When she put it down, it tipped over and the contents poured out all over the pavement. I said to her:
'Do pick it up...'
Her answer came straight back: 'I don't have to any more...' And she went back inside.
Chaos reigned.
My first direct confrontation with the new regime came a few days later when I went into the Bank to find that every wall was covered by political posters. They pictured a hammer and sickle with star, and a slogan:
O DIFICIL E LUTAR QUANDO O DESISTIR É FACIL!...
('It is difficult to fight when it is easy to give up!')...and it was signed CELULA DO BANCO INGLÊS and PARTIDO COMUNISTA PORTUGUÊS.
I immediately had the doors locked, called a meeting of the whole staff (about 40 people), and asked who was responsible for the posters. After some initial shuffling about, two young men stepped forward: Ferreira and Viana by name. Ferreira was small, bearded, cunning and furtive; Viana was large, open-faced, slow-witted and embarrassed. It was they, it turned out, who made up the 'Portuguese

Communist Party Cell of the English Bank'. The posters were duly removed.

A week or so later, the walls were once again plastered with identical posters, now about half the size of the originals. I summoned Ferreira and Viana and told them they must be removed.

This game continued until the posters measured only five and a half by seven and a half cm; they were, rather forlornly, secured to the walls by one drawing-pin each. I ordered that they also be taken down (keeping one as a souvenir) and there were no more incidents of this nature.

Towards the end of the working day, I began to notice the Bank emptying rather earlier than usual until, on several occasions, I found myself alone in the premises. I asked Fonseca, the accountant, where everyone had gone, and he answered that the staff were having meetings with the *commissão de trabalhadores* ('workers' commission'). I found out where the meeting was taking place and went in. Ferreira, who seemed to be chairing, saw me and came down from the dais:

'What are you doing here?'

I replied: 'I am the manager of this branch. I am *also* a worker'...and sat down at the back of the room. Shortly afterwards, discussion flagged and the meetings were called off.

Although Ferreira never stopped being a problem, Viana became an ally for rather an odd reason.

Angelika's grandmother, 'Omi-Omi', had passed away in Berlin, and I joined her sister there to help tidy up the estate. One day, just before I returned to Oporto, Ingrid and I took some time off, hired a car and drove through Checkpoint Charlie into the Russian zone of East Berlin for a cup of tea. The following Friday, back in Oporto, I found myself sitting next to Viana at a Bank party. He was lecturing about the wonderful state of affairs in East Germany, which he planned to travel to as soon as he could afford to do so. When I mentioned to him that I had been there only a week before, Viana looked at me with wonderment, his face broke into a broad smile and the battle was won.

Security was nothing like what it is these days. However, we did have a procedure for bomb threats. One day I was passing the little room where Dona Alda looked after our PBX, and over-heard her talking on the phone, in Portuguese:

'Where have you put it this time, dear?'

Pause.

'I see. But last time you put it there too, and I couldn't find it.'

Pause.

'How big is it?'

Pause.

'I see. In a brown paper parcel.'

Pause.

'All right. Thank you for letting me know, dear.'

She hung up. I went in and asked her: 'What was all that about?'

Dona Alda turned on her famously warm smile and replied: 'Oh. That was a lady who has been phoning me for weeks to tell me there is a bomb in the building. I didn't want to bother you.'

She was right, of course. The Portuguese would never activate a bomb if there was any danger of anybody getting hurt.

It was in Oporto that I experienced my first (and only) run on the Bank. Before the Revolution, BOLSA probably had not much more than 2 per cent of all deposits in banks in Portugal. Afterwards, depositors began to remove their money from the Portuguese banks and redeposit them with the *Banco Inglês* (together with the *Crédit Franco-Portugais* and the *Banco do Brasil* which were, then, much smaller entities). Very soon the ratio of our deposits to our 'dotation capital' went sky-high, and I visited the *Banco de Portugal* (the note-issuing authority) to explain to them that stability could only be maintained if the Bank continued to take deposits. The Acting Governor took note (but issued nothing in writing). BOLSA business volumes grew exponentially, with hundreds of new accounts being opened every week. Cash deposits increased at the same rate, and enormous amounts were redeposited with the Central Bank every day. We found it hard to keep the right amount of cash on the premises to match withdrawals.

Then someone started a rumour that we were short of cash, which was, in one sense, true, as we were geared to a much lower cash turnover. Hundreds of account-holders stormed the Bank in an attempt to get their money back.

When I sent messengers across the square to obtain more banknotes, the communists spotted an opportunity for disruption and put a picket on the gates: large men with helmets and iron bars. BOLSA staff were hindered from going through the doors of the *Banco de Portugal*. All that could be done was filter customers, letting them in as slowly as possible. By the end of the day, the Bank was down to coin only. It was not fun.

That evening, I put into motion an exhaustive public relations exercise to persuade the public that their money was safe. The panic abated, and we in the Bank had an impromptu celebration.

On another occasion, Pinto, one of the chauffeurs, phoned me at home, before I set out in the morning, and told me not to go to work - it was too dangerous. Trusting Pinto entirely, I put on some old clothes, borrowed a car from a neighbour, and drove past the Bank. There was a picket on the front door, with the same helmeted louts and their iron bars. I didn't try to enter the bank, but, instead, let it be known that I had taken a week's holiday. Christian Courtois, my colleague at the *Crédit Franco-Portugais*, just up the *Avenida dos Aliados*, was not so lucky: he tried to get through and ended up in hospital.

Pinto was small and unobtrusive; he had the habit of *being* there whenever one needed him. During the spring and summer of 1975, road communications between Lisbon and Oporto - and even between Oporto and Vila Nova de Gaia on the other side of the Douro - had become very difficult. Road-blocks had been mounted to hinder alleged anti-revolutionary demonstrations and 'marches on Lisbon'; these impediments tended to be left in place. I remember vividly, on one occasion, as Pinto was driving me across the *Ponte Dom Luís I*, being stopped by a drunken soldier who held his primed G3 in one hand, and a bottle of beer in the other.

Pinto appeared one day in my office and suggested driving me around on the Bank's Vespa, as we would much more easily get round the road-blocks; there was only one thing, he said: would I mind if he did not wear his chauffeur's cap? The idea was adopted forthwith and we were able to deliver the Port Wine companies' salaries by scooter – on which Pinto turned out to be a Whiz Kid. He didn't wear a cap, and I didn't wear a suit.

The Vespa was used for servicing the agency at *Pinto Magalhães*. And it was at the agency that we were to experience the only real violence of these troubled times. In a surfeit of zeal, and under pressure from the mob, some left-wing army officers, in the name of the Revolution, had been handing out G3s to anyone who wanted one. There was not too much ammunition about, but one could only ascertain whether or not the things were loaded if one was too close for comfort.

In any event, one afternoon, I received a telephone call telling me that the agency had been held up by three men brandishing G3s. I leapt into a taxi, which took off up the *Avenida*. In those days, there was one lone traffic-light, just past the town hall, where we had to pull up, as the traffic-light was at red.

I noticed that a police car had pulled up beside us and, on impulse, lowered the window and asked the driver if he was going to the hold-up. He nodded, looked at me, did a double-take, jammed his foot on the accelerator, started the siren and shot off at great speed. It was that sort of revolution.

The dreaded Ferreira had his comeuppance. There were on one occasion more than 200 very angry workers shaking their fists, shouting and blowing whistles, outside the Bank. They had marched to Oporto from a steel foundry, where they were employed, in an outlying town, and were demonstrating because they hadn't been paid for months. Their lawyer brought a cheque into my office, drawn on another bank, and demanded that it be paid. I refused. However, just in case there had been some genuine confusion, I took the cheque to the photocopying machine and made a copy, forgetting to retrieve the original from the machine. When I went back a few minutes later, it had gone. I summoned every single member of the staff and told them to find the cheque, even if it meant turning the place upside down.

It was found under a pile of papers on Ferreira's desk. What can he possibly have wanted to do with it? In any event, he suffered such a loss of face that he was never a problem again.

One late summer's day, Amaro, who had since asserted himself as the president of the *commissão de trabalhadores*, which still held sporadic meetings, was waiting for me in my office. All the other members of the commission were standing outside and came in after me, without an invitation. They stood there rather awkwardly until they were invited to take a seat. They refused. Amaro was clearly quite embarrassed. Then he started to speak:

'Senhor McCammon, we have to tell you something.' I waited.

'We have come to apologise to you.'

'Whatever for?'

'We want to apologise for having inconvenienced you.'

'I still do not understand.'

'We want to apologise for the revolution. It is all going wrong.'

'You really have no need to apologise to me. I have no connection with your revolution. I have not been unduly inconvenienced. I do not accept your apology because, as far as I am concerned, you have nothing to apologise about. However, I note what you have said and I am grateful for the courage you have shown in coming here.'

The door was not shut and I saw Ferreira walk slowly past, and then back again. Although he had resigned from the commission, when it became clear that the Bank was largely staffed by liberal thinkers, he quite obviously still wanted to know what was going on, so that he could report to *his* bosses.

The group still stood in the office, shuffling feet. Amaro cleared his throat.

'We wondered...' I waited. Amaro braced himself. We wondered if you...' He looked across expectantly. I took the bull by the horns:

'You have apologized to me. You did nothing wrong. *Others* have been doing things. You have done *nothing at all*'.

Amaro glanced at his team and smiled. Was there on his face the shadow of an embryonic idea? They all shook hands with me, patting me, in the Portuguese way, on the back, and filed back to their desks. They held another meeting that evening, and evidently resolved to attack the root of 'the problem'.

Ten days later, Amaro brought in a copy of the *Diário da Assembleia Constituinte* (a sort of Portuguese *Hansard*), number 67, dated 22 October 1975. It recorded a letter being read out to the Assembly, where it had been greeted with cries of '*muito bem*' and applause from the members. It read (freely translated):

Most excellent Prime Minister,

The majority of the workers of the Bank of London & South America, Ltd, Oporto, alarmed by the tendentious programming of the RTP [Radio Televisão Portuguesa], which has allowed itself, in an ostensively divisionist attitude, to present programmes where the dominant tone has been a miserly and counter-revolutionary attack on the 6th Government, PS [the Socialist Party], PPD [the Popular Democratic Party], and taking into account that:

1. The RTP belongs to the people and should serve the people;

2. The vast majority of this country gave its support to the 6th Government and the measures taken by it, and unconditionally supports, as it has already proven, the performance of the commander of the Military Region of the North;

3. This same people is fed up with paying to look at programmes where torpid insinuations, insult and calumny are the constant words of order; demands from Your Excellency a firm attitude which leads to an immediate repositioning [read: sacking] of the staff responsible for such shameful and wicked programmes.

Oporto, 16 October 1975. Signed 'with tens of signatures'
[Amaro's headed the list.]

It was a brilliant letter, couched in language which the Prime Minister himself could have no objection to - politically or ideologically. It frontally attacked the most important vehicle of the extreme left. And it was the first time that something constructive had been read in the Assembly, which was not a bland and unspecific message of support for the government. The timing was good: one month after the left-leaning Prime Minister Vasco Gonçalves had been replaced by the independent José Pinheiro de Azevedo.

The members of the staff of the BOLSA's branch in Oporto - with one exception - walked tall.

Just over one month later, on 25 November, came the counter-revolution.

This is the story of one small contribution to the beginning of the end of communism in Western Europe.

ATLANTIS IN A WINK

Anti-heroes in the James Bond industry have often exercised as much an attraction for the buffs as does 007 himself. My son wept when Jaws - a massive, rather disagreeable character with steel dentures - fell out of an aeroplane; so Mr Broccoli very shrewdly brought him back into the next movie, as if nothing had happened. You can be sure that *Superman III* is the sequel to *Superman II*, and, sooner or later, *Arachnophobia IX* will follow *Arachnophobia VIII*.

But the system can go wrong. *George III* was changed to *The Madness of King George* when American audiences began to complain that they had not seen the previous two instalments. William Shakespeare showed that he had recognised the power of this gimmick, when he wrote *Henry VI* in three parts, followed closely by *Richard III*. Then he confounded the critics by penning *Henry IV afterwards*, and in only two parts. But a pattern had been set. Milton eventually got the hang of it and, having written *Paradise Lost*, left his public on tenterhooks for ten years or so before coming up with *Paradise Regained*.

But let us break the sequence, and sail, irrationally, across the deep and the obscure, from Paradise to Atlantis.

In the early 1800s, George III set a trend, and madness became quite fashionable. Sensing a market niche, William Blake developed his own response to *Paradise Lost* and its author, when he wrote *Milton*, a poem in two parts, which was prefaced by 'And did those feet in ancient time...' popularly known as *Jerusalem*. Blake's work, which included *The Marriage of Heaven and Hell* (a book of paradoxical aphorisms), has been related to Neoplatonic tradition, Jungian, Freudian and Marxist theory, and Christianity. This stretches the imagination.

Wordsworth's reported verdict, after Blake's death, was: 'There is no doubt that this poor man was mad, but there is something in the madness of this man which interests me more than the sanity of Lord Byron or Walter Scott.' Wordsworth himself wrote things like '...the flowers/that in Madeira bloom and fade', without ever having been there. Not without good grounds was he known as 'Wordswords' by a number of his later critics, and it is one of these – George Bernard Shaw – who at last disembarks with us in Madeira (Atlantis?), for it was there – believe it or not – that G.B.S. learned how to dance; in fact he even went so far as to leave a portrait photograph to his dance-master, immodestly inscribed 'to the only man who ever taught me anything'.

'Willy, Willy, Harry, Stee; Harry, Dick, John, Harry Three...' generations of British schoolchildren used to chant, in order to memorize the names of British kings and queens; and much of the monarchy was condensed into a forlorn little poem, to which silly stanzas are still being added. Then along came 'instalments', and history became far less chewy and much more swallowy. Even myth has somehow become far less remote. Take the Dragon Tree.

Hercules was quite a god. In fact he was almost super-human. And he didn't just spend his time godding about on Mount Olympus: he had Things To Do. The twelfth of his labours was to fetch golden apples from a mysterious tree on the island of the Hesperides ('daughters of the evening'), at the world's end. The tree, needless to say, was guarded by a fierce dragon.

Millennia later, Ptolemy described an island in the Atlantic which he called *Erythria* ('red island'), after a dye which was extracted from a tree there. Pliny all but echoed his words, writing of the 'purple islands'. Later still, St Brendan was believed by early Christians to have inhabited a holy island off the coast of Africa, together with a colony of saints.

From the fifteenth century, sailors who happened upon the precipitous north coast of the island of Madeira, with its mountain-tops lost in cloud, believed they were looking at the Mouth of Hell – but changed their minds as soon as they had sailed around to the southern lushness of Funchal. They were then convinced that they had discovered part of the lost continent of Atlantis. And perhaps they had. For, even today, you can see, scattered about the island, a few specimens of the Dragon Tree, with its pithy trunk and bizarre, upside-down appearance. The vivid red sap was prized by early settlers as a dye and an essence with magical healing powers. And who knows if the floods which have periodically washed great slabs of Madeira into the ocean were not the same waters as those which inundated Atlantis?

There is a little Madeiran village called Faial, perched on the north-east corner of the island, where, some 300 years ago, the local *morgado* (first-born) used to ride his horse into church and make it kneel at the elevation of the Host. On his demise, he was granted a decent burial – only because he owned the place. But it was after his tomb had been washed out to sea during a torrential rain-storm, that the locals felt that divine justice had at last been done.

Machico, in the south-east, is not a good place to build churches. Fire and flood have taken their toll since the *Capela do Cristo* (Chapel of Christ) was first constructed, in 1420, by João Gonçalves 'Zarco', the one-eyed adventurer who, with his co-navigator Tristão Vaz, rediscovered the island for the Portuguese. The whole church was washed into the Atlantic in 1803. Some weeks later, the crucifix from the high altar was discovered floating many leagues away by the crew of an American galley who returned it to the populace of the ravaged village, its delicate Gothic carving wondrously preserved. Subsequently the edifice was rebuilt and appropriately renamed the *Capela dos Milagres* (Chapel of Miracles). Although assaulted by floodwaters twice more, it still stands, and the crucifix heads a proud, festive procession round the village every 6 October.

It is recorded that, in the same flood of 1803, 'the home of the Tatlock family (who were having a dinner party at the time) was washed out to sea in its entirety, where, every window ablaze with light, it went down like a large ocean liner'.

The construction of an English church was financed by a voluntary levy on Madeira wine exports, and a subscription fund which was supported by – among others – poor, batty, King George III. The handsome neo-classical building was designed by the then British Consul at the cost of £10,000 – 'an unconscionable sum of money' at the time. A large masonic eye stares down from the dome. There is a bust of Philippa of Lancaster in the garden and two towering magnolia trees. In the English Rooms library nearby, a cross nestles coyly on the shelf between Crime and Adventure.

Matins was led by two incumbents, the one with an engaging uphill-downhill voice, befitting the island perfectly. The lilies,

123

painted around the arches above the recessed altar, seemed to bow down, the better to enjoy the message of 'Solomon in all his splendour'.

'He shall lead me into green pastures,' we chanted, and the palm-trees rustled their assent. A dog barked its way into the responses as if to tell us that it, too, knew the story of the *morgado's* horse.

We, the Holy Trinity Church congregation of Madeira, then marched our way through 'Onward Christian Soldiers' in this off-shore relic of the erstwhile diocese of Sierra Leone, in step – or so it seemed – with generations of New World discoverers, and monarchs of poetry and prose.

Everything fell into place. Zarco and King George, unlikely allies, merged into one; and as, with insane gusto, we pitched into Blake's *Jerusalem,* the solitary eye, high above us, imperceptibly winked.

* * *

This essay was penned after a fascinating trip Angelika and I made to this charming island at a time when I was involved with the Port Wine trade. It is in memory of the late Richard Blandy, one time British Honorary Consul at Funchal (Madeira), who was a perfect host, and gave me some valuable counsel. My mother Gwynneth had visited the island in 1928, on her way to Durban with the *Kenilworth Castle.* This was three years after George Bernard Shaw's visit; five years after Agatha Christie had passed through; and six years after the exiled Karl I von Habsburg, last Emperor of Austria, Hungary, Croatia and Bohemia, had died there.

* * *

The following three Oporto stories stand in for all those situations which had nothing or little to do with the business in hand. The first and third were recounted to the bank manager (me) by one of the two twins and Miss Tait respectively; I chose to deal with the man from Lincolnshire myself.

TWINS

There were two ladies, in their 60s, who regularly put in an appearance at the Oporto Cricket and Lawn Tennis Club, a bastion of stability during the Revolution. They were identical twins. And they went to the Club, it was said, to use the shower facilities.

One summer afternoon, one of the twins was walking home from town, when she chanced to go past the Communist Party headquarters, with its loudspeakers blaring out the music of the *Internationale*. There were decks of carnations outside the door: this was, after all, the 'Carnation Revolution'.

She stopped and picked one, whereupon a little man with a beard came rushing down the steps:

'You cannot steal our carnations!'

'I am not stealing your carnations.'

'I saw you distinctly taking one.'

'I did indeed take one. Are you not communists? Doesn't everything belong to everybody?'

And she turned away from him and ambled off home.

The following day, her twin sister happened to take the same route, past the Communist Party headquarters, with its loudspeakers still blaring out the music of the *Internationale*. She was admiring the colours of the flowers as she walked past. To her surprise, a little man with a beard came rushing down the steps, and handed her a bunch of carnations...

THE MAN FROM LINCOLNSHIRE

The story was that he had got into a taxi from one side at exactly the same time as she had got into the same taxi from the other side. That was how they had met. They had done a business transaction and he owed her £20 (which was worth more then than it is now). He had at least the same amount in a Building Society in Mablethorpe and would we please arrange for this amount to be transferred to him as soon as possible? He had a thick Lincolnshire accent, and his nose dripped.

Such a request was, in those days, not as easy to satisfy as it sounded, and I warned him that there would be bank charges.

They both came into the Bank every day of the following week to see if the money had arrived. On the tenth day (a Monday) they asked for me at Reception. He needed, he said, another £10 to 'take care of her time during on-going negotiations'.

What we couldn't tell him was that we knew the lady quite well. She visited the Bank every month to receive an allowance due to her from a former member of the staff of the Bank, who had got her into the family way. In fact she was very well known around town.

We allowed the charade to continue: bank secrecy.

Then the money arrived. I handed him the equivalent in escudos of only £25 (£30 less £5 charges). He counted it punctiliously. Then he stared at me, the dew-drop quivering, tantalisingly, at the end of his nose, and asked:

'Are you from Lincolnshire too?'

I took it as a rhetorical question.

MISS TAIT

Miss Tait had lived in Oporto for as long as anybody could remember. She was well into her 90s when I got to know her. She liked a good chat and treated bank managers as people to whom she could turn, in complete trust, for any reason at all. One was torn between being very comfortable with the notion that one was so completely trusted; and being slightly displeased in the knowledge that one might be importuned at any time of the day for an indefinite time and asked for a cup of tea.

Actually, she was very good fun. There was only one problem. She was very ancient and looked exceedingly brittle. I was always nervous that she might keel over and break something (a bone, say) on my large cast-iron radiator. But thankfully, it never happened.

One day, during a particularly turbulent period of the Portuguese Revolution she came into the Bank in high dudgeon.

'I am very annoyed.' I sat her down as quickly as I could.

'Good morning, Miss Tait.'

'Yes. I am very annoyed.'

'What has happened?'

'Last night, I had a bullet through my drainpipe...'

'How terrible. Nobody was hurt, I trust.' She didn't hear me.

'You know, I was in Petrograd once.'

'Petrograd? When were you in Petrograd?'

'It was during the Kerensky rebellion. I was standing by a window and a bullet went past me. Buried itself in the ceiling. Couldn't find that one either. I'm very annoyed.'

That evening, I visited her at her property, overlooking the Douro. She showed me where the bullet had perforated her pipe. There had been shooting nearby and she was lucky not to have been hurt. She had hoped to find the bullet so that she could give it to her adopted daughter.

Her family later told me that she had indeed taken part in the Kerensky rebellion, as an ambulance driver. This had been in the autumn of 1917, when Alexander Kerensky, supported by Russian and foreign counter-revolutionaries, made a vain attempt to regain power after the Bolsheviks had overthrown his Provisional Government in Petrograd. At the time she must have been in her early 30s.

BUSYBODY

This story dates back to the days when I had nothing whatsoever to do with the British Consulate in Zürich. In retrospect, had I had more consular experience, it would never have happened.

We had an elderly babysitter at the time. She was Swiss and lived nearby. I remember being enormously impressed on one occasion, when she proudly announced that she had never been abroad. There was no need to, she said. Switzerland had everything that anyone could wish for. She may well have been right. She was stern but never lost her temper. One Christmas, back in the 1960s, she gave us a crib, which we have to this day. It was a very honourable relationship.

Once, as she was leaving, she asked me casually if I would help her find her sister.

'Where was your sister when you last had contact with her?'

'She was in England.'

'No address?'

'I no longer have an address.'

'No other indications of where she might be?'

'Absolutely none.'

She spoke quite a challenging dialect of Swiss German, but her last reply (*garrrrrnüüüüt*) was so clear and definitive that I now know that I should have stepped out of this conversation at that point in time.

But I didn't: 'Do you have anything at all that might help me to find her?'

'I have a photograph of her.'

The next time she came to us, she brought the photograph with her. It showed a stately young woman in the clothes and with a hairstyle which suggested the 1930s. There was the name of a professional photographer on the back, and the faint trace of what seemed to be the name of a town in the British Midlands.

There was no Internet in those days; no Web. All my detective work was done by letter or by phone. It became an obsession. I contacted mayors, policemen, lawyers, jury service clerks. Gradually a picture of the sister's life began to emerge, and eventually I found her, living with her daughter, a stone's throw from where the picture had been taken. I proudly wrote down the address and gave it to our baby-sitter.

A month or so later, there was a letter for me in the post from the UK. I opened it. It began:

'Dear Busybody...'

* * *

Many years later, I was brusquely reminded of this experience at the British Consulate:

Honorary Consul: 'I have heard that your daughter has disappeared. Please let us know if you need any consular assistance.'

British citizen: 'May I trouble you, Sir, to mind your own business.'

HOLY MOUNTAIN

It was April 1982, and I had been invited to accompany an old friend, Michael Sternberg, then Consul General of the USA in Thessalonika, on an official visit to Athos. There were to be a couple of diplomatic/consular engagements in Thessalonika itself, after which we would leave for the Holy Mountain.

Michael felt that it would facilitate the issue of a visa, as well as the entry to certain diplomatic engagements, if he could introduce me with a consular title (which, of course, at the time, I did not have). We settled on 'Honorary Consul at Lugano' - it might just as well have been Plaza-Toro. Some time later, I chanced to meet the real British Honorary Consul at Lugano, Lancelot de Garston, and came clean. He took it very well.

The formalities in Thessalonika included a diplomatic do, during which a Swiss functionary eyed me a little curiously, and a basket-ball match between Greece and the United States, where we were the shortest people in the building. We lived in Michael's official residence, behind bars and padlocks under extraordinary security, and sped around the city, shadowed by armed bodyguards in jeeps.

Then it was time to leave for Ouranopolis, where we took a small boat to Daphne. Our spectacular visas, signed by the Administrators of the monasteries of Vatopedi, Koutloumousiou, Karakalou and Stavronikita, were issued at Karyes, and our passports impounded.

Our visit to Athos was a wash-out: it rained for the four days we were there and, because one has to walk everywhere, we spent our time soaked to the skin. No matter. For those 96 hours we were transported back to Byzantium. The Classical Greek I had studied at school miraculously matched the lingua franca spoken there by Bulgarians, Russians, Serbs, Turks, Americans and Greeks. We saw treasures in the libraries; we debated and prayed with the monks. We were back with the dates and times of the Julian calendar. And the Byzantine flag fluttered proudly. We were called to prayer early each morning by the clop-clop of the hammer on the wooden *semantron.* And we fell into bed shortly after sundown.

We lived on rice and pickled cabbage; cheese and biscuits, boiled egg, yoghurt and cold squid; tomato-juice, dried fruit and sugar-water. The tables were laid with food ready for the next meal, it must be said, *after* every meal, and, by the time we all sat down again, the plates were black with flies: it was disgusting.

In our wet boots, we visited Koutloumousiou, which purportedly houses the largest relic of The True Cross, and has been burnt down only once in the last 800 years; then north-west to the tenth-century Zografou, where one of the 12 Bulgarian monks in residence showed us a selection of the 400 manuscripts – mainly in Slavic – and 8,000 books, which had evidently been protected by the monastery's remoteness in the hills. Two icons of St George may be viewed, one of which is believed to be 'not fashioned by the hand of Man'. The story goes that a doubting priest placed his finger on the icon to establish if it had really not been made by Man's hand. The finger stuck to the icon: we could still see it forlornly hanging there, like a black chipolata sausage.

Then we trudged back southwards to the ten-monk monastery of Dochiariou of the Serbo-Moldo-Wallachian tradition; Xenophontos, sacked and damaged, over the centuries, by many incursions of pirates; and the green-roofed Russian St Panteleimon, founded in the eleventh century. What one now sees, however, was constructed 700–800 years later. On the track

Athos: Simonos Petra, 1982.

back up towards Karyes, we passed the Skete of St Andrew, built in the mid-nineteenth century with monies provided by the Russian Tsars. In the early 1900s, the complex, the site of the largest church in Athos, housed 700 monks; when we went past, there were less than ten. Because the Statute of Athos does not countenance the building of new monasteries, later structures must be styled 'sketes'.

We were greeted with water and Turkish Delight at Stavronikita, where we were to spend two nights. During our stay, we were permitted to view the monastery's most famous relic. The mosaic icon of St Nicholas Streidas, when discovered in the ocean, was found to have an oyster embedded in the image's forehead. After the oyster had been removed, blood reportedly oozed from the crack. Here, we received a message from the Holy Administration in Karyes, that our passports had been mislaid (do nothing; they want a bribe, said Michael).

We dropped in for lunch and an introduction to miracles at the Georgian Iviron, which houses the best known icon of Athos: the *Panagia Portaitissa*, which, according to tradition, was painted by St Luke the Evangelist. We re-crossed the peninsula to the spectacular Simonos Petra, which had burnt down in 1580, 1626 and (completely) in 1891; it was during the last conflagration that the extensive library was destroyed. We spent our last evening there, after a protracted theological discussion, during which it was announced that our passports had been found again (told you so, said Michael). The excursions along a rickety platform, high above the terraces, to visit the loo, were daunting.

According to the monasteries' way of life, each is categorised as either cenobitic or idiorrhythmic. In the former group, everything - roof, work, food and prayer - is regarded as communal; in the latter, roof and prayer are communal, whereas work and food are left to the initiative of the individual monks. Of the monasteries we had visited, only two - Dochiariou and Iviron - were idiorrhythmic.

We were hosted at Simonos Petra by an American monk, who was wearing the same walking-boots as I was. They were decorated with little metal trefoils. When we first met, I noticed that one of his was missing, and joked with him about it. Just before we caught the ferry from Daphne back to Ouranopolis, I noticed that one of mine was missing.

Suddenly, the Byzantine chimes metaphorically struck midnight, and it was time for the British Honorary Consul at 'Plaza-Toro' to return to the real world.

COUSIN CHERRY

Cousin Cherry (name *not* changed: her father and my late mother's father were brothers) merits a biography just for herself. But she'll at least get a mention here.

In February/March 2010 we were in Sydney to celebrate her 100th birthday. One hundred guests were invited. And what a day it was, with Cherry on sparkling form in the sub-tropical heat ('What a sissy – he is not coming to the party; says it's too hot for him; he's only 96'). There was a soirée of zimmer frames parked in the hall and the buzz of conversation did credit to her extraordinarily wide-ranging life, and her vast net of acquaintants. She is a networker par excellence, and very good at family history: I once asked her where my maternal grandfather (her uncle) had been born. After a moment's reflection, she answered, 'I know it was on land...' After another moment, she continued, '...but somewhere I have a copy of *his father's* marriage certificate.'

Lewis Davies, her grandfather, had been a sea-captain whose life has been documented in Welsh-language sources, and of course one of my ambitions for this trip to Australia, was to obtain a copy of the said marriage certificate; and Cherry let me have one. The stately hand-written document, in Latin, shows that the marriage took place in Braila, a port on the lower Danube, in 1860, in the presence of the Secretary of the Acting British Consul there.

* * *

I was in the VIP room at Zürich airport with the British Ambassador 140 years after this marriage had taken place. We were meeting Prince Michael of Kent who was passing through on business. I was aware that Prince Michael knew Cherry and, during a lapse in the conversation, asked him if he had received her Christmas card that year (picturing Cherry, at the age of 92 or so, seated on the pillion of a swarthy Sudanese tribesman's motorcycle). Prince Michael chuckled: yes, he had received her card. What a woman! They had not so long ago visited the library of St Catherine's monastery, Mount Sinai, together.

At this point in the conversation – as if to underline the esoteric nature of the occasion – we were approached by Andrew Tesorière, HM Ambassador at Tirana, also passing through Zürich, but with an Albanian ministerial trade delegation in tow. He had recognised Prince Michael. He told us that, since being accredited to Albania, he had been living in a two-roomed flat with his wife and (if my memory serves me right) four militia men.

I stepped back from the distinguished throng and mused that Marie Christine, Princess Michael, née Marie Christine Agnes Hedwig Ida von Reibnitz, whose mother was also an old friend of Cherry, had been born in Karlovy Vary in what is now the Czech Republic, only a stone's throw up-river, in cosmic terms, from where my maternal great-grandfather had been married. But how did Albania fit in to all of this?

Cherry was at it again.

PLAYING AT GOD

'The name of this new town is Ksamil,' she said, giggling, 'and it is the only town in our country without a cemetery...because nobody has died yet!' This was the sort of statistic, we all thought, which would be more appropriate in Transylvania. But then – the train of thought continued – surely there was not much difference between Count Dracula and the ever-present – if dead – Enver Hoxha (rhymes with dodger). As we had heard that there were no churches whatsoever in this strictly atheistic land, the cemetery anecdote took us by surprise.

The trip from Corfu had been unexpectedly rough once we were free of the narrow channel between that island, where Odysseus had briefly courted Nausicaa, and mainland Illyria, known to its people as Shqipëri, 'the land of the eagles', once ruled by King Zog, 'the bird'. Our destination was Albania.

Once visas were to hand, we had to deal with the Custom-House Declaration where *Mblemer* (shades of emblem) means 'surname', and a question is asked which, by its spelling, betrays nothing but isolation: 'Do you posses any of the goods mentioned below, transmiter and eceiver radio sets, Camera Recorder, Television set, Refrigarator, ashing machine, and other house Comodities, watches Drugs, Printed metter cuch as leters, Books Magazines, Different currencies, explozives [*sic*].'

As the good ship *Petrakis* set course for Sarandë, past the one-monk monastery of Pantocrator, perched on the highest peak of Corfu, now literally straddled by a horrendous television pylon, we had time to muse on what had gone before.

Anyone who has been to Corfu will know that required reading for the island is Lawrence Durrell's *Prospero's Cell*, and one can still visit the house where he wrote it, now, and possibly already then, a sturdy but scruffy *taverna* with a splendid view across the bay at Kalami. In fact it is three books in one: the history which Ivan Zarian was longing to write but couldn't; the volume which Count D. should have written but was not inclined to; and the account, in diary form, which was eventually published.

Durrell tells the story of the Cypriot shepherd, later St Spyridon, who saved the island on many an occasion, and after whom most Korfiote males are named Spyros. He also records the Count's erudite theory that Corfu (Corcyra) was the island of Prospero in Shakespeare's *Tempest*, hence the title of the book. *Twelfth Night*, after all, was set in Illyria.

Another cruel little tale is of two lovers during the Turkish occupation, he an Albanian Muslim, she a Greek. During a political crisis they were separated but regularly signalled to each other, respectively from Cape Stiletto and the islet of Govino. Then, following her sudden death, the girl's fire was no longer lit. For many years thereafter, on the second Sunday of every month, the boy's faith flickered across the bay to the unresponding Govino headland... so near and yet so far.

First impressions, as we arrived at the port of Sarandë, were of hundreds of little boys (not one little girl to be seen) staring at us from the beach and the harbour walls: stares which were neither friendly nor unfriendly; primitive, animal stares: beings unaware that they were staring. Massive, shiny, blue speedboats of the *sigurimi* (security police) were set apart from the rusting hulks of everything else. There were dozens of posters with exhortations of (the late) Enver Hoxha and his successor Ramiz Alia, crudely designed to render morality and religion superfluous: the wayside calvary of Christendom transformed into a maxim of the Thought Police.'

The head customs officer, a handsome, sinister individual, relieved some of us of the odd newspaper and novel ('to be returned after I have read it'), and we stepped ashore.

Our link-person from Albturist was Miranda, a pretty blonde English teacher from Tirana, in her early 20s, with the bloom of guileless humour in her eyes. She steered us with great charm around ancient Buthrotum (Butrint), with its timeless stoneworks changing shape under the successor cultures of Corinth and Corcyra, Rome and Byzantium. 'It's all Greek to me!' and: 'This must be a statue of the goddess Miranda,' she chuckled.

She told us how the latter-day Italian occupiers had begun excavation in order to prove that Albania was part of the Roman heritage; but, on discovery of Illyrian inscriptions carved in Ancient Greek characters, had only succeeded in enhancing Albanian nationalism.

Grubby little boys, muttering 'goom' (for chewing gum, we supposed), and 'stilo' (pen), hung about.

We were shown a group of 'volunteer students', hacking painfully away with picks and shovels at an ancient provisions room in part of the sprawling archaeological complex. After we had passed, I crept back to see what they would do unwatched: they were already packing up and moving off – possibly to the next heroic demonstration.

'We have a problem,' said Miranda enigmatically, as our vintage Albturist bus wound its way north up the single track road back to Sarandë, 'Nobody in Albania may own a car.' Bicycles may be bought with *leks*, the local currency, but motor-cycles may only be purchased with foreign currency sent from relations abroad. 'Everybody in Albania travels by bus.' A glance at the town bus terminal later in the day, replete with its creaking and clanking Russian and Chinese leviathans, bore this statement out. 'Our problem,' I said to Miranda, who had never been outside Albania, 'is that *everybody* seems to own a car.'

Diminutive peasants, straight out of the nineteenth century, idled under scrawny roadside olive bushes, themselves a contrast to the 500-year-old gnarled monsters, regimentally set out under the Venetian olive-planting initiative in Corfu, only four km across the narrow channel to the west. Fields of sweetcorn and tomatoes stretched out around Ksamil, which also produces water-melons, 'for export,' said Miranda proudly; wooden mussel-farms in the upper waters of Lake Butrint; 'the lower levels are contaminated by natural gas,' she remarked innocently; rice paddies along the banks of the Pavllo, south of Butrint: 'our country is self-sufficient in food,' she recited.

A ten-course meal, obscenely extravagant and inappropriate in a country of subsistence diet, awaited us back at the Hotel Butrinti in Sarandë, accompanied by the nostalgic singing of two supremely unspoilt tenors, straight out of the 1960s or earlier. The high point of the entertainment was a dance group, with the men cavorting beautifully and vainly through traditional country dance routines. Initial impressions of effeminate gestures were gradually suppressed by the realisation that one was watching something in character with 450 years of Ottoman occupation, after the death of Skanderbeg, the national hero, when men – not women – were the flaunted sex. The women dancers provided little more than modestly decorative accompaniment.

A walk around Sarandë, the purchase of a loaf of bread and a souvenir box – the only things our *leks* would buy from the otherwise empty shelves – and our visit drew to a close. The whole town, it seemed, waved us away from the quay.

What were we left with? How could such a culture-gap be bridged? A scenario of no religion, no logic, no morality, with the artful Hoxha in the role of God Almighty... There was a link; Miranda supplied it: the 'Christian' name of her companion, our Greek/Italian interpreter – a member of the Greek minority in the south of the country – was Spyros. 'And Miranda,' she told us with pride, 'was, of course, Prospero's daughter.'

Angelika and I had one day in Albania in the autumn of 1990. We had been spending time in Corfu with some old friends in the United States Foreign Service, Dorothy and Vernon Penner. Neither the United Kingdom nor the United States entertained diplomatic relations with Albania at the time. Whereas I then had no connection with the Foreign Office, Vernon was posted to the NATO Defense College at Rome, and, for obvious reasons, could not come with us.

THE MAHARAJAH OF JAIPUR

There was shouting outside my office.

'Bloody disgrace. You should be ashamed of yourselves. You have no idea how to treat customers. I always thought a British passport meant something. Until now, that is.'

I opened the door, and was accosted:

'Who do you think *you* are?'

There were two ladies: one younger, 50s, doing the shouting; and one older, 80s perhaps.

Both were tanned and fit. The younger one was very angry; the older one, looking this way and that, just nodded. I had got back that morning from a business trip to India. It had been the usual rush. I had travelled the previous day from Jaipur to Bombay and flown straight back to Zürich. I was tired; and this was the last thing I wanted. I told her who I was. She shook my hand reluctantly but imperiously, and introduced her mother, who smiled.

'Ah. Well what do you say to this? We were sent to the wrong address. Well...? Can't you see my mother is old? How can you allow such a thing to happen...to me - us - of all people?'

Colonial. Rude. The worst sort. Used to bullying underlings. I apologised to her and explained that we had only just moved to the new address. I asked her how I could be of assistance.

'Why were we not received by you? I phoned yesterday and asked for an appointment. They told me you were not there. Where were you?'

'I was returning from a business trip, Madam. Now, how can I be of assistance?'

'I asked you where you were...'

'Actually, Madam, though it is none of your business, I was in India...'

'Where in India?'

'Yesterday I was in Jaipur, before returning to...'

'Oh!' Her countenance changed completely...

'How's the Maharajah?'

I had no idea how the Maharajah was; I had not been to see him. But I told a little white lie:

'Quite well, actually. Now, what can I do for you, Madam? Time is getting short.'

Our social positions were suddenly reversed. Here was somebody who had been (she thought) with the Maharajah of Jaipur only yesterday. She apologised for her brusque behaviour; told me she did not want to waste my time any further, bid me goodbye and left. Her mother followed her out of the office but, as she was going through the door, turned to me, smiled again, and gave me a scarcely perceptible wink.

* * *

While little white lies should not be over-used, I take refuge
in what Sir Henry Wotton, James I's emissary at Venice, once
wrote in a German Gentleman's notebook: *Legatus est vir bonus,
peregrè missus ad mentiendum Reipublicae causâ,* which has been
translated: 'An ambassador is an honest man, sent to lie abroad
for the good of his country.'

I thought of Rudyard Kipling's 'Elephant's child – who was
full of satiable curtiosity.'

THE BAOBAB AND THE THUMB-PIANO

The clatter of the sugar-cane mill must have been music to the ears
of Thomas Murray MacDougall, when he finally got it started on
his estate in Triangle (in south-eastern Rhodesia, now Zimbabwe)
on 11 September 1939. It had been an extraordinary feat to get the
heavy, secondhand equipment up from Natal. Roads had to be
cut, and drifts constructed over rivers. It took 'Mac' half a year to
find part of the load which he had had to abandon in the lowfeld
bush when the rains came. But at last it was ready.

Half a century later, as guests of a very dear niece, who used
to live there, Angelika and I pay a quick visit to the Triangle
Memorial Chapel, erected by the Lowfeld Community in 1991.
Leadwood trunks are set into the walls of the chapel, around
the mahogany pews. There are stained-glass representations of
a hippo, a sable, a dove, a ground hornbill, a baobab tree, cattle,
a butterfly, sugar-cane and – most important – water. There is a
picture of George Cantuar, and another of the Right Reverend
Jonathan Siyachitema, Anglican Bishop of Central Zimbabwe. St
Andrew's in Zürich is a million miles away.

Later we learn about the mopane tree with its butterfly-
shaped, high-protein leaves, on which the mopane worm – a
Bushman delicacy – subsists. There is the marula bush, reputed to
make elephants intoxicated; the rain tree, inhabited by the cuckoo
spit insect, which exhumes its nourishment as fast as it takes it in,
causing a 'rain' to fall; the sausage tree under which one stands
at ones peril: the fruit, which has been known to fall on unwary
picnickers, can weigh up to 4 kg.

Then there is the baobab, referred to by Dr Livingstone as 'that
giant, upturned carrot'. Young baobabs are difficult to spot, with
their small, simple leaves; only years later do these leaves become

'palmately compound' with up to seven distinctive leaflets. This has given rise to the Bushman belief that there is no such thing as a young baobab, and that mature specimens are flung from paradise, landing topsy-turvy, with their roots in the air. Someone asks if zebras have black stripes, – or white.

As two red lechwe bucks face off, their horns clashing in light-hearted combat, a German tourist, forgetting for a moment that he isn't watching television, remarks that it is all 'just like real life ...'

All too soon, magically, we are in a canoe in the Okavango Delta in northern Botswana, peacefully navigating the waters which rush down the mountains in south-eastern Angola, and disappear into the desert. We are surrounded by papyrus reeds, which hide the mysterious Zambezi sitatunga, a marsh-deer with thick, spiral horns. This timid beast is known to submerge itself in the water if danger threatens. Wielding the paddle of the canoe is Letter.

Letter is a Bushman, who has migrated northwards from the depths of the hot, silent Kalahari. He is tiny, with a little, squashed, wizened face. Letter isn't his name actually; but it is as close as anyone can get to the first two syllables of it. The rest is made up of the characteristic clicks of the Bushman tongue. He will not tell anybody what his full name is.

When Letter came to Okavango, he walked but he mainly ran. He does not know how many weeks it took him. He enjoyed the journey.

He left most of his meagre possessions with his family, and brought with him only his giraffe-hide sandals, duiker-skin hunting trousers, a penduline tit nest (woven with wild cotton and animal hairs) to keep his tobacco dry, a digging stick, and his favourite thumb-piano, fashioned from bits of woods and flattened fencing wire.

In his eyes, as we drift idyllically about in the canoe, we see his little legs carrying him steadily across the vast, dusty reach towards us, to the rhythmic, metallic melody of the trusty little musical instrument, which fits snugly into his minute palm, with nobody within miles to hear his tune. We, his enchanted audience of two, cannot hear the music either.

When we wake up, we are back in Zürich.

GREENERY

The last two periods of my working life, after I had left the Lloyds Bank Group, were as accredited Representative of Cater Allen Bank and as British Honorary Consul at Zürich. These were straddled by my activities in environmental studies, and Angelika's inventive efforts with 'Art Ventures', which she first created to assist young musicians visiting Zürich to get to know something of the cultural scene while they were here. Her little organisation, which operated on a very modest budget, expanded its activities to such an extent that she hosted groups from places as far afield as Vancouver and Cape Town, Tomsk and Buenos Aires.

At the same time she found the energy to look after the Zürich Conservatory Orchestra on excursions to Hamburg, New York, Paris and Shrewsbury. Latterly, she has become an interpreter, accredited to the Canton of Zürich, for social service cases – many of them very challenging – where Portuguese, Spanish or English needs to be simultaneously translated into German or Swiss German, and vice versa. Her experiences here, we both agree, have been not unlike many of my own experiences as Honorary Consul. It has been a privilege for me to share them with her.

My own focus in the environmental field, in these cradle years of ecology, was to try to defuse the charged atmosphere which tended to prevail whenever, say, a banker found himself stuck with an environmental scientist. I came in from the banking side. I had one theme only: the title was always 'Who pays?' With time, I found that bankers and environmentalists were able to set up valuable associations, and that bankers and insurance executives began to provide substantial financial support to environmental causes.

My interest became more defined in the mid-1980s when an old university chum, Robert Goodland of the World Bank, introduced me to Professor Nicholas Polunin, a fascinating man who first became famous with his works on Arctic Botany. John Buchan wrote the foreword to his first book, *Russian Waters* (1931). Polunin claimed to be the last man alive to have added major islands to the world's map; these were later renamed Air Force Island, Prince Charles Island and Foley Island, all north of Hudson Bay. He held various academic appointments at the Universities of Oxford, Yale, Harvard, McGill, Baghdad, Geneva and Ife, Nigeria. He created the Foundation for Environmental Conservation in Geneva, which, during our association, I represented at environmental conferences and conventions.

Later, I had the privilege of being asked to join the Board of the Foundation by Nicholas Polunin Junior.

One of my proudest achievements – I have no qualms about recording this – was winning the Foundation's 'Best Paper' prize for the year 1995, for a research article entitled 'Banking Responsibility and Liability for the Environment: What Are Banks Doing?' This exercise was later taken over by the Durrell Institute of Conservation and Ecology at the University of Kent.

My first conference, in April 1991, *Banking, The Environment and Education*, took place at the University of Sussex. Then followed, thick and fast, *The Ecological Market Economy* (at Olten, Switzerland); and the *CMDC World Clean Energy Conference* (Geneva). After my presentation at the CMDC meeting, a Greenpeace representative asked me a question:

'What would a banker suggest as a solution to the problem of the Maldives?'

My reply was, perhaps, not very diplomatic, but it did lead – rather unexpectedly – to quite a constructive discussion and a fruitful relationship with Greenpeace:

'If you are referring to global warming and rising sea-levels, I would suggest emigration.'

In November of the same year, I sponsored and organised a one-day conference in Zürich on *Banking and the Environment*. One of the most remarkable things about this meeting was that a large Swiss bank sent, as its representatives, two electricians; the same bank is now one of the 'leading lights' in environmental applications...

UNCED in Brazil (see below), was preceded by an invaluable briefing sponsored by the Swiss Science Writers' Association (Geneva) on the importance of commas and brackets in UN negotiations.

In January 1994, I was invited to speak at *The Hague International Model United Nations 26th Annual Session*, which looked at the problems of Indigenous Peoples, a new venture for me; the charming, ill-fated Ken Saro-Wiwa, of the Nigerian Ogoni People, was one of the other speakers.

The *Bankakademie, Hochschule für Bankwirtschaft* (School of Finance & Management) in Frankfurt got in on the act six months later, when I took part in a seminar there entitled *Doing Justice to the Environment in Business.*

In December 1994, I attended an advanced and down-to-earth course on *Environmental Protection in Banks* put together by the *Institut für Management und Umwelt* (Institute for Management and Environment) in Augsburg, Germany. In 1995, during a visit to Zimbabwe, I held informal discussions with the Lowveld Conservancies to get to know about their 'Campfire' programme. This numbered among its strategems such intriguingly simple and sensible guidelines as: 'a live rhinoceros is worth infinitely more to villagers than a dead one.' The subject tied neatly into the revenue side of my 'Who Pays?' theme.

April 1996 saw me in New York for the 4th Session of the UNEP Commission on Sustainable Development.

As time went on, banks and insurance companies in developed countries became more aware of their ecological responsibilities. They began to translate such terms as 'Environmental Impact Assessment' (EIA) into their own language, and transcribe them into their own procedures manuals. There seemed to be little left for me to do in this arena. I therefore began to concentrate on so-called 'microcredit', and, later still, on water.

MICROCREDIT

It was Dean Jonathan Swift, contentious Irish nationalist and author of *Gulliver's Travels* and many other historical and political tracts, who provided the inspiration for the Irish Loan Funds of the eighteenth to twentieth centuries. He had, from his own pocket, established a revolving loan scheme of £500, to support tradesmen in Dublin who had fallen on hard times. Thomas Sheridan, Swift's god-son and biographer, recorded that it was his maxim that 'anyone known by his neighbours to be an honest, sobre and industrious man, would readily find security, while the idle and dissolute would by this means be excluded'.

After Swift's death, this maxim was adopted by the Dublin Musical Society which, in 1768, raised enough money from its concerts to provide an average loan of £4 10s (today's equivalent to about £300) each, to some 6,000 'poor but industrious tradesmen'.

Serendipitously, there is a diplomatic connection: Swift's employer and patron, in his early life, was Sir William Temple, an Irish parliamentarian, who had been employed on various diplomatic missions. It was he, as Ambassador at The Hague, who successfully negotiated the marriage of Prince William of Orange and Princess Mary of England, as well as the 'Triple Alliance' (between England, the United Provinces and Sweden).

Swift's method of lending to poor people was dusted off and re-introduced into developing countries in the late 1960s; it commenced in earnest in Bangladesh in the mid-1970s. Grameen ('rural') Bank was at the forefront of the system's modern beginnings. The objectives included wresting credit-giving away from local moneylenders (with their outlandish interest rates), and counterbalancing the influence of traditional male social dominance in Bangladesh, a country with an inherent (lay and religious) resistance to female entrepreneurship.

The 13 principle features of 'Grameencredit' were, and still are (in summary):

- Credit is promoted as a human right
- Credit is aimed at poor families, particularly women
- Credit is based on trust not collateral
- Credit is aimed at the creation of self-employment and housing; not consumption
- This was started as a challenge to conventional banking which regarded the poor as not creditworthy
- Credit will be offered at the door-step
- Loans will only be granted to a group of members ('loanees')
- New loan(s) will be available after previous loan(s) is/ are repaid
- Loan repayments are in weekly or bi-weekly instalments
- More than one loan is possible
- There are obligatory and voluntary savings programmes
- Loans are usually granted through non-profit organisations
- A social Agenda is modelled on Grameen's so-called '16 Decisions'

The 16 'Decisions' are (in summary):

- We shall follow the principles of Discipline, Unity, Courage and Hard Work

- We shall bring Prosperity to our Families
- We shall look after our Houses
- We shall grow and eat Vegetables and sell the Surplus
- We shall plant as many Seedlings as possible
- We shall keep our Families small, minimise Expenditure and look after our Health
- We shall Educate our children and ensure that they can earn to pay for their education
- We shall keep our children and our environment Clean
- We shall build and use Pit-latrines
- We shall drink water from Tubewells; if it is not available, we shall boil it or use alum
- We shall not take a Dowry at our son's wedding nor give one at our daughter's wedding
- We shall not inflict Injustice on anyone nor allow anyone else to do so
- We shall collectively undertake bigger Investments for higher incomes
- We shall Help each other
- We shall restore Discipline in any centre if there is a breach
- We shall take part in Social Activities collectively

Now, resisting the temptation to criticise the simplistic style of some of these tenets, let us look at some Grameen Bank figures (Bangladesh alone) as at the end of 1976:

Disbursements (loans): $1,000
Members (Loanees): 10 (of which 20 per cent female)
Villages involved: 1

But see below.

In February 1997, I travelled to Washington DC for the first *Microcredit Summit*, sponsored by the RESULTS Educational Fund. Useful but inconclusive work was done on bridging the financial gap between, say, $1,000, the statutory maximum that a microcredit institution could advance, and $100,000 which was the minimum amount that commercial banks were prepared to lend. The chief executive of Monsanto and Hilary Clinton were prominent; but Professor Muhammad Yunus, founder of Grameen Bank, whom I met and chatted to for the first time, was, for me, the star. He was awarded the Nobel Peace Prize in 2006.

A Worldwide Inventory of (nearly 1,000) *Microfinance Institutions,* created in or before 1992 and serving at least 1,000 members, had been carried out by the World Bank as of July 1996. The list covered 45 countries in Africa from Algeria to Zimbabwe; 28 in Central and South America, from Argentina to Venezuela; 17 in Asia from Bangladesh to Vietnam; and 8 in Europe from Albania to Russia. Of these institutions 206 completed a survey which showed that about $7 billion was reaching more than 13 million individuals and groups as at September 1995. Of these figures, Grameen Bank now accounted for about $1.1 billion lent to 2 million individuals.

The World Bank did report that

> Most of the 206 institutions in the said survey were created recently. This is partly due to a profound interest in microfinance in the 1980s and 1990s combined with the fact that most of the programs created in the 1960s and 1970s for microlending disappeared due to dismal repayment rates, corruption, and heavy subsidisation leading to a 'grant mentality' among clients. As the 1980s progressed, more and more microfinance programs were created. This trend continues in the 1990s.

Despite this shaky start, Grameen Bank figures (Bangladesh alone) as at the end of 2009 (to be compared with the figures on the previous page) had grown to:

Disbursements (loans): $8.7 billion
Members (Loanees): 7.9 million (of which 97 per cent female)
Villages involved: 83,458

Bangladesh and India are the two countries with the largest number of microcredit members: nearly 30 million each. Regrettably, at time of writing, threats to this admirable financing system are coming from politicians in Andhra Pradesh who, for example, not appreciating the real costs to providers of bonafide microcredit operations, want to cap interest rates, and are encouraging loanees to default. Simultaneously, potential loanees (particularly in India) are being pressed by ruthless for-profit moneylenders, some of them linked to the State government, to take on multiple loans which have led to large-scale bankruptcy. Traditionally excellent recovery rates have plummeted from 98 per cent to as low as 20 per cent. Some larger institutions, with star-studded share registers, have even made enough money out of microcredit operations that initial public offerings (IPOs) are beginning to appear. Worst of all is the increasing pressure Muhammad Yunus has to face from Bangladeshi politicians, who are jealous, it seems, of his Nobel Prize, and do not like his candour.

Nevertheless, microfinance has proved to be a hardy system, and seeds have been sown.

Interestingly, average loans today are of approximately the same magnitude as they were in Jonathan Swift's time.

WATER

If one lives in Switzerland, one can safely drink tap-water. So, what *else* do you know?

Here are some random 2010 Press headlines:

'Are we threatened by climate wars?' (*Neue Zürcher Zeitung*, 22 July) - Water shortage as a catalyst for war in North Africa and Southern Europe.

'Bitter Toll' (*Economist*, 3 April) - Millions of animals die in drought in Mongolia.

'Chattahoochee Blues' (*Economist*, 18 September) - Water wars between Georgia, Alabama and Florida.

'Fishy Business' (*Economist*, 27 March) - Correspondent excluded from Japanese-hosted meeting at the Convention on International Trade in Endangered Species of Wild Flora and Fauna (CITES), where portions of the critically endangered bluefin tuna were pointedly served at meals.

'Groundwater is disappearing, the seas are rising' (*Neue Zürcher Zeitung*, 20 October).

'Operation "Clean Water" in muddy waters' (*Neue Zürcher Zeitung*, 4 February) - Russian drinking water in danger.

'Power and the Xingu' (*Economist*, 24 April) - Plans to build the world's third-largest hydroelectric station in the Brazilian Amazon.

'Rising Seas and a Looming Catastrophe' (*The New York Times*, 22 November) - Collapse of ice sheets in Greenland and Antarctica, following Global Warming, threatens coastal cities.

'Severe Drought Puts Spotlight on Chinese Dams' (*Science*, 12 March).

'Tap that Water' (*Economist*, 8 May) – The argument for dam-building in Africa.

'The Drought Ends, The Shouting Starts' (*Economist*, 24 April) – Should Australia save its farmers or its rivers?

'Who owns the Water Supply?' (*Engineering and Technology*, 24 July–6 August) – Water shortages predicted as catalysts for twenty-first century conflicts.

'Yemen in a Water Emergency' (*Neue Zürcher Zeitung*, 17 June.)

Conflict – international or intra-national – over water shortages in Iberia, in the Middle East, in California; squabbles over marine territory in the Arctic, in Central America, in the South China Sea; deep-sea mining rights; fishing wars everywhere? None of these are figments of our imagination: they are real issues.

What is known, for example, about the rivers which happen to have been mentioned in this short book?

The most recent case of pollution of the DANUBE was in October 2010, when seven people were killed and dozens left with serious burns. Lasting damage to countryside and wildlife has not yet been properly assessed.

The eastern part of the DOURO river basin is increasingly prone to water shortages.

The level of the MADEIRA river in the upper Amazon region can drop by as much as 20 metres in times of drought.

The MOSCOW river is heavily polluted by industrial waste.

The NILE may well stop flowing into the Mediterranean within the next five years.

Pollutants are still being released into the Great Lakes and ST LAWRENCE basin.

New dams are planned for the TIGRIS, both in Iraq and Turkey.

The Amur, USSURI and Sungari river basin is dangerously polluted by toxic chemical residues.

The YONGDING river no longer flows.

To end on a more optimistic note, Father THAMES, after being known as 'The Great Stink' in the mid-nineteenth century, when cholera was rife in London and Queen Victoria found no bathrooms when she moved into Buckingham Palace (that same River Thames which had featured in my school report all those years ago), is becoming a success story.

While on the Board of the Foundation for Environmental Conservation, I played a modest part in the publication of *Aquatic Ecosystems*, which, in the light of the above, I regard as one of the most important environmental books to be published this century. Although my own involvement, as my late mother used to say, was 'as a pimple on a pumpkin', please search out the book and give it to a school or university library near you.

This essay - and all the others which are on environmental or developmental subjects - might be seen as intruders in a description of the activities of honorary consuls. The fact is, though, that any Consular Corps can be a worthy forum for such concerns. I never missed an opportunity to discuss them then; nor will I miss this opportunity to reach a wider audience now.

UNCED (UNITED NATIONS CONFERENCE ON ENVIRONMENT AND DEVELOPMENT)

Scene 1

I never did find out what was in the package awaiting me on registration, because the smart RIO '92 carrier-bag, sponsored by the City Council and Tourism Authority, disgorged its contents down a drain, through an ill-glued bottom, just as I was boarding an airport bus. Charlie Chaplin couldn't have done it better! My neighbour for the ride, a charming and finely-adorned representative of the 'Women Studies' NGO from Omdurman, Sudan, was a fitting reminder that the World was coming to Rio. Somehow, we found ourselves talking about the indigenous Brazilian word *abacaxi*, which, strictly, means pineapple, but is also slang for a muddle or a mess. She saw a similarity with a Sudanese word *bakash*, which has the same connotation. We both knew that many thousands of people were descending on this beautiful, dangerous, steaming, teeming city at the same time, and the symbolism of our discussion was lost on neither of us. What sort of an *abacaxi* awaited us?

Excellent Organisation and Security

Although certain of the more militant NGOs may not agree, I believe it was a brilliant feat of organisation to arrange for the Global Forum to be well-separated (30 km or so) from the formal UNCED proceedings. If this had not been the case, present and future agendas would have become impossibly entangled, and security - for everyone - would have become a nightmare. As it was, our Brazilian hosts coped - in both 'centers' - with the most esoteric of problems in a human way that only those nations with real problems can accomplish.

While registration at the Global Forum was simple, UNCED security at *Riocentro* was superlative. Brazilian military forces, in sundry shades of khaki and green, lined the route, only a few yards apart. There were army vehicles, even tanks, strategically placed. Gun-barrels (unprimed, we later read) were symbolically pointed at the *favelas* and serious crime became, for two weeks, a thing of the past. Our own sense of well-being was enhanced by the delight of the *Cariocas* (the people of Rio) at being able fully to enjoy their marvellous city, for the first time in years.

Outside Flamengo Park, forgers and sneak-thieves were doing a roaring trade in Global Forum passes, shoulder to shoulder with peddlers and musicians. The atmosphere was festive.

Inside the enormous, oblong, green park (soon, to the alleged delight of the critics of green movements, enthusiastically trampled into a uniform, brown expanse of dust) there were 35 structures, to be used day and night for meetings, conventions, rallies and exhibitions. There were also (we were assured) no fewer than 675 prefabricated stalls for NGOs. The sheer numbers and the variety of persuasions of the delegates present, their intoxicating enthusiasm, their sense of common interest; all this and more made Flamengo Park a fairground with a purpose. Film-stars were photographed looking earnest about this and that. An Amerindian arrived from the Amazon with a Jaguar (*Felis onca*) skin for sale...

Healthy Rivalry Predictable

While the zaniest pressure-groups somehow got away with their crazy contentions, a number of better-known names nearly tipped the occasion from the sublime into the ridiculous. A sense of Global Forum *versus* UNCED began to be cultivated: them against us. Shortcomings and delays in the ongoing negotiations at *Riocentro* were headlined: demonstrations and marches were organised.

BUSH GO HOME said a banner, behind which tramped a small group of angry-looking people, before the United States President had even arrived. I found myself thinking - and even saying - that it was sad how certain NGOs did not have more pride. It was, after all, due to pressure from many of them that UNCED was taking place at all.

Meanwhile, at *Riocentro*, square brackets for insertion and deadlines to meet were the order of the day. A senior Swiss delegate has since told me that all the important discussions took place in closed session. But I am not so certain: *Riocentro* is an immense exhibition area, which was transformed for the duration into an alternative UN complex. Logistics, timing, organisation - all were impeccable. The lowliest helper inevitably offered to take one there rather than point out the route. The President of Brazil, in spite of gathering political clouds, did not put a foot wrong. In the main exhibition hall there were nearly 200 booths for Sovereign States and other entities. But for the heat, this was an ideal place for lobbying. Common refrains were 'Where is Nepal?' or 'What is Belarus?' Civil servants, ambassadors and ministers scurried about.

The Plenary Hall was air-conditioned, and one occasionally had the impression that some plenipotentiaries were exceeding the seven-minutes' rule in order to avoid - so to speak - the 'greenhouse effect'. For reasons of diplomacy, the President was only able to remind subsequent speakers to keep their presentations short. But speak they did, and soon it seemed that Biodiversity, Climate Change and Sustainability were second-nature to them. If over 100 Heads of State from North and South can be persuaded to bone up on such subjects, then real progress *has* been made.

Scene 2

The concentration of senior politicians and diplomats which characterised this extraordinary event can seldom - if ever - have been matched. On one memorable occasion, during an interval between speeches to the Plenary Session, I found myself in a small ante-room with six other people. An embarrassed George Bush Senior was there, in one corner of the room, with an aide - embarrassed because he had very nearly rubbed shoulders with an equally embarrassed Fidel Castro, who was placed in another corner with *his* aide. Helmut Kohl, Chancellor of Germany, stood, blinking, near the door. The sixth person, tallest of them all, squarely in the middle of the room and smiling broadly at this uncomfortable vignette, was Ratu Sir Kamisese Kapaiwai Tuimacilai Mara, the first Prime Minister of Fiji, wearing a splendid formal jacket with matching *Sulu va Taga* (resembling a skirt) and sandals.

Had UNCED been a dismal failure, I would have rated it a success - if only because I had been privileged to witness this bizarre scene.

It was an honour to represent the Foundation for Environmental Conservation (Switzerland) at the United Nations Conference on Environment and Development (UNCED), which was held in Rio de Janeiro, Brazil, 3-14 June 1992, and in the '92 Global Forum, also in Rio de Janeiro, 1-14 June 1992. While this was the first time that the *E* and the *D* of *UNCED* were on the world's stage at the same time, it turned out, generally speaking, that the (then) developed World wanted to talk about its own *environment*, and the (then) developing World its own *development.*

But what, *exactly*, took place in Rio?

It is a hard task to list the achievements of this enormous meeting of the minds. Some 35,000 people went to Rio for both events; 9,000 journalists kept the world informed. Of the 180 member states of the United Nations, over 100 heads of state or government took an active part. A cynic's bottom line for all these statistics might be that there would be at least 35,000 different opinions about such a list of achievements; and 9,000 different journalistic view-points. And, judging by the diversity of interests of those present at the conference - particularly at the Global Forum - this might not sound unreasonable.

The 1,420 accredited non-governmental organisations (NGOs) stretched from the Africa Harvest Mission (Nigeria) to the Zambia Alliance of Women; from the Arab Thought Forum (Jordan) to the World Muslim Congress (Pakistan); from the All Japan Seamen's Union to the Wilderness Society (Australia); from the Academy of Sciences of the USSR (Russian Federation) to the YWCA-YMCA of Sweden; from AEK-Pemasky (Panama: representing the Kuna indigenous community) to the Sociedad Pachamana (Peru); from the American Bar Association (USA) to the World Leisure and Recreation Association (Canada).

How could there possibly be an all-embracing view about *anything?*

But help was at hand.

Well in advance of the conference, participating countries had been asked to provide National Reports, following certain guidelines and more or less standardised formats. These reports were to include data on each country's perspectives, experience, policies, activities and issues, set in the context of their interpretation of the two key words: environment and development. Impressively, no less than 169 country reports were received in French, Spanish, Arabic and Russian, as well as English, by the UNCED Secretariat.

Reports were also received for certain country and island groupings; these included the European Community (EC), the Organization of Eastern Caribbean States (OECS), the Pacific Island Developing Countries (PIDCs), the Southern African Development Coordination Conference (SADCC). The Reports are a snapshot of the world in 1992.

The various national teams, so to speak, were now on the field, waiting for the referee to blow his whistle.

Just before 'kick-off', the Royal Society of London and the US National Academy of Sciences jointly issued a report (*Population Growth, Resource Consumption, and a Sustainable World*), which began as follows:

> If current predictions of population growth prove accurate and patterns of human activity on the planet remain unchanged, science and technology may not be able to prevent either irreversible degradation of the environment or continued poverty for much of the world.

This unequivocal and unique communiqué – the first ever to be issued jointly by these highly respected institutions – stood behind every single mission statement, made during the proceedings of this vast event, and provided timely food for thought at the Global Forum. Following their initial jockeying for attention, delegates became conscious of the limited time they had to take and draft and re-draft decisions, and get business done.

The phrase 'sustainable development' began to be accepted as an integrating concept. The climate treaty was signed by 154 countries, including the United States of America. The Earth Summit's 'polluter pays principle' was affirmed in the Rio Declaration, together with the 'environmental impact assessment'. The role of women was asserted, as was the identity, culture and interests of indigenous people.

The North agreed to make new and additional resources available to the South. All states were to address the eradication of poverty. And so on.

Most of us, I believe, suspected that many of these resolutions would turn out to be wishful thinking. Economic downturns inevitably throttle munificence. Most of us admired the stand of The Netherlands, for example, when the Dutch delegate announced his country's preparedness to raise assistance to developing countries to 0.6 per cent of GNP, *as long as other countries would follow suit.* Few were surprised when none did. And there was no US Signature on the Convention on Biological Diversity...

Nevertheless, it was a start.

Having aired my own theme of 'Who Pays?' to generally receptive audiences, my objective had been achieved, and I came away feeling elated and satisfied.

According to the old maxim, Rome wasn't built in a day...

...Nor was Rio!

CHERNOBYL

In February 1994, at the invitation of Victor Danilov-Danilyan, Russian Minister of Environmental Protection, I took part in a conference in Russia and Ukraine with the Citizen Ambassador Program of People to People International (based in Spokane, Washington). This visit was divided between Moscow, Kiev and Chernobyl, where one of the nuclear reactors had blown up eight years previously. This turned out to be a very exciting expedition to two countries which were in the process of re-defining themselves, at a time when Russian and Ukrainian experts were falling over each other to be as frank as possible about the dreadful state of the environment of the former Soviet Union.

Some of the presentations were quite shocking, and it seemed almost normal, while leaving the only reactor at Chernobyl which was still partly in commission, to be told that I had a trace of radioactivity on one of my overshoes, which was then unceremoniously thrown into a rubbish bag by a controller; almost normal to learn from our guide that the officer in charge of the control room there, who seemed to be slurring his words during his brief presentation, was drunk.

During this conference, I was thrown together – the only British citizen – with distinguished representatives from a wide variety of environmental disciplines of the United States. These ranged from studies of Agent Orange to Carcinogen Risk Assessment; from Drug Abuse to Geodesy; from Photogrammetry to Radiation; from Superfund to Teaching; from Toxicology to Waste Water Treatment. Our leader was a veteran of the 1979 core meltdown at Three Mile Island, Pennsylvania.

Grand phrases were uttered by Russian experts:

'Without proper assessment, no-one has the right to finance.' (Danilov-Danilyan)

'Planned: environmental passports for industries; toxic pollution certificates for drivers.' (Sevastianov, Deputy, Moscow City Duma)

'There is now an Environmental Centre at the Ministry of Defence.' (Grishin, Environmental Impact Assessment expert)

'One hundred and sixty scientific ecological programmes all work at different levels via 38 different ministries and departments.' (Vedenjapin, technology/environment expert)

And some disturbing admissions were made:

'In Cherogovka (a town 65 km from Moscow) no chemical facilities have waste disposal; everything goes into the town sewage.' (Ponomarev & Gorelyov, 'Adequatization')

'Hydrology maps are no good; Chernobyl may be called the map reflecting our disasters.' (Yakovlev, Head, Directorate General for Hydrogeology & Geoecology of the Ukrainian State Committee on Geology and Utilization of Mineral Resources)

Anecdotes abounded. On arrival at the Ukraina Hotel in Moscow, I was in the bar one evening, listening to a discussion between two scientists. The American was, among other things, an expert in fish diseases. He was explaining to his Russian colleague that he was particularly interested in a fungal condition which occurred in flat-fish, and drilled neat, round holes right through the body. The following exchange ensued:

'Are you aware if any fish have been found with this condition in the Moscow river?'

After a moment's reflection, the Russian replied:

'No, this condition is unknown here.' Pause, then, 'There are *no* fish in the Moscow river.'

Later the same evening a member of our group, from New Mexico, asked me to come with him to another bar to meet a new friend. As we entered the room, we were approached by a ruffian in a greatcoat, with a remarkable scar from above his left ear, across his face, to somewhere below his right ear. He held out his hand and announced himself as a Chechen. Then he threw himself into an armchair and his coat opened, revealing an enormous automatic pistol, stuck in his belt. I got up and left. The next morning, I told my colleague that he was a bloody fool getting into such company. He agreed and we still correspond.

The second night in Moscow, one of our delegates, a specialist in imaging research, had too much to drink. He was on the other side of Moscow. The Minister himself was alerted, and, at 2 o'clock in the morning, *walked* him back to the hotel (in the company of his bodyguards), so that he would be sober enough for his presentation the next morning.

It had been from the grounds of the Ukraina Hotel that the House of Councils (the 'White House') had been bombarded only 14 months earlier, and politics, for foreigners, was still taboo. Possibly the most illuminating - and unexpected - answer I received from our guide to one of my questions about Michail Gorbachev, as we stood by the Tsar Bell in the Kremlin, was:

Outside Chernobyl, author on left with dark glasses, 1994.

'He gave us back our religious rights.'

We all sat down to dinner on the first night at our hotel in Kiev and partook of a dish of meat and veg. Nobody could tell what sort of meat it was: beef? pork? mutton? It could also have been fish or fowl. I plumped for foul and raised a laugh from my American colleagues. We were drinking Georgian mineral water which smelled of rotten eggs, and didn't taste much better. 'No wonder,' said one of our number, 'look at the readings.' Compared to the Swiss *Henniez* which shows 7 mg/l for sodium and 392 for bicarbonate, *Borjomi* measures, respectively, 1200-2000 mg/l and 3500-5000 mg/l!

The proof of the pudding, on this occasion, was in the drinking.

Russia and Western Ukraine are very different countries. The obtaining of a visa for Russia involved two visits to Berne and several bureaucratic stages where consular staff were effectively controlling each other; I have no idea what caused the severe delays we encountered at immigration in Moscow.

It took ten minutes to obtain a visa for Ukraine, with the sole consular officer in Berne issuing it then and there. On arrival in Kiev, we were greeted by an immigration officer who stamped our passports as we were leaving the plane. At time of writing, I fear that the immigration process will soon be taking longer again.

VALENTINE'S DAY

The year was AD1281. It was 'Naming Day' in Paradise. Most of the Saints had come to the party, and there was quite a hubbub in the stratosphere. Martin, Patron Saint of drinking and tavern keepers, had brought a consignment of VAT 69 as an aperitif, and *Chateauneuf-du-Pape* to go with the main course. There were the usual jibes about his cellar being next door to 'the other place', but Martin didn't mind really; and His Eminence's Choice was regarded as the most fitting Port Wine to accompany the St Ilton. Even Katherine, whose arthritis was nagging her, remarked that it was going to be a heavenly occasion. 'Divine,' retorted Agnes, not to be outdone. Cecilia would be in charge of the music: 'For all the Saints...' was an old favourite.

Visibility was not at all good, but Nicholas had brought a selection of eye-glasses and ear-trumpets, so all would be well. The balcony was packed, and *there* was Valentine, with his trestle table, at which wagers would be made. Betting was of course frowned on, but, once every few years, a little flutter with the Peter's Pence was tolerated - Naming Day was a *very* special occasion. Saintly High Society was well represented. Antony and Benedict were there, Andrew, David, George and Patrick had shared coracles; Elizabeth had come with Jude; Osmund and Quentin had travelled down from Francia; Rosalie and Teresa up from Sicilia and Iberia respectively. There were two Zoës, four Irenes, seven Lucians, masses of Hilarys, Johns and Stephens. And no less than 65 Saints named Felix had arrived by saintmobile, including the Zürich Felix: he was easy to pick out as he had Regula on one arm and his own head under the other.

For obvious reasons, the party was usually held over Roma. But this time, because of a feud about the crown of Sicilia - a great embarrassment to Rosalie - the cardinals' conclave was to take place in the nearby castle of Viterbo, seat of the late Pope Nicholas III. Simon de Brion (sometimes called Brie or Mompitié), the front runner, had, as papal legate, conducted negotiations towards the assumption of the crown of Sicilia by Charles of Anjou, whose support he now enjoyed. But that didn't make him very popular in Italia. Of the names he might choose, MARTIN II was odds-on favourite.

Seven hundred years later, Angelika and I were in the ancient French city of Tours, in order to put together a concert programme for the Youth Orchestra of the Zürich *Konservatorium*. There is not such a thing as a typical French city, though some characteristics are common to all of them. Tours has its own *voie semi-piétonne* (which conjures up visions of people hopping along on one foot) and masses of examples of that unique, untranslatable signpost: *Toutes Directions*. Announcements for the forthcoming visit of John Paul II were all over the city, and he has since been there, in order to inaugurate *l'Année Martinienne*: the 1,600th anniversary of the death of St Martin, Bishop of Tours.

The Pope has also celebrated an open-air mass in Rheims to commemorate the 1,500th anniversary of the baptism of Clovis, so-called founder of modern France. In Tours, a very Gallic campaign of 'de-baptism' has been gathering pace, in the hope that parishioners will remove their names from baptismal registers, to protest against the Pope's Clovis initiative. Just about every aspect of the poor man's existence, it seems – including his very baptism – is disbelieved by somebody somewhere.

One newspaper has called Clovis's conversion 'little more than a pragmatic decision by a pillaging polygamist to win church approval'. In whatever context, such as taxpayers' money being used to build a podium for the holy visitor from Rome – not to mention the perceived threat to French secularity – this whole to-do amounts to a jolly good excuse for a demonstration. But that is another story. Or is it?

Martin's mausoleum in Tours is a very solid affair, erected 100 years ago by Cardinal Archbishop Meignan, who now kneels in Vosges marble, admiring his own handiwork. *Hommages* and *dédications* on the yellow sandstone columns include words from as far afield as Algeria, Peru and Pannonia (now in Hungary), where Martin was born, of heathen parents, in AD316. After becoming a catechumen (a sort of religious apprentice) at the age of ten, he reluctantly joined the army, and it was while he was stationed at Amiens that he divided his cloak with a beggar and had the vision which was to change his life. On the vast wooden doors outside his mausoleum, a centurion's helmet and an archbishop's mitre testify to his metamorphosis. A sword divides the words ROBUR (strength) and CARITAS (charity) on the wrought-iron gates nearby. Martin was a remarkable man who, according to Gregory of Tours, performed 206 miracles *after his own death.* Under the arch, in our full view, like a question mark, as near as possible to the tomb of his very own Patron Saint, stands a contemporary *clochard,* swigging surreptitiously.

Back in Paradise, the atmosphere above Viterbo was now quite tense. For the occasion, the cardinals – though they did not know it – were called 'the field'. Appearances were very important, and just being able to talk about 'favourites' and 'outsiders' and 'evens' and 'on' made the Saints feel almost mortal again. A hot tip had now elevated MARTIN II to the favourite's position on Valentine's betting board. This was deemed to be the most likely name for Simon de Brion, if he were elected.

But the field was still wide open, and the Italian cardinals were known to be plotting something. So it might be any of the other names shown: HONORIUS IV? INNOCENTIUS V? BONIFACIUS VIII? LEO IX? GREGORIUS XI? Even JOHANNES XXII figured, but as an outsider of course. Which name would the new man choose? Three bells sounded, signalling the departure of all unauthorised persons from the conclave, and 'the field' was 'away'!

The Saints were exhausted by the time the race reached its conclusion, five months later. What a party it had been! The longer the cardinals took to make up their minds, the more fun the Saints had. In fact they did not know – until afterwards – what the rules of the race were. This was the first time the fixture had been at Viterbo. The contest usually took place by secret scrutiny; otherwise there was acclamation (unlikely on this occasion). So it had probably been compromise. It didn't matter really, and it had been an exciting occasion, with the Italian cardinals putting up a spirited defence against their French counterparts, until most of the former fell at the last fence, and Simon de Brion romped home. Betting had closed of course but Martin was still doing a brisk business in pick-me-ups. He himself had put a shilling or two on MARTINUS II, and he was confident of winning something now, but the newly elected pontiff still had to choose his name.

When the result was finally announced, a gasp went up from the assembled throng. Simon de Brion had declared himself to be not MARTINUS II but MARTINUS IV! The Saints later learned that the papal chancery had misread the names of two previous Popes named Marinus as Martinus II and Martinus III. So these two names had been disqualified. Helier was furious: having expected to be able to invest his winnings in a nice off-shore account, he now saw all his hopes disappear, so to speak, in a puff of smoke. And the three Hilarias didn't think it was funny at all. Someone else made a remark about cardinals not knowing their cardinals from their ordinals. But, apart from this, the occasion passed off with the gravitas due to it. After all they had the next party to look forward to. It was winner-take-all, so no bets were won; but Valentine, the bookmaker, made a killing.

* * *

Conventionally, the Papal Nuncio is widely accepted as *Doyen* of the Diplomatic Corps (CD). The Consular Corps (CC) in each city has a seniority list, based on dates of accreditation, which is strictly respected. While I was Secretary of the Zürich Consular Corps, the senior Consul General of a large oriental land presented me with a problem when he told me that he was not prepared to become the *Doyen*, as was the convention. We had no Papal Nuncio we could fall back on, and I had to seek guidance from my Ambassador. As things turned out, I managed to persuade the second most senior Consul General to side-step convention and become the *Doyen*.

The only time I have met a Papal Nuncio was at UNCED in Brazil in 1992. He was scurrying around the immense conference centre, his robes flying, doing his best to sabotage any initiative which could, in any way, be related to population control. The effect was comical.

The above tale is compassionately dedicated to him. Readers may be assured that every effort was made, in the writing of it, to conform to those relevant historical records which are open to the public eye.

THAT ALL THINGS ARE CHANGED, AND THAT NOTHING REALLY PERISHES, AND THAT THE SUM OF MATTER REMAINS EXACTLY THE SAME, IS SUFFICIENTLY CERTAIN

Spare a thought for the controllers of immigration in the 1790s, in Australia.

Barnard Walford, an engraver, is believed to have been the first Austrian to have settled in Australia. He could later claim to have been the first Jew who landed in Tasmania (together, oddly, with the first Muslim, Jacob Sultan). Walford had somehow arrived in London from Vienna when he was a 14-year-old. Seven years later, he was arrested and tried at the Old Bailey for having stolen a basket of laundered linen. Disproportionate penalties were being dispensed at the time and he was sentenced to seven years, with transportation to the colony of New South Wales. He was embarked on the *Active* with the 3rd Fleet, which arrived at Port Jackson in 1791, after 183 days at sea. He and his 174 fellow-passengers suffered appalling privations which left 21 dead.

Jane Mulloy (or Molloy), from Middlesex, had earlier been transported with the *Neptune* of the 2nd Fleet, after being convicted of stealing '16 yards of printed cotton', and was also sentenced to seven years. She had had an unspeakable time during the fleet's 159-day voyage via the Cape of Good Hope. On arrival, 258 of the 1,017 male and female convicts who had been embarked on the 2nd Fleet's three ships, were found to have died. Of the 759 who disembarked, more than 500 were sick or dying of scurvy, typhoid, smallpox, starvation or mistreatment. For this black chapter in Australia's early settlement, the Master and Chief Mate of the *Neptune* were later tried for murder.

After this almost inconceivable introduction to their new homeland, where there were, of course, *no* immigration officers to greet them, and no such thing as a social service, Barnard and Jane steeled themselves to their new existence, settled down together and raised a family. Barnard was first given an allotment in Norfolk Island, and later a 90-acre grant in Van Diemen's Land (Tasmania). Their daughter Mary Walford's second husband, John Sparke, provided stability. They had six children, one of whom, Edward Joseph, was my maternal great-grandfather.

Two hundred years later, my mother Gwynneth Linda Sparke Huelin (née Davies, later McCammon), then in her mid-80s, wanted to pay a last visit to the country of her birth. For most of her life, there had been no such thing as an Australian passport and she had travelled there and back dozens of times, either with no passport, or with a British passport, or a British Indian passport (stamped, grandly, on the cover: INDIAN EMPIRE), or a Jersey passport. On this final occasion, she applied, as had become mandatory, for a visa. The Australian consular section at the High Commission in London ruled that, because she had been born in Australia, she could now only travel there on an Australian passport. The application process took so long that, by the time she received the passport, the date of her planned departure had long passed. She never made it back to her homeland.

The title of this essay was written by Francis Bacon, in Latin, in the 1590s, 200 years before Walford's arrival in Australia. It might have been rendered: *Plus ça change, plus c'est la même chose.* Some, who do not want something, get it with a vengeance. Others, who do, do not.

SNORING

For those aficionados of Lawrence Durrell who have wrestled unsuccessfully with *Justine, Balthazar, Mountolive* or *Clea,* there can only be one word of advice: read *The Black Book: An Agon.* It was published 19 years earlier than *Justine,* in Paris, when Durrell was 27 years old; it is the 'Alexandria Quartet' in embryo. Better still though, seek out Durrell's 'Sketches from Diplomatic Life', in particular *Esprit de Corps*, in which you will find a tale about a Japanese diplomat, who waltzed his wife with ever-increasing gusto out of a New Year's Eve party in Prague, through the French windows and into a pond at the end of the garden, the butler - inexcusably - having substituted second rate Scotch whisky for the *sake*.

Half a millennium ago, in Swaffham, Norfolk, there lived a peddler, John Chapman, who dreamed one night that if he were to go to London Bridge, he would hear some good news. It took him a long time to reach his destination and, when he got there, he paced the span, wondering what to do next. He told a shopkeeper about his dream. The latter said that he, too, had had a dream: that if he (the shopkeeper) were to go to a little place called Swaffham, in Norfolk, and were to dig under an apple tree, he would find a treasure. He had no intention of allowing his dreams to dictate to him, and strongly suggested to the peddler that he return home and go about his business.

John, containing himself with difficulty, thanked the man for his advice, retraced his footsteps, and set about digging down into the flinty soil under the apple tree in his own garden. His spade soon struck a large brass pot, which turned out to be full of gold coins. An acquaintance deciphered an inscription on the pot, which indicated that there was a second - much larger - vessel, buried even deeper. John the peddler carried on digging and - hey presto! - there it was. This hoard was used - as this story goes - to rebuild the parish church.

Another son of Swaffham discovered another treasure in another era, and arguably became the most famous archaeologist of all time. A tantalising, water-stained label in the Swaffham Museum reads: 'Specimens of natural flint "eyes" found on the Sybian Hills near Thebes, used by the ancient Egyptians for their [illegible]...' And a diary entry for the '11th Month November 1922 5 SUNDAY...21 after Trinity' announces in a very down-to-earth manner: 'Discovered tomb under tomb of Rameses VI. Investigated same, found seals intact.'

Howard Carter had just found the lost hoard of Tutankhamun.

'Wonderful things,' he replied when Lord Carnarvon asked him what he could see.

We were on our way to a wedding in Great Walsingham.

Little Walsingham, now the greater of the two, is 'England's Nazareth'. The shrine of Our Lady of Walsingham was the brainchild of one Richeldis de Faverches, lady of the manor in the mid-eleventh century, who, after having three visions of the Virgin, was convinced that she should build on her own land a replica of the home of Mary and Joseph, which she had seen in Nazareth. The simple structure was to attract pilgrims in their thousands. Even the likes of Sir Walter Raleigh were moved:

As you came from the holy land of Walsinghame,
Met you not with my true love by the way as you came?

With the Reformation, Walsingham slid into oblivion as Henry VIII became 'the pope, the whole pope, and something more than the pope'. His sovereign ruthlessness is shown up by Anne Boleyn's initials on the majestic oak screen, given by her spouse to King's College Chapel, Cambridge, not so far away, and the off-hand remark in a modern brochure that this *opus magnum* of 'Philip the carver' could thereby be dated to 'between 1533, when Henry married her, and 1536, when he had her executed.' This dreadful deed was curiously intensified, in starkly symbolic fashion, by an unfinished jigsaw puzzle, which we later saw lying on a side-table in the royal drawing-room of Sandringham, some miles to the north.

Now, centuries later, the Walsingham shrine has been reconstructed, and bridges are being built between dogma and tolerance, and, to the delight of the townspeople, pilgrimages are stretching the car-parks.

The wedding was a splendidly happy occasion, the groom Scottish, the bride Japanese. A Highland piper at the door of St Peter's Church, Great Walsingham, was a reminder that this, too, was the country of the Northmen, from whom deliverance was no longer necessary. Kaleidoscopic kilts, outnumbering morning coats, complemented the exotic eastern presence. The groom beamed and the bride shone shyly. Her father spoke movingly, in Japanese, about planting a cherry tree. Somehow, everyone understood. The groom's father, with a twinkle in his eye, talked of an arranged marriage. Then the ceilidh was announced and this dichotomy of cultures joined in a oneness which only dance can create. The Gordons were Gayly gallivanted; the Eightsome Reeled; and the White Sergeant Dashed. Too soon, the happy couple were piped away under the stars, and it was over.

We spent the night in Great Snoring, smaller - by a whistle - than Little Snoring, just down the road, the latter boasting a St

Andrew's Church with a rare, detached, round tower, made of flint. The word 'Snoring', according to Those Who Know, has nothing to do with sermons, but comes, rather, from a name dating back to the first wave of Saxon invaders, just as the Romans were leaving, with the unlikely meaning of 'swift', 'bright' or 'alert'. This dictum is, however, belied by the number of Gotobeds in the local telephone directory... Our kindly hosts were to give us breakfast at a table which had once belonged to a distant forebear, one Charles Dickens: such generous portions where Oliver Twist had been conceived?...

On the cosmopolitan tartan of Walsingham, one particular memory went around and around, as sleep overtook us in Great Snoring. It was the Durrellesque vignette of the bride's father, suddenly transformed into a whirling dervish, orientally content, completely out of control, but, time and again, finding himself hooked and steadied by a friendly arm at the very last moment, as he gamely skipped about, Stripping the Willow.

The Moon's the same old moon
The flowers exactly as they were
Yet I've become the thingness
Of all the things I see.

(*Satori* poem by Shido Bunan, seventeenth century)

SMASHING CHINA

In June 1996, Angelika and I travelled to Beijing, to attend *ENERGEX '96*, as guests of the Chinese State Planning Commission and others. While alternative energy was the thrust of this seminar, it very soon transpired that the Chinese Ministry of Coal Industry (which had been abolished in 1988, brought back in 1993, and was to be abolished again in 1997), said to be the biggest employer in the People's Republic, was also a 'sponsor' of *ENERGEX*. It may or may not be coincidental that the main marketing material of the larger participants, exhibits and so on, concerning alternative energy products, were said to have been 'lost at the Customs'; they reappeared on the last day of the conference. Luckily, my own contribution, 'Who Pays?' had by then been committed to memory, and my presentation did not suffer.

Facts are difficult to get hold of in China. Apart from the blatant embroidery of the truth which one gets from members of the Party, veracity tends to get mixed up with wishful thinking. This can be followed by an oriental type of justification which can be perplexing for westerners. In an idle moment in the Xian Museum shop, I was flipping through a 'book' of GENUINE CHINESE COINS, when I spotted, embedded into page 2 a very bad imitation, which I pointed out to the Chinese attendant. She looked at me po-faced and said, 'One imitat-i-on.' In page 3 there was another fake: 'Two imitat-i-on.' We got to 11 fake coins, with the attendant responding to my questions without a change in her tone, until the absurd dialogue was terminated, angrily, by our guide (whose name, incidentally, was Cloud).

Six years later, in Zürich, I had the honour of being invited to the *Forschungsstelle für Sicherheitspolitik und Konfliktanalyse* at the *ETH* (Research Centre for Security Policy and Analysis of Conflict at the Federal Institute of Technology), on the occasion of a speech by the Chinese Ambassador. It was an enjoyable occasion, but I had one problem. The Ambassador peppered his speech with statistics: minorities allowed to have three children; 300 Uygur incidents in the PRC last year; 30,000 mosques; 30 million children saved from neglect and so on. In China, '3' is considered a lucky number, as it sounds similar to the Chinese character for 'birth'. Many of the other statistics he gave consisted of the number 3 multiplied - randomly it almost seemed - by a power of 10. I simply *did not know* whether I could believe the distinguished gentleman or not.

Another souvenir of our 1996 visit to the Middle Kingdom was my unexpectedly gaining an interview with the Minister at the National Environment Protection Agency in Beijing. I felt I needed a new suit to meet this important member of the Party, and managed to have one made in a day at a large store in the capital. Unfortunately, on the way back to the hotel, I took a taxi which had just driven through a car-wash with its windows open, and sat down in three inches of water. It was a trebly sobering experience as, the following day, and now dry again, it was only with the intervention of my large chauffeur, who carried an early model mobile phone, that I got past a gun-toting guard and was able to meet the Minister for what turned out to be an anodyne (read: useless) exchange of opinions.

Outside the walls of the 'Neiborhood [*sic*] of Beijing International Convention Center', it was impossible to believe that the phrase 'environmental protection' existed at all, in spite of the 50 million new bicycles which were hitting China's roads every year at the time. Here is one little story to illustrate this.

THE LUGOU BRIDGE

It was 740 years ago that the 17-year-old Venetian Marco Polo set out from Acre with his father and uncle. After reaching Ormuz, centre of the thirteenth-century spice trade, the three travellers struck through the middle of Persia and on to the entrepot of Balkh, a still active caravanserai in what is now northern Afghanistan, which I passed through in 1963. Then, undaunted by names like Kashgar, Yarkand, Khotan and the Gobi - which the young man called the 'Desert of Lop' - the Polos reached the realm of the Kublai Khan at Shangtu. It had taken them three years.

The Marco Polo Bridge, 1996.

Still in his early 20s, Marco studied the languages of the Great Khan's subjects and, becoming a civil servant, journeyed widely in the Chinese provinces. 'Ten miles after Cambulac [Beijing],' he recorded, 'the traveller reaches the wide river Pusilanghin, on which tradesmen sail with their wares down to the ocean. A fine stone bridge crosses the river; in the whole world there is no other bridge to compare with this one.'

Incredibly, the Lugou Bridge, better known in the West as the 'Marco Polo Bridge', still stands, some 15 km south-west of the centre of Beijing. It was here that Genghis Khan made the first breaches in Peking's defences, 100 years after the bridge had been built. And a war memorial nearby graphically testifies to the fact that it was here, too, that the bloody Sino-Japanese War broke out in the night of 7-8 July 1937.

The fine stone structure is 266 metres long and nine metres wide. Each side is lined by hundreds of unique stone lions, some of which go back to the twelfth century. The structure was restored in the fifteenth, seventeenth and twentieth centuries, and is now bounded by two road bridges and a viaduct. But, some 20 years ago, a dam was built upstream, to divert water to Beijing, and the Yongding river (as it is now called), known to the Kangxi Emperors as the 'Everlasting Permanence', this river which surged down from the mountains 500,000 years ago, when Peking Man lived in his cave in the Dragon Bone Hills, abruptly died.

When I remarked to our young guide that no water was flowing under the 11 massive arches, she looked at me in surprise, glanced at the bridge and went off to find out what had happened, and - who knows? - to get the authorities to turn the water on again for us. She hadn't even noticed that the river-bed was dry.

OTHER ELEMENTS

In July 1996, Königswinter, Bonn, was the venue for a seminar on *Environment and Financial Services,* sponsored by the German Ministry of the Environment, under a 'green' and very personable

Angela Merkel. The event was almost hijacked by the Deutsche Bank, which had suddenly become interested in the subject, and felt it should be playing a leading role; the bank in later years *did* play a leading role. In November 1996, The *Observatoire de la Finance* saw the year out with a short convention on *Financial Performance/ Socially Responsible Investing* in Fribourg, Switzerland.

In February 1997, I travelled to Washington for the *Microcredit Summit* (described above).

There then followed *Clean Energy 2000* (Geneva, January 2000) and the Foundation's *5th International Conference on Environmental Future* on the subject of the *Future of Aquatic Ecosystems* (Zürich, March 2003); this became the meat of *Aquatic Ecosystems*, the book.

I had already attended sundry conferences which had been organised by the British Embassy, often in conjunction with the British Council. Two stand out in my memory: an *Air Traffic Control* seminar held provocatively at Zürich airport, only a few months before the collapse of Swissair; and *Not for Sale*, a shockingly topical seminar held at the University of Geneva in February 2004, about the trafficking in cultural artifacts stolen from Iraq, Afghanistan and elsewhere.

In September 2002, however, I was surprised and delighted to receive an invitation from the British Embassy to a conference in Berne on *Private Finance and Sustainable Development*. Other such conferences, for example on *Energy Emissions Trading* and *Corporate Social Responsibility*, were to follow, and I trust the powers that be will excuse me for feeling a tiny bit responsible.

GOD'S PLAN

According to the Old Testament, 1992 will be approximately the 7,000th anniversary of a serious environmental problem in Iraq. Over-population was already causing concern and God was regretting that he had ever created Man. He didn't like the look of the Earth either; it was corrupt and rotten. So he decided to have a flood. He didn't want to wait for 'global warming' to melt the polar ice-caps because that would have taken too long. He wanted to have a good, quick cataclysm, so he decided that he would make it rain for 40 days and 40 nights. That should do the trick, and he could start all over again.

But then he had second thoughts: if all living things perished, his work in the heavenly laboratory would have been wasted and Haydn wouldn't be able to compose *The Creation*. So God looked around for a worthy, experienced and mature human, and found someone who at that time was over 500 years old.

'Noah,' he said, 'do you know anything about Conservation or Sustainability?' And Noah was obviously a good candidate, having only had two sons in 480 years. So Noah built a Biocube. This was not unlike the Nordic Gene Bank in Spitzbergen or Biosphere 2 which the Americans have recently constructed in the Arizona Desert, but it needed to float. In those days, Biocubes were always made of gopher wood and pitch (an old name for tar, a product of crude oil), as you will see if you read verse 14 of chapter 6 of the *Book of Genesis*.

By the 17th February of the year in which Noah became 600 years old, he had begun to collect his immediate family and one pair of all other living things into the Biocube, and the rain began. The rest of the story you know.

Noah's experience was traumatic, it is true, but God's plan was in fact carried out without the use of acid rain or toxic fumes or radioactivity or any other of the dreaded agents which we are getting to know as environmentally unfriendly. There was a minimum of bureaucracy; politics were suppressed, at least during the voyage; and finance was, it seems, unnecessary, as Noah's sons were well connected to the local saw-mills, and had access to an oilfield in the Land of the Kurds. There was food to a Darwinian degree. It was a Utopian situation and a very good way to begin the Bible.

You can be certain, though, that, as the flood subsided and became a sea, and the sea became a river, Noah once again found himself to be drifting towards the banks...

This article was read at UNCED, as an introduction to a 'Who Pays?' presentation, only months after the last of over 700 burning oil-wells had been extinguished in Kuwait.

OMAN

During the 1970s, I had been twice to Oman on business. On the first occasion, just after Sultan Said bin Taimur had been deposed by his son Qaboos, Main Street Muscat was lined with Land Rovers and, at the Muttrah *souk*, I managed to find some time off to purchase a beautifully fashioned *khanjar*, made of melted down Maria Theresia thalers, with its sheath and belt of webbing worked in silver thread. I also brought home a few twigs of the *neem* tree, used as tooth-brushes, and some blocks of frankincense to burn in the barbecue. During my second visit, Toyota Land Cruisers were in the majority, and the alleys were full of cheap imitations of this stately Arabian dagger, with their hilts made of sandalwood, marble or even plastic; the *neem* and frankincense had been driven off the stalls by shoddy household goods, made in China. On the earlier occasions, I was unable to visit Salalah in the south, as it was being shelled by Dhofar rebels. Yes, this medieval world was changing fast; but something in Oman was immutable: it was difficult to define. I determined to take Angelika back there with me, one day.

Opportunities arose over the year-end 2004/5 and 2005/6, and, both times, we stayed at the Hyatt Hilton in Muscat. I had been furnished with a letter of introduction to Clare Douglas, HM Consul there.

* * *

The SS *John Barry* under Captain Ellerwald never arrived in Dhahran. It was carrying a cargo of 3 million silver Saudi one-riyal coins, minted in Philadelphia. The currency was destined for Aramco, the Arabian American Oil Company, for the payment of salaries. In 1943, Washington was worried about the adequacy of its oil reserves and gave high priority to the securing of additional supplies for its war effort. Hence its interest in the Aramco operation. The problem was that Saudi Arabia was running out of coins, and paper money was not yet in use.

The first consignment of coins minted in Philadelphia arrived safely in late 1943. By 1945, 49 million riyals had been shipped. The only cargo missing was that of the *John Barry*.

What had happened was that a German submarine, U-859, under the command of Captain Lieutenant Johann Jebson had picked up the trail of the *John Barry*. Two of the three torpedoes he fired scored direct hits and on 28 August 1944, the ship went down. Amazingly, only two crewmen were lost in the sinking: 39 crewmen and the entire armed guard were rescued by the Dutch freighter *Sanetta* and the US Liberty Ship *Benjamin Bourn*. Captain Jebson and most of his crew died one month later when U-859 was sunk by the British submarine HMS *Trenchant* off Malacca.

A mistaken rumour that the ship's cargo was worth $26 million caught the attention of two treasure-hunters, Brian Shoemaker and Jay Fiondella, who, with two Washington lawyers, obtained the rights to salvage the ship with a bid of just over $50,000, through their company, the newly-formed John Barry Group. But there was one problem: the hulk had sunk just off the coast of Oman, not in the sultanate's territorial waters but definitely inside its declared economic zone. They needed Omani participation.

This was forthcoming from a British salvage expert Robert Hudson and Sheikh Ahmed bin Farid al-Aulaqi, who was originally from the Upper Aulaqi Sheikdom of Said, a constituent territory of the Aden Protectorate, latterly part of the Federation of South Arabia and Yemen. They did more than participate: they bought the salvage rights from the John Barry Group, reportedly for $750,000, and recovered nearly half of the cargo of coins in October 1994.

While rumours persist that al-Aulaqi financed the commissioning of the Muscat Hyatt Hilton (our hotel) with his profits from the salvage operation, there are other rumours that he sank some $10 million into preparations for the venture. In November the following year, the coins failed to sell at auction in Geneva when they were put up as a single lot. It is not publicly known how many of the one-riyal pieces have since been disposed of.

* * *

Angelika and I duly paid a visit to Clare Douglas at the British Embassy, a short walk down the beach from our hotel. It was being guarded by an Omani gun-boat, off-shore. Clare gave me a fascinating exposé about Oman and the line of succession to the throne. This information is no longer restricted: if the Royal family cannot agree, the Defence Council will take a decision, based on two names, which the childless Sultan Qaboos has placed in sealed envelopes.

The second time round, we managed to see Salalah. It was just after the 2004 *tsunami*, which had deposited some fishing boats, peremptorily, in the garden of our hotel.

The coin salvage operation was exciting enough. The Omani succession - not to mention those of Oman's large neighbours to the north and west - promises to be more exciting still.

Notwithstanding the current poignancy of politics in the region, I cannot resist re-telling the story of the British Consul General in Muscat who, in 1960, sent a dispatch marked Confidential, in reply to an enquiry whether a B flat clarinet score was an accurate rendering of the National Salute to the then Sultan. Such is the erudition of consular life.

II

And What it Led To

APPOINTMENT

My first formal acquaintance with consular affairs was through the HONORARY CONSUL'S SAMPLE LETTER OFFERING APPOINTMENT. It was the intention of the FCO to close the Consulate General in Zürich and appoint an honorary consul, to be responsible for the German- and Romansch-speaking eastern cantons of the Swiss Confederation. His or her duties would include:

> Notarial acts;
> The levying of consular fees;
> The protection of British nationals;
> The relief and repatriation of distressed British nationals;
> duties under the Merchant Shipping Acts. [Switzerland, incidentally, though irrelevantly here, *does* have a navy.]
> Assisting Commercial Officers from HM Embassy at Berne, and visiting British businessmen.

Further headings in the letter took in financial provisions (an annual honorarium plus the entitlement to reclaim actual incurred expenditure on certain items); accounts; duration and leave.

In a covering note, HM Consul wrote that the sample letter of appointment 'gives a flavour of what might be expected'. It became evident that he had chosen these words with great care.

Then I received a letter from the Deputy Head of Mission at Berne, asking for my formal acceptance of the job of honorary consul, *should it be offered to me.* I readily accepted.

During my working life, I have been a clerk with an accounting firm, a bank employee and representative, holding various positions in Brazil, Portugal, Spain, Switzerland and the UK (with ancillary activities in Austria, Bahrain, Beirut, Denmark, Dubai, Germany, Iran, Italy, Kuwait, Lebanon, Saudi Arabia and Yugoslavia), correspondent for a Calgary newspaper, consultant for environmental studies, honorary dish-dryer and gardener at various addresses, assistant librarian at the British Institute of Persian Studies in Teheran, and a linesman 2nd Class for Walsh Canadian in Quebec Province, Canada.

The above FCO job description sounded like something new. Five years, the initial term of the contract, seemed reasonable.

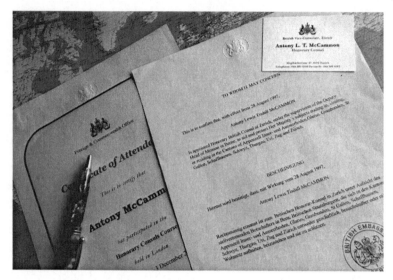

Tools of the Trade.

The very modest honorarium also seemed equitable as I felt that, after a lifetime of living abroad, with the backing of my British passport, pay-back time had arrived. Nevertheless, when I became Honorary Consul at Zürich, I had not the faintest idea that I was embarking on an occupation which would be the most enthralling and challenging of them all.

HORSES FOR COURSES

'How could you have let them abuse my daughter?'

Yes, it was only a training exercise, but it was pretty challenging all the same. This particular session was to teach us how best to deal with the Pakistani parents of a young British citizen who had been killed in a traffic accident. Her body had been preserved for some days in freezing storage until a post-mortem had been performed by a male pathologist – all without the Muslim parents' knowledge or consent.

I took part in two Foreign Office consular courses: one in Copenhagen, one in London. The whole spectrum of consular situations was covered, from trivialities to disasters, from oaths of allegiance to divorce, from robbers to fraud victims, from pregnancies to post-mortems. Patrick Murray, the actor, once defined life as being 'the ever-dwindling period between abortion and euthanasia'. By this definition, we covered every chapter. Under 'prisoners', we learned to distinguish between on-the-run, suspected, detained, escaped, arrested, investigated, sentenced, jailed, released, repatriated and deported, and we learned how to converse with them. We were taught about nationality, passports, visas, dual nationals. Time was spent on affidavits, assaults, changes of name, custody of children, death, funeral directors, matrimony, paternity suits, pets, rape (both sexes) and the Press. There were practical exercises, like the one above, with professional actors taking part. Every situation was based on a real case. The last day was taken up in a 'disaster' scenario, involving us in a coach crash with casualties, somewhere abroad.

There were valuable opportunities to spend time with Honorary Consuls from other parts of the world and professional staff from the FCO in London.

After completing the London course, I had a day to spare, and happened to go for lunch at the 'Shakespeare's Head' in Holborn. There was a seat near the entrance, and I asked a man, sitting alone at a nearby table with a beer, if he would be good enough to watch my coat while I ordered a plate of food. He nodded his agreement. When I returned to the table with a tray, I thanked him and sat down.

'I 'ope you don't mind me asking...' said the man, with a pronounced Cockney accent,

'Are you from round 'ere?' I explained that I was visiting for a few days.

'Oh, where you from then?'

'Zürich.'

'Is that in Europe?' I nodded, my mouth full of scotch egg. 'Never been there. Is it far?' Our conversation continued for a few minutes. Then I asked him: 'Are *you* from round here?'

'East End, Guv. But I only came out this morning.' Warning lights flashed.

'Where were you?'

''er Majesty's Prison in Brixton.'

'How long were you there?' (We had been taught not to ask, *How long did you get?*)

'Six months...this time.'

We chatted for nearly an hour, until I had to leave for another appointment. He was a bachelor, in his 50s, and he enjoyed a flutter on the horses. I wondered if this was the reason for his life of petty crime. He told me he always got nervous when he was let out. He was frightened of the real world, and was often tempted to do something so that he could go back inside.

As I rose to go, he got up too and handed me my coat. 'I 'ope you don't mind, Guv. I'd really like to thank you.'

'Whatever for?'

'For talking to me. You wouldn't believe it, Guv. Most people just don't know 'ow. You can't imagine. I really enjoyed our mee'ing. Thank you.' He waved to me as I left the pub.

*   *   *

It is an odd thing but, many years ago, I was on a banking course in a hotel near the Aldwych. It was painfully boring, and, once or twice, I seized an opportunity to slip away and have a quiet drink in the bar at the Savoy Hotel, where there were, in those days, enough dark crannies for one not to be noticed. On one occasion, I was sitting at a corner table with a *Tio Pepe*, minding my own business, when a man came up to me and said, 'Excuse me, are you Mr Cox?' I told him I was not Mr Cox.

Ten minutes later, another man came up to me and said: 'Excuse me, are you Mr Pippin?'

From that day to this, I have wondered if I was not, unwittingly, playing a part in some elaborate MI5 ritual with the code-name 'APPLE'. In any event, the experience provided food for thought.

I do believe, though, that the Holborn cockney was for real.

LAST WORD ... FIRST

'Don't forget...'

It was an exhausting session. Our instructor had been discussing particularly gruesome cases of murder, manslaughter, GBH (grievous bodily harm) and dead bodies in general.

'...Battle-scarred veterans can quail at the sight of a lifeless baby.' He looked at us, slowly and compassionately, one by one.

'Don't try to be heroes. When you are trying to comfort a bereaved BC, there are few things more embarrassing than passing out or bringing up your breakfast.'

'If you are asked to visit a mortuary with the family of the deceased, and if - for any reason - you feel uneasy about it, ask the pathologist or the mortician if you can go in there on your own, beforehand. Have a glass of water ready, or something stronger. The first time *anybody* views a corpse can be - usually *is* - a traumatic experience. And violent death can be...' he searched for a word, '...soul-destroying.' One could tell he was speaking from bitter experience.

Someone asked, nervously, 'What is a BC?'

'British citizen...' The instructor continued without a pause...

'And one final thing: grown men and women will be frightened of sharing certain secrets with their doctors or their ministers or their shrinks or their spouses. But they won't hesitate to pour out their troubles to you. I cannot explain it; perhaps it is something in the word consul...Just be prepared.'

What valuable advice that turned out to be!

AMBASSADORS AND CONSULS

Sir Ernest Satow, HM envoy extraordinary and minister plenipotentiary in Japan (1895-1900), quoted Émile Littré's dictionary:

> The diplomat is so-called, because diplomas are official documents (*actes*) emanating from princes, and the word diploma comes from the Greek (*diplóō*, to double) from the way in which they were folded. A diploma is understood to be a document by which a privilege is conferred...

It was the French who appear to have used the word *diplomate* for the first time in the modern sense, in the late seventeenth century.

As regards the word 'ambassador', Satow cited other sources:

> The derivation of the word 'ambassador' seems to be as follows: Fr. *ambaxadeur* (15th century), OSp. *ambaxador*, It. *ambasciatore*, from *ambaxade*, OSp. *ambaxada*, It. *ambasciata*, all these from *ambactiáre*, a word not found but inferred to have existed, and this formed on *ambactia*, *ambaxia* in the Salic and Burgundian laws [eighth-tenth centuries], meaning charge, office, employment, name of an office formed on *ambactus*, a servant...

Foreigners living in ancient Greek city states were permitted to choose representatives to act as intermediaries between them and local authorities. In early Roman times, *consoles* (later *consules*) were two, annually elected, senior magistrates, also called *praetores*, who supervised the Senate, commanded armies and governed provinces. They took over on the death or expulsion of the king. Later emperors of Rome either recommended candidates or, more commonly, took care to hold the title themselves. This consular office, largely an honorary one in the time of Pliny the Elder, lasted for about 1,000 years.

The word *consul* was used by the French in the Middle Ages for a municipal magistrate. Napoleon Bonaparte was made one of the three *consuls* of the new regime after the coup of *Brumaire* (November, 1799), before becoming *premier consul* for life. He then became emperor, but the word *consul* stuck.

Meanwhile, in England, the word was used from the thirteenth century as a synonym for 'count', and subsequently (early seventeenth century) employed by Shakespeare and others as an appellation for sundry foreign officials. As to the activities of latter-day consuls, Satow cited Talleyrand (1837):

> *Après avoir été un ministre habile, que de choses il faut savoir pour être un bon consul! Car les attributions d'un consul sont variées à l'infini: elles sont d'un genre tout différent de celles des autres employés des affaires étrangères. Elles exigent une foule de connaissances pratiques, pour lesquelles une éducation particulière est nécessaire.*

Talleyrand's *précis* has, in my opinion, not been bettered, and I have left it untranslated.

The first British consular officer to be appointed in Zürich was an anglophile Swiss national by the name of Heinrich, later Sir Henry, Angst. He became honorary British vice-consul in January 1886, and was raised to the rank of consul in June of the same year. In 1896, he was further promoted to consul general, still honorary, and represented Their Imperial Majesties Victoria, Edward VII and George V for nearly 30 years.

Angst's long tenure as consul general cannot have been easy for him. During the Boer War, for example, his neutrality (as a Swiss citizen) was often called into question by supporters of Paul Kruger, fifth president of the South African Republic. One incident is described in a biography by Robert Durrer, when the British Secret Service intercepted some maps of the Transvaal, which had been ordered by Kruger; they had been drawn by the *Topographische Anstalt* (Topographic Institute) *Schlumpf* in Winterthur, which happened to be in Angst's consular district.

Angst was the first director of the *Schweizerisches Landesmuseum* (the Swiss national museum) and was awarded honorary membership of many learned British societies. He was a close friend of Sir Richard Burton, the orientalist and explorer, as well as Edward Whymper, who was the first to climb the Matterhorn.

From 1915 to 1917, when Switzerland found itself in the German ambit, the Zürich consular district was looked after by Sir Cecil Hertslet, Consul General for Belgium, at Antwerp.

'After the occupation of Vichy France,' Arnold Lunn noted,

> the Germans refused transit visas even to British diplomatists accredited to the Berne Legation. Today [January 1944] Switzerland is more inaccessible to Englishmen than Thibet [*sic*] to Gibbon's contemporaries.

(Arnold Lunn also recounts the story of Edward Gibbon, historian and Member of Parliament, who, himself, had had a similar problem 200 years previously, when the French did not allow him to travel through *their* territory to reach Switzerland; he solved the problem by posing as the Swiss companion of two Swiss officers - a solution which would be well beyond the reach of a modern British MP.)

Hertslet was succeeded by Lord Acton. One of the more colourful characters to have occupied the position, he was in Zürich for five months in 1917. He was then transferred as HM Ambassador to the newly independent Republic of Finland where he was perceived to be of German descent, made public his views about the inevitability of communism, escaped an assassination attempt, and was withdrawn.

I took over as Honorary Consul from David Bell, the last career consul general in Zürich. Having dismantled and unceremoniously disposed of the tall aluminium flag-pole on the old building, I mounted the Royal Arms on the gate-post of the Cater Allen representative office in Minervastrasse. Sadly, this handsome brass plaque was stolen, shortly before the Consulate was moved, for reasons of security, round the corner to Hegibachstrasse. David had had a staff of 30 people; counting the Pro-Consul, I had a staff of one.

HONORIFICABILITUDINITY

...is said to be the longest word in the English language. In *Love's Labour's Lost* (V.i.45), Shakespeare gave it a 'grandiose extension' – but in Latin. It means 'honourableness' and is as good a word as any to introduce a short essay on the origins of honorary consuls and the apparent anomaly between the words 'honorary' (meaning 'unpaid') and 'honorarium' ('a voluntary payment made for services where no fee is legally required').

It is generally recognised that the *Report from the Select Committee on the Constitution and Efficiency of the Diplomatic Service (1861)* – more than any other initiative – established the foundations of the Diplomatic Service, as we know it today, based on open examination, apprenticeship and regular structures of promotion, salary and pension.

But the modern honorary consul, who has, *de facto*, the same responsibilities as career consular staff, is subject to no open examination, receives no apprenticeship, is no longer promoted, is paid not a salary but a modest honorarium, and has the benefit of no pension (outside that which he would normally receive from his separate professional life). And there's the rub.

So, what happened before 1861?

> Edmund Hammond, the permanent undersecretary, when asked by the chairman [of the said Select Committee] what changes had taken place in the service during his thirty years at the Foreign Office, knew of no other than that several missions had been established in South America, that there were more paid attachés and that their salaries were charged on the general diplomatic fund, nor did further questioning appreciably stimulate his memory.

If a senior civil servant at the Foreign Office knew so little about British representation abroad, how could he possibly have had any idea about the duties and rights of a mere honorary consul?

But we should not be too hard on the said undersecretary, for we learn that a diplomatist, down to 1850 or thereabouts,

> often found it convenient to take abroad with him a young son or nephew, or a friend's son, who thus got the opportunity of acquiring Continental 'finish' under a paternal eye. These 'attachés' shared their patron's house and table, and in return assisted with the secretarial work of the mission. They took their duties light-heartedly, the more so as few of them intended to make a diplomatic career. So soon as they had gained whatever insight into public business their simple routine afforded, or had seen enough of the world, they returned home and diplomacy knew them no more.

These unpaid attachés – the practice continued well into the period of Hammond's responsibility – were described by George Canning (the Foreign Secretary) 'as a couple of dozen young men, scattered over Europe; owing no allegiance and taking diplomacy only as subsidiary to amusement'. Choosing a more literary turn of phrase – officially the Foreign Office knew nothing about them – Lord Bulwer-Lytton (Secretary of State for the Colonies) styled these dilettante diplomatists 'mere saunterers'.

However, whether they were of the eighteenth or the nineteenth centuries,

> The British tax-payer could owe [the said attachés] no grudge; they were unpaid. Society could expect nothing of them but

> amusement and a disposition to enjoy themselves; and they had no responsibilities, unless it was that of not misleading the chief by a wrong decyphering, or an incorrect translation.

The large majority of them had nothing to lose, as they were heirs-apparent with a pre-determined future – with or without the benefit of their service abroad. A number of them made well. Charles Bankhead, of modest means, son of the personal physician of Lord Castlereagh (Canning's predecessor) and a distant relation, by marriage, of the McCammon family, found a wealthy patron and rose to be British Ambassador to Mexico. Other senior outsiders were also given preference: for instance, Austen Henry Layard, archaeologist and politician, whose 'Nineveh and Babylon' appears on my bookshelves, was summarily made Ambassador to Madrid, to the annoyance of a number of career diplomats.

As Honorary Consul (a good century and a half later), I was blessed with the assistance of a willing and capable Pro-Consul, who was of enormous help in the niceties of translation to and from German and Swiss German, French and Italian, as well as the interpretation of certain obscure aspects of Swiss politics – quite apart from her able handling of sundry consular cases.

(The closest we got to decyphering was the use of ancient telegraphic code-books necessary for the identification of the monosyllabic ideograms which make up Chinese proper names, in the days when we assisted the Visa Section in Geneva. Précis-writing, the other important and time-consuming responsibility of earlier attachés, had been overtaken by the typewriter in the 1860s, and, much later, by the computer and its accoutrements.)

In my time, there was indeed the odd, grumpy junior officer at the Embassy in Bern, who seemed to object to the presence of an amateur among career consular staff. This attitude is of course no less prevalent in industry, commerce or insurance; and I must confess to having had similar feelings, during my 30 or so years in banking, about certain know-all trainees, computer buffs, money-market wizards, and hedge-fund merchants, not to mention latter-day chartists, who were regularly inflicted upon us.

Down to 1852, the incumbents at important embassies lost their positions with every change of government, their influential connections, for instance, with a Foreign Secretary, having lapsed. Since then, diplomacy, depoliticised, has steadily become a profession.

Times have moved on from the days when a diplomatist's only motive for engaging an attaché might have been to reassure himself that the eligible young man in question would be a worthy enough partner for his own unmarried daughter.

Already in 1814,

> ...heads of missions appear to have drawn a practical distinction between these 'dandies' and the more useful 'careerists'. We find [Ambassador] Clancarty at Frankfort...using the phrase 'my working staff' as distinct from the others, one of whom *could not even write*[my italics].

And, at the other end of the scale, times have definitely moved on from the days when a diplomatist was given an ambassadorship in distant South America because the King saw in him a rival for the favours of a royal mistress (read: 1826, Lord Ponsonby, Buenos Aires, George IV, Lady Conyngham).

Nevertheless, we now have the honorary consul being appointed by the ambassador, with only token approval from London, 150 years, it seems, after an all-but-identical practice had been snuffed out by the controllers of the Foreign Office. Admittedly, circumstances were very different then. Henry Angst in Zürich, mentioned above, had started out as vice consul, and was promoted to consul, and later consul general; but all of his titles were strictly honorary ones.

Modern honorary consuls are surely more mature - certainly better informed - than the junior attachés of the eighteenth and nineteenth centuries had been. And their modest honoraria now come out of the embassies' own budgets. Many a British Honorary Consul has provided valuable ancillary services in the promotion of investment from their host country into the UK, or the furthering of British exports.

For comparison: among my foreign colleagues in the Corps Consulaire in Zürich, only a few operated in the same way as we did, with strict control over every centime which came from consular services. In some cases, accounting seemed to be relatively lax; and in others, it seems to have been understood that any such income would accrue to the consul himself. Such practices, which used to be wide-spread, now tended to fuel rumours that some appointments were even sold to the highest bidder as a business proposition. One colleague, who had represented a Latin American country for 30 years or so, was abruptly removed from the Post (which he had inherited from his father), having *not once* visited the country he represented. I often wondered how certain Pacific island states could support consular representation *anywhere.*

Be that as it may, by the 1850s and 1860s, British consular services were organised enough to accommodate a new type of mission, nominally diplomatic, but designed primarily for the protection of British subjects, and the furtherance of British industrial and commercial interests. This focus continues.

Probably the first British Consul anywhere was a local man who served in Florence when England opened a legation there in 1456. The first Crown appointment was in Pisa in 1485. An English consul became active in Aleppo (then in the Ottoman Empire) in 1583, after that city had become the principal market for goods from the East. Then it was Madeira (1658: wine), Salonica (1724: carpets, raw silk), Oporto (1753: wine again) and Rio de Janeiro (1808: sugar, cacao, rubber etc.) eight years before the first British Consul was appointed in the USA (at Baltimore, an early railroad hub). All of these consuls – and many more – effectively held honorary positions. A British 'career' Consular Corps, in fact, only dates from 1825.

And there we have it: the position of an honorary consul (though not the title), with its attendant duties, rights and honorarium, is centuries older than Graham Greene's creation. The word 'honorary' (first found in literature in 1614, according to the *OED*) preceded 'honorarium' (1658).

The honorarium is indeed modest, but, as John Nicols has put it, the honour is considerable.

The essential difference between a career consul and an honorary consul nowadays is that the latter can no longer aspire to the highest post at an embassy. That said, proximity to this post was as much as I could have handled.

THE PARABLE OF THE TSAR'S FINGER

'What *exactly* do you do here?' The question was calculated to be offensive. Married couple: British, retired, late 60s, self-appointed Guardians of the Privy Purse. (In the course of swapping yarns with my consular colleagues, I had discovered that every Post was plagued by at least one such couple.) Then, looking pointedly around the empty reception area: 'The old Consulate General was such a *busy* place, wasn't it Mildred? Whatever happened?'

'Good morning, Sir. Good morning, Madam. How can I help you?'

'Oh, we are just paying Her Majesty a courtesy call. We can wait if you are too busy.' Heavy irony. 'We can take a seat, can't we Mildred? – and await our turn.'

At that very minute, the door opened, and in walked five Somali would-be immigrants, with an East African *Schlepper* ('people-smuggler'), who was already known to us. They were followed by a British family: mother, father and three small children (Dad had left his attaché case, with all the passports, lying on the luggage trolley at the main railway station, and it had disappeared). Our little reception area was suddenly filled with the agitated chatter of 11 people. The retired married couple, who had been making a show of sitting down in the corner, thought better of it and left, with their noses in the air. They never again visited us.

The real irony of this tale is that, had I taken proper notice of the question which this tiresome pair had originally asked, and had I, perhaps, made a few notes at the time, and not just relied on a leaky memory, the writing of these memoirs would have been a lot easier.

During my tenure, there were, in my consular district, some 5,000 British passport-holders – far less than the 25,000 or so in French-speaking Switzerland. While a higher proportion of those in the Lausanne-Geneva region were retired people, permanently resident, I was responsible for more businessmen and -women and their families. Moreover, I had far more cases which concerned British and Commonwealth citizens and others, who were passing through Zürich airport and the main station. There was, for example, a flourishing business in stolen

British passports which commanded a premium among travel documents in the black market: at one time, they were said to be worth tens of thousands of Swiss francs each. Well-disguised and very professional pickpockets, believed to be largely Colombians or Kosovo-Albanians, roamed the arrival and departure zones. Photo-substitution (in the old-style passports) was commonplace, and, composite travel documents, skilfully stitched together and re-bound, also came to light. From time to time, we would pick up from the airport police a dozen confiscated passports which had been tampered with in some way; and those were just the British travel documents.

There was the occasional professional problem, such as the distraught circus clown, who claimed to have been physically assaulted by a bullying impresario after he refused to resign ('Look, he hit me here'), and thrown out of the Big Top by a strongman. There was the computer programmer who asked for protection, not only from his Russian girlfriend, who was threatening him with terrible things, but also from his wife back in the UK, who, after she had found out about his new liaison, threatened him with unimaginable things. He went into hiding somewhere and I began to get calls from both women, as well as his mother ('Whatever happens, please don't tell *her* anything') and his employer. Our lawyers' list was well thumbed.

We quite often had visits from parents, accompanied by children, who - as children will - ran riot and screamed and vomited. For these occasions we had a little toy chipmunk, which wiggled its bottom and sang a song, falsetto and rather loud; our neighbours, a firm of executive-search specialists, sporadically looked round the door to see what was going on. Again and again, we faced trivialities, and it was often very difficult to remain patient. 'Would you be good enough to translate this for me?' from a British resident of 30 years standing, who proudly boasted that he still couldn't 'speak a word of this damned local lingo' (Swiss German). What he wanted to show me turned out to be a speeding fine. There was almost always a funny side.

There was tragedy too. The worst cases, for me, involved children: victims of road accidents, distant plane crashes, natural disasters. Child abduction (commonly perpetrated by one of the parents, usually the mother) is an appallingly complex matter, and I was grateful for the assistance received from the FCO child abduction unit. Prisoners of all categories were a significant part of our brief. While we could take no part in the legal proceedings, visiting and reporting back to the Embassy in Berne, and the FCO in London (as well as sundry other Consulates who were, on occasion, also involved) was of foremost importance. Thankfully, one could call upon someone at the FCO for help in any conceivable situation, from detention right through to repatriation (where there was always a social worker/adviser on hand) and prison transfer (after a statutory period, back to an institution in the UK).

'Human rights' popped up regularly, but questions usually came to us in the heat of the moment after, say, a sacking, at a time when the victim should have been talking to a lawyer and not wasting his - and our - time threatening to sell his story to the Press. It was nevertheless comforting to know that the human rights section in London was always on hand.

One thing was drummed into us during consular courses: we should treat the Press with kid gloves and every time refer questions from, say, a British provincial newspaper - always hungry for news - to the Press Office at the FCO, where Press releases were scrupulously updated. The occasional correspondent did not always play by the unwritten rules (even going so far as pretending to be a member of the victim's or the prisoner's family). Such caution was well-based, but I was still able to cultivate close relationships with members of the Zürich Press Corps, who, in my experience, never abused their positions, and were often very helpful.

Security considerations were dictated by the FCO's own threat level classifications: 'low', 'underlying' (a low level of known terrorist activity), 'general' and 'high', and the Embassy kept me well informed. Protection from the Swiss side was provided by the *Festungswachtkorps* (literally, the 'fortress watch', a body dating back 100 years to the first official defence of the St Gotthard Pass); the *Sicherheitsdienst* (security service) of the Zürich police force, and the Swiss Army. The drilling of platoons of army recruits in our courtyard at first caused some consternation among the neighbours, but later became popular when it was noted that the volume of burglaries in the area had sharply declined. Once or twice, because of ardent young men with guns, I had difficulties getting into the Consulate myself. Sydney, our *Grosser Schweizer Sennenhund* (very large Swiss farmers' dog) did not like the uniforms one bit.

Apart from a series of demonstrations in the early days, which all passed off peacefully, the detention of a few troublesome parties (often mentally disturbed), and the usual plague of letters containing some mysterious powder – one couldn't take chances – there was no serious embarrassment. For the eventuality, we had goggles, industrial gloves and helmets in reserve.

...All of which still leaves the enigmatic title to this essay unexplained.

The appearance of a mere honorary consul in lieu of a professional consul general naturally caused some perplexity among members of the British community, particularly the older members, who were used to benefiting – at least on the occasion of the Queen's Birthday Party (the 'QBP') – from a small corner of the incumbent's entertainment allowance. With the helpful assistance of the Zürich regional chairman of the British Residents' Association (the 'BRA') and others, the Union Jack was kept flying, but we were, I admit, 'on our inners'. The celebration of Her Majesty's Golden Jubilee in 2002 was a tight squeeze indeed. However, at this moment in time, it must be admitted that (*pace* the then local employees!) the cost-cutting exercise which led to the closure of the Zürich Consulate General, now looks very timely indeed. If it hadn't happened then, it would certainly be happening now.

It is extraordinary what a sensitive subject 'entertaining' can become. Reciprocity, in some form, is a must, and sometimes this is not as straightforward as it might seem. The post of honorary consul certainly has a cachet of its own. Angelika and I were invited to sports events: swimming, golf, the Zürich Open women's tennis tournament, and international youth football competitions; *Knabenschiessen* (an annual Zürich shooting contest, now for boys *and* girls, despite its name); cultural engagements at the Opera House, and the *Tonhalle* (Zürich concert hall); and national days of other members of the Corps Consulaire. There were recitals of the Salvation Army brass band, countless other charity get-togethers and international school events.

Private invitations addressed to the Honorary Consul needed special care. I remember sitting on a tram once, in front of an English lady who was talking to her friend about a planned dinner party. I had no idea who she was. At one stage of the conversation, she said:

'Oh, *do* come; the British Consul will be there. I'd really like you to meet him.' I made a mental note not to accept should I ever receive an invitation from her, but I never did.

The re-jigging of the consular district for which I had responsibility also had its repercussions. I learned that an Anglo-Swiss club in an outlying canton had objected because the respective canton was now no longer part of the responsibility of the Zürich Consulate, and I asked the Deputy Head of Mission in Berne what – if anything – I should do. He said: 'Tell them about the Tsar's finger.' He was referring to the story (probably apocryphal, nobody really knows; there are several versions of the tale) about Tsar Alexander III marking down on the map the route for the Trans-Siberian railway. His finger (or was it his thumb?) overlapped the ruler as he was tracing the line, and produced a 'bump', which, it is said, caused engineers to question the logic of such a large diversion. As it happened (or so the sequel to the story goes), there turned out to be a very good reason for the diversion: Lake Baikal.

This parable was duly recounted after a dinner hosted by the said club, there were chuckles all around, and the matter was diplomatically resolved.

LA DIPLOMATIQUE

Satow (1917) makes the point that *la diplomatique* is the term used in French for the art of deciphering ancient documents...

If you walk into our house, you are quite likely to spot imitations of the Rosetta Stone, or the Phaistos Disk, or the Runestone of Jelling. And on the book-shelf, you might see a copy of *Système*

Hiéroglyphique (Champollion), or a *Glossary of Anglo-Indian Words* (Yule-Burnell, a must), or *Geschichte der Schrift* (Faulmann, another favourite). Angelika has been striving to keep the dust off these relics for years. But that is not the half of it: other books on languages are there in abundance. There are tomes on Chinese, Danish, Hebrew, Hindi, Malay and the patois of Trinidad and Tobago; as well as Pidgin and the Vulgar Tongue; Assyrian, Middle-English and Sanskrit; and so on. I have been lucky enough to study Ancient Greek and Latin (at school), French (at the Sorbonne), Spanish (at the *Centro de Estudios de Español* in Málaga), Russian (at McGill University), a little Persian, Portuguese and German (at courses sponsored by the Bank of London & South America (BOLSA), Japanese (at the *Reisehochschule*, Zürich) and Arabic (at Berlitz).

The 'direct method' German course (one-to-one basis, just talking, no grammar) took place in 1968 at an institute near Lambeth Bridge, among Foreign Office staff learning exotic Far Eastern languages. Before taking the course, I drove Omi Omi and a friend, Trude Piwowar, around West Berlin in my mother Gwynneth's battered Morris Oxford. I thought I was making headway when Trude taught me my first German phrase *immer geradeaus* ('keep going straight on'). She made me repeat the words over and over again, until I realised that the exercise had nothing to do with linguistics: she hadn't been in a motor car for years and simply wanted me to drive in a straight line for as long as possible. *Rechts* and *Links* came later.

Actually Angelika is a far better linguist that I am: she natters away in French and Italian without any formal training at all, and now makes a living translating from German and Swiss German into English (a foreign language for her), Portuguese and Spanish. My sons and their families, who are all bi- or trilingual, have also brought Dutch and Braille into the family.

One of the most forbidding tongues is represented on my shelves by Sir Charles Bell's *Grammar of Colloquial Tibetan*. Only in the language itself can certain Tibetan expressions be fully appreciated. Colonel P.T. Etherton, 'late HM Consul-General in Chinese Turkestan', recorded the following salutation, which gives a flavour of the idiomatic niceties of this enigmatic land:

'Have you slept well,' is the universal greeting, sleep being an all-important necessity for the snow dweller.

'Good morning,' would be classed as redundant and strictly untruthful when the wind is howling, and a snow storm swathes everything in gloom.

There have been other linguists in our family. My father ('Tony') spoke Hindustani (Urdu). His father ('Pop') had 'lower standard Urdu' and 'higher standard Baluchi'. My mother was fascinated by languages and spoke fluent French. In addition, she struggled with Spanish and Portuguese and made every effort to reciprocate when my German mother-in-law, Liselotte Meissner, learned English. I have no doubt that many early Davies's and McCammons were bilingual (Welsh and English; English and Gaelic). Another relation who distinguished herself in this way was Emily Elizabeth Sparke, née McKellar, the wife of Edward Joseph Sparke, my maternal great-grandfather. She put together a short but erudite dictionary of the Australian aboriginal tongues: *Kamilaroi, Yaraldi* and *Wiradjuri.* Though I have not seen the manuscript, I understand it has been tentatively dated (by the Mitchell Library in Sydney) to 1900.

Language is at the point of entry to all cultures. The FCO has recognised this for years, and now has some of the best language scholars in any diplomatic service. The four ambassadors, to whom I worked in Zürich, were fluent, respectively, in Greek, Arabic, Chinese and Hungarian as well as a number of other 'easy' languages.

I do not pretend to be in that league. But, in spite of enormous pressures only to converse in the Queen's English, and notwithstanding an unfortunate experience I had with a French consular colleague (see below), I have always believed that foreign tongues should be given a chance too. After all, it was the opinion of the great Samuel Johnson that 'languages are the pedigree of nations'.

CONTRASTS IN STYLE

From Her Britannic Majesty's Ambassador to Switzerland, at Berne:

> Be it known to all to whom these presents shall come that, by virtue of the powers vested in me by Her Majesty's Commission, I do hereby constitute and appoint Antony Lewis Tisdall McCammon to be Honorary British Consul at Zürich with full power and authority, under the superintendence of Her Britannic Majesty's Consul at Berne, by all lawful means, to aid and protect Her Majesty's subjects trading in, visiting or residing in Switzerland.

> Witness my hand and seal of office...

* * *

From the Swiss Federal Department of Foreign Affairs, Berne:

> *La circonscription consulaire de la Section consulaire de l'Ambassade est modifiée par adjonction du territoire des cantons de la circonscription consulaire de l'ancien Consulat général de Zürich, étant donné que ce poste est dorénavant subordonné à l'Ambassade. Sa catégorie est donc celle d'un Vice-Consulat et M. Antony McCammon a le titre de Consul honoraire ad personam...*
>
> *Le Département saisit cette occasion pour renouveler à l'Ambassade l'assurance de sa haute considération.*

These words from Berne subtly altered the terms of reference applied to existing British Honorary Consuls in Switzerland, with the Swiss head of protocol preferring to apply a more rigorous interpretation of the relative section of the *Vienna Convention on Consular Relations* of 1963. Usually, though not in the case of the United Kingdom whose honorary consuls are nominated by Her Majesty's ambassadors, credentials are signed by the head of state of the sending country. It is then on the back of credentials thus signed that an *exequatur* is issued by the receiving country. Though my function was theoretically identical to those of all the other (23) honorary consuls in Zürich - not to mention the 40 consuls general and honorary consuls general - I was not entitled to an *exequatur* and my title had to be *ad personam.*

194

ROBERT LAMBERT CBE (1921-97)

What follows is taken from an obituary I penned for Robert's children after his death in 1997. Robert was very supportive during my early days as Honorary Consul, and made me promise to purchase a copy of Satow's *Guide to Diplomatic Practice* - an acquisition which I have never regretted. Robert was a remarkable man and a very good friend.

Robert's achievements began at an early age. Captain of the Oppidans at Eton, he was an Oppidan Scholar, and was awarded the top scholarship to Magdalen, Cambridge, where he gained a double first in Classics and Modern Languages. As well as being an elegant master of the English language on all imaginable occasions, he was also fluent in French, German, Spanish, Italian, Russian, Greek (Ancient!) and Latin. His memory was infallible.

During the war years, he was with the London 90th Regiment RA, where he became very involved in maps, bearings, codes and security in general. Many stories about him have passed into Army folklore. On one occasion, when an enemy shell landed uncomfortably close to one of his gun crews, he quelled the confusion with a 'Come along Gentlemen, please, business as usual'. After landing in Sicily, he bemused his men by reciting to them long passages of Homer's *Odyssey*, in Greek, from memory. He insisted on shaving in his landing craft on D-Day in order to set a good example to his troops.

He returned to England to work with the Bank of England and then Barclays Bank where he was appointed European Representative based in Zürich.

While cherishing his British background, Robert loved living in Switzerland, and after 20 years based in Zürich, he successfully applied for Swiss citizenship. The erudite range of his interests stretched to memberships of the Bembridge Sailing Club and the Kandahar Ski Club.

Sadly, his wife Ann predeceased him in 1988.

Kindness and fortitude were Robert's watchwords. But he tempered these with his invincible good humour. When confronted with his own impending death, he said he wanted to be buried with his wife but wondered how a second gravestone could be placed on the same plot. 'Perhaps we should engrave the other side, and just put PTO under Ann's name,' he remarked, inimitably.

COMMUNICATIONS

I haven't heard from our Ambassador to Spain [William Carmichael] in three years. If he doesn't contact me in the next year, I intend to write.

George Washington

* * *

'I am afraid, said a woman on entering a shoe-shop, that one of my feet is larger than the other.'

'Oh no, Madam, exclaimed the salesman, if anything, one is smaller than the other.'

That man, Ladies and Gentlemen, is consular material.

From a consular course

* * *

An honorary consul should be a person who can tell you to go to hell in such a way that you actually look forward to the trip.

Anon. (also applied to ambassadors)

GURKHAS AGAIN

'Excellencies, Ladies and Gentlemen...'

It was a hot June afternoon in 1999 and, together with sundry members of the *corps diplomatique* and *corps consulaire*, I was attending the unveiling of a memorial, in the verdant grounds of the Cantonal Hospital in Zürich, to 'His Majesty...Svasti Sri Giriraja Chakra Chudamani Narayanetyadi Vividha Virudavali Virajamana Manonatta Parama-Ojaswi-Rajanya Parama Projjwala-Nepal-Tara Parama-Pavitra-Om-Ram-Patta Parama-Jyotirmaya-Subikhyata-Tri-Shakti-Patta Parama-Suprasiddha-Prabala-Gorkha-Dakshina-Bahu Mahadhipati Shriman Sri Sri Sri Sri Maharajadhiraja Tribhuvan Bir Bikram Jang Bahadur Shah Bahadur Shamsher Jang Devanam Sada Samaja Vijayinam...', 1906–55, King of Nepal 1911 to 1950 (when he was deposed) and 1951 (when he was restored) to 1955, when he passed away, at the said hospital. It was my first such engagement.

Our host, the Ambassador at the Permanent Mission of Nepal (to the UN) in Geneva, was addressing us in English.

Stealing a look at my fellow-guests, I saw that several were already beginning to sag in the heat. I moved closer to the ornate metal plaque, affixed to the solid, square, polished, black-granite plinth. Above, carved into the stone, was the dedication to HIS MAJESTY KING TRIBHUVAN OF NEPAL. But it was the ornate royal coat of arms which caught my attention.

'...Honorary General, British Army, Colonel-in-Chief the 1st Gurkha Rifles, the 3rd Gurkha Rifles, the 4th Gurkha Rifles, the 5th Gurkha Rifles...' the ambassador was ploughing valiantly through the late king's biography just as my eye alighted on the crossed *kukris* at the centre of the royal crest. They appear above the sword (representing Katmandu) and hexagram of two superimposed triangles (broadly symbolising Hinduism and Buddhism).

I still have my father's steel *kukris*: the general purpose (*budhuni*) version, with two miniature blades (probably intruders) tucked into the wood and goat-skin sheath; and the slender, ceremonial (*siropate*) fighting-knife, which fits snugly into a scabbard faced with finely-carved silver panels on black velvet. The *budhuni* is very sharp; the *siropate* is terrifyingly so. There is a notch at the base of the cutting edge which is said to be there to allow blood or sap to drop away from the blade rather than running on to the buffalo-horn handle, making it slippery or sticky: a potentially fatal situation in the heat of battle. It also delineates the cut-off point of that part of the weapon which needs to be sharpened.

Contrary to popular belief – helped along by Hollywood – the *kukri* is not thrown: a Gurkha would never let go of his knife. Nor is it designed for slitting throats. It is, rather, a tool for chopping and stabbing. There are also those who believe that a *kukri* should be replaced in its scabbard only after it had been blooded. Not so: anyone who has withdrawn a *kukri* from its close-fitting sheath will know that the blade must be kept extremely well oiled and that the accretion of any foreign substance – such as blood – could have catastrophic consequences.

Not that such superstitions do not come in useful sometimes – particularly if there are, say, grandchildren about. We used to display these instruments of war proudly on the wall. Nowadays, needless to say, they are kept well hidden.

'... The Most Illustrious Order of the Three Divine Powers... the Order of Om Ram Patta...the Order of Supreme Sun of Afghanistan...GC of the Order of Merit of the Republic of Italy... Legion of Honour of France etc., etc....' Some of the Excellencies were looking at their watches; others were drifting away from the memorial. But the speaker was steeled in his resolve to complete his address.

Until I met the Nepalese Ambassador – himself of Gurkha origin – at the Zürich ceremony, my mother, Gwynneth, had been my only other source of information about these tough little men and the battles they were fighting on the North-West Frontier. In his correspondence, my father scarcely mentioned them. He alluded to the odd *havildar* (sergeant) and *naik* (corporal); to 'bearers', 'orderlies' and 'sweepers' and, now and again, to 'the man'. He occasionally touched on such events as '...this damned *Dussera*'(a noisy Hindu party) and 'the *Nautch*'(originally a sort of Indian ballet, later a dance attended by expatriates). There was the screaming of 'jacks' (jackals) around the perimeter fence and the 'breath of death' (a desert wind).

But only rarely did he refer to Gurkha officers. Superior status was, rather, reflected, as in his throw-away remark that it was '...awfully bad for the horses not to be ridden by a sahib occasionally...'

He made one mention (in a letter dated 1 December 1935) of a '*khudd* race for recruits', which tied in with something my mother once told me: she described an exercise she once witnessed where Gurkhas, practising ambush techniques, '...poured, like water, down a cliff-face'. A history of the 6th Gurkha Rifles confirms that 'every year from 1934 to 1939 the 2nd Battalion won the Gurkha Brigade Hill Race'.

My father's regiment was formerly known as the Cuttack Legion (after an area in Orissa State) and the Rangpur Light Infantry. By 1886, it was made up exclusively of Gurkhas and became the 42nd Gurkha Light Infantry, later the 6th Gurkhas. The first battalion made its name at Gallipoli. A second battalion had been raised in 1904. Much reduced, the 6th is now part of Queen Elizabeth's Own Gurkha Rifles.

Gwynneth also told me that the Gurkhas had a very strange sense of humour, deriving, for example, enormous pleasure from chasing each other around with the head of a water-buffalo, which had been detached, in competition, by the smallest number of *kukri*-strokes (two-handed knives were allowed). She was in awe of these strange, loyal little men, preferring the company of her elderly Sikh dentist, who, with his treadle drill, fixed her post-pregnancy teeth so well that some of his fillings lasted until her death, 60 years later.

I only ever heard from her one tale about the enemy tribesmen who confronted my father's regiment. They were known not only for their extraordinary accuracy with their (single shot) muzzle-loaders, but also for their great stealth. So addicted to silence were they, indeed, that, in order to preserve the inviolability of their own ambush positions – which they held unseen for days at a time – 'they even pee'd down straws'. I have no idea how my mother got to hear about this nicety, nor whether she was disgusted by it, or impressed.

'...Excellencies, Ladies and Gentlemen,' the ambassador broke into my train of thought, 'Thank you all for coming.'

A BOTTLE OF WHISKY

A memo to the Embassy in Berne:

1. I believe (though I cannot find chapter and verse in DSP [the FCO book of rules], that I must report to you any gifts I have received as Honorary Consul here.
2. On the occasion of the visit of Glasgow Celtic Football Team on 2 and 3 November 1998, I was presented with a bottle of Glenlivet whisky by the Operations Manager as a token of the team's appreciation for my assistance.
3. Sorry to miss you on the night. It was so cold and damp that I wished I had had the bottle with me.
4. Amazingly, not one supporter turned up at the Consulate next morning, having mislaid his sporran.

Berne's laconic reply:

Noted. Enjoy.

CONDOLENCES

For some reason, whisky made me think of condolences. Perhaps it was because one of my responsibilities was the death of the Queen Mum, who was partial to a tot - though her favourite tipple is said to have been gin and Dubonnet. At our little Consulate, sympathetic words in her memory filled four books, which were duly forwarded to Clarence House. This was more than Princess Diana, who was my very first such case. The events of 9.11 occasioned a special visit to the United States consular agency. No words were necessary: everyone was in a state of shock.

There was a strict procedure in the Consular Corps, with a standard form of communication for current and former heads of state. I clearly recall my visit to the Austrian Consulate General, when Kurt Waldheim died; and to the Croatians when Franjo Tudjman, the country's first president, passed away. A buffing-up of the respective country's history does not go amiss.

My most memorable condolence occasion - for quite the wrong reason - was when I went to sign the book at the Nepalese Consulate following the tragic massacre of the royal family by the crown prince. There was an extraordinary glass structure, lying at an angle in the hall. I took it to be a crooked pagoda - some sort of oriental sign, symbolising the fall of the royal house. Weeks later, I asked Ueli Vetsch, the Honorary Consul, to explain it to me.

At first he was puzzled by my question. Then his face lit up and he began to laugh.

'Oh that!' he said. 'That was just a chandelier which, for some reason, detached itself from the ceiling of the top floor just before you walked in, and crashed to the ground. I heard the commotion but I didn't know what it was. You were quite lucky, you know ...'

A SECRET

That morning, the telephone never stopped.

'British Consulate, good morning. How can I help you?'

'I wonder if you would be good enough to help me find someone.'

'Of course. Please let me have some details and I will see what I can do.'

'I am rather worried actually. We have had regular contact, by letter and by phone, for quite a long time.'

'Are you missing a member of your family?' I knew this question may not have been appropriate, but one has to start somewhere.

'Not exactly. She's a very old friend.' *Old* friend or *old friend?* – difficult to decide at this stage. 'We have known each other for nearly 70 years...'

'Are you able to travel?'

'Not really. I am bedridden. I just have...' he paused for a few seconds '...my telephone now. I hope you don't mind me calling you. I have your number from the Foreign Office.'

'Of course not. Give me your full name and telephone number; and please let me have your friend's full name, telephone number and address if possible.' He slowly obliged.

'... Very happy years. I hope you understand. We only ever met once...' I said nothing.

'...In Switzerland. I went on a walking tour; near Mürren. We met there. It was a long time ago. Do you know Mürren?'

'I have ski-ed there a few times, Sir.'

'Have you met the Lunns?'

'I recall being introduced to one member of the family, Sir. He had a thick beard...' At that moment, some more visitors walked into the Consulate. '...I must hang up now. I will drive out and look for your friend, and let you know what has happened as soon as I can.'

'Thank you. Goodbye.'

His lady-friend, I quickly discovered, had died two weeks previously. I found out where she had been laid to rest, phoned him and passed this on. He was not family, so I felt I could do this myself. He received the news calmly.

'I hope you don't mind me telling you this, but I already knew she had died. I just knew. I wanted to send her some flowers, but I didn't know how. Thank you for your help. It was nice talking to you.'

I know how elderly people love having a good chat. For many weeks, *I* felt like calling *him* back. But that (I quickly learned) is not what honorary consuls are for.

A DEAD MURDERER

It was summer 1998. A stalwart of the British community paid me a visit. He was the resident expert on everything, and a nuisance. He lost no time in seizing the initiative.

'You heard about Hume?'

'Sir Alec?

'No, not him: Donald Hume.'

'Who's he?'

'You mean to say you have never heard of Donald Hume, the murderer?'

'I can't say I have.'

'…the man who knifed and dismembered people…?'

'No…'

'…with a German SS dagger…?…A British Consul who has never heard of someone who dropped body parts from a helicopter into the English Channel? I can't believe this…'

'Mr Bright, please enlighten me. I do not know who this Mr Hume is. Are you here on consular business?'

'I am indeed.' He seemed less sure of himself. 'I thought you should know that Mr Donald Hume has just died.'

'So, you have come to report a death. Are you related to Mr Hume?' Mr Bright now looked uneasy. He glanced around and his voice dropped to a whisper.

' Don't you keep tabs on people?'

'What on earth do you mean?'

'Files…you know…on convicted murderers and so forth…' I looked at him intently. 'I don't mean *me*, I mean Donald Hume.' I reflected for a moment.

'So you want to know whether we have a file on this Donald Hume…who is now dead? Even if we had one - which I don't think is the case, I still don't see what business this is of yours.'

'But this man…' Mr Bright was trying to win back lost ground - shot two people in your consular area.' I picked up my pen.

'When did this happen?'

'About 40 years ago. I thought you would know about it.'

'Mr Bright, I have been Consul here for one year. Is - was - Mr Hume British?'

'Of course...otherwise I wouldn't be here...' I decided to give him some rein.

'Tell me about him.'

And he did. Donald Hume had stabbed a Jewish partner-in-crime to death in London, and had indeed tried to dispose of the victim's dismembered body from a helicopter. On a technicality he avoided being sentenced for murder, but pleaded guilty to being an accessory after the fact. After eight years in Dartmoor, he took to bank robbery and shot a Midland Bank teller. He moved to Zürich and shot two more in another robbery attempt. Sentenced to life in 1958, he was released and repatriated in 1976 by the Zürich authorities, who believed he was insane. Mr Bright had read in a tabloid newspaper that morning that the body of 79-year-old Donald Hume had been found at a hotel in Basingstoke; it had been identified by fingerprints on file in Broadmoor, where the man once known as the most dangerous man in Britain had subsequently spent 15 demeaning years.

My visitor's smugness, as he left, was trying. But at least we *both* knew that the case of the dead murderer did not concern the Consulate.

A CONVOLUTED LIFE

From a note to the file:

Young British married woman left UK for Middle East, met Egyptian, got pregnant, married under Islamic law; he divorced her under Islamic law. She had baby in Dubai, went home to her British husband and persuaded him that baby should take his name. She then divorced British husband who later provided letter of rebuttal re baby's parentage, mother having decided that baby should change name to that of real (Egyptian) father. Latter had in meantime come to Switzerland to work (hence our involvement) and had married a Swiss woman. We were requested by British Embassy Cairo to arrange for father (who had subsequently taken Swiss nationality) to come to Consulate and sign a paternity declaration. He wavered but remained well-disposed towards us. After much unpleasantness from mother (who had moved back to UK) to all parties, she finally engaged two (lady) lawyers, one British, one Swiss, and forced father to have a blood test. On day he was to sign paternity affidavit, father's Swiss wife appeared in Consulate, wanting to know what was going on; and Swiss lawyer contacted father and advised him not to sign as mother had not been paying her legal bills. After a last argument about who should take original of paternity document, he finally signed. Mother's efforts to change the birth certificate continue. Case duration (so far): 30 months.

PORTRAITS

She was blonde and *very* pretty; beautifully coiffed with an urchin haircut; long graceful hands; dressed unusually in a silk blouse and skirt. She was not the sort of visitor honorary consuls often receive.

'How can I help you?'

'Lost my passport.' The voice spoiled the effect, slightly.

'Where might you have mislaid it?'

'Know exactly who took it...'

'Oh?'

'Vere was two of 'em.'

'Where did this take place?'

'Night-club...'

'And when?'

'Free o'clock vis morning'...and she gave me the name of the establishment.

'Vese two black blokes wanted me to show 'em a British passport, so I did. But vey wouldn't give it back to me. Ven vey ran off. So I chased 'em; didn't catch 'em vough. What a lovely view you have.'

'You chased them at 3 o'clock in the morning?'

'Anyfing wrong? I took my shoes off.'

'Can you describe them?' She handed me two fine pencil sketches.

'Did vese on my way here; fought you might need 'em. I'm a portrait-painter...'

BOXING...

I had been invited to the *Kantonspolizei* headquarters to help identify a thick-set young man, who was accompanied by two very solid policemen. His stance seemed, in some way, familiar. Going to shake his hand, I saw that the man was handcuffed.

'Would you mind taking those off him, please?' The police obliged.

'Are you British?' The man nodded. The nod was somehow familiar...'Would you please give me your date and place of birth?' He shook his head. That shake, again, rang distant bells... According to the police, he had earlier claimed to have been born in Hackney. 'Were you born in London?' No reaction; his eyes ranged around the room. His face was glum. 'Do your parents live in Britain?' He seemed about to say something but then stopped himself. 'Why did you come to Switzerland?' He looked out of the window. Then the penny dropped: he was a boxer; that's what it was. 'Do you box?' An enormous grin appeared on his face. 'Tell me where you box. Which club?'

'Hackney...' And that was all he would say.

Later that day, after I had returned to the Consulate, I received a telephone call. It was the *Kantonspolizei.* Just after I had left the station, the man stood up, floored the two policemen (straight-lefts to the jaw?), trashed the office and sat down again. Reportedly, he still had an enormous grin on his face as they put him back into the cells. He refused any further consular assistance.

...AND TENNIS

He wore immaculate tennis gear, and carried a sports-bag which contained two rackets. The police brought him to the Consulate, as, they said, he was suspected of various misdemeanours but claimed to be British. Could I help? We all sat down.

'Where are you from?'

'I'm from Britain.'

'Were you born there?'

'Yes, absolutely.'

'What is your date of birth?'

'I've lost my passport.'

'What is your date of birth?'

'I don't 'ave it.'

'Would you please give me your date of birth?'

'I 'ave been born at Buckingham...' I was having difficulty placing his accent.

'The date in my passport is... May I 'ave a piece of paper? And he wrote something down. Somehow his writing and his tennis garb were incongruous.'

'Buckingham is a big place; can you be more precise?'

'Precise?' He wasn't fully understanding the questions, it seemed. '... Palace.'

'I beg your pardon?'

'Palace. Buckingham Palace.' The accent was definitely French.

' *Vous parlez français.*' It was a statement, not a question (an old trick). His face lit up.

'*Bien sûr!*'

QED, thought I.

Shortly after the police had taken him back to their headquarters, they phoned the Consulate to say that he was now claiming to be from St Lucia, where French was still spoken; and St Lucia was, in those days, the responsibility of the FCO. So back he came, with his police escort but without his tennis bag.

'So, where *were* you born?'

'Buckingham Palace, I 'ave told you.'

This visit lasted less than five minutes.

Some days later, the police phoned to say that he had changed his story yet again: he had become a Nigerian, so nothing more to do with the British authorities. It finally turned out that he was from Senegal; but, by the time that this had transpired, he had managed to stay the minimum time in Switzerland to qualify for an application for refugee status.

CRIME IN ZÜRICH

I attended a talk, reported in the Press in early May 1999 by the retiring senior state attorney in Zürich. Here are some of the points he made at the time:

Foreigners make up a much larger percentage of the criminal class than is first evident. Swiss residents are easier to catch. Statistics are based only on solved crimes, or some 6 per cent over all.

Liberal/left-wing lawyers have seen to it that the burden of proof is now much greater. *Datenschutz* (protection of personal data) and other wheezes are constantly used to delay proceedings until it is too late. If (his example) four Kosovo Albanians are arrested in a room with $100,000 in their collective pockets and six kilos of raw drugs on the table, simple denials will almost certainly be enough to get them off the hook. From one minute to the next, fluent German-speaking foreigners can only express themselves in their own language, and translating/interpreting is (e.g. with Albanian) an easy road to the statute of limitations.

Figures from *Poeschwies* (prison, near Zürich) show that up to 90 per cent of detainees are classed as 'foreigners', largely because they have no fixed abode. It costs Sfr. 300.- to 400.- per day per head, with serious cases up to Sfr. 1000.- Standards of accommodation are so high that a delegation of Russian prison officers recently would not believe that they had been shown a real penal institution.

After sentences are completed, it is almost impossible to get rid of habitual offenders; the nominal salary received in prison is easily enough to support an average-sized family in, say, Serbia. Even when there is a common language, simple dialogue is problematic. Detainees from the former Soviet Union and the Balkans are suspicious of Swiss-style interviews: they expect to be ordered around and knocked about a bit.

No figures about British detainees; they are not among the larger groups. *Poeschwies* statistics, however, show that 6 per cent are English-speakers.

LEGS

He was suddenly there: very tall, with remarkably long legs; lightly dressed, stout walking-shoes. Small rucksack. Large, pleasant face.

'I seem to have lost my passport, and will need a new one – and some visas. I have just arrived in Zürich from Paris and am on my way to Madrid. I walked here.'

'Did you come from the main station?'

'I walked here.'

'Yes but did you walk from the main station? The airport?'

'I told you I walked here.'

'Yes but where from?'

'Paris. I always walk.'

'And where will you go next?'

'Madrid.'

'Walking?'

'Of course. I walk everywhere. I don't like cars; I don't like trains; I don't like planes. I sometimes do boats.'

I fixed him up with an emergency passport and gave him information about obtaining visas. And then, suddenly, he was gone. Yvonne (the Pro-Consul) and I looked at each other. Then he was back, accompanied by one of our neighbours, a career-planner, who seemed puzzled.

'Sorry. I tend to take wrong turnings.'

We took him downstairs, and waved him away. He didn't see us: his seven-league boots had already taken him round the first corner, on his way to Barcelona and Madrid.

CONVENIENCES

A treatise on urinals cannot usually be found in decent literature. The subject, however, certainly merits a passing thought. For those readers who are interested in a bit of history, one has to go back to the Roman Emperor Vespasian, who might have been amused (or perhaps not!) to know that his name has been perpetuated in the word *vespasiano,* a modern Italian sobriquet for the *pissoir.* Vespasian is known to have raised a tax on public lavatories. The name *vespasienne* was created in 1834/5 for a revolutionary new public urinal installed in Paris by Claude-Philibert Barthelot, Comte de Rambuteau, *Préfet de la Seine,* who was an early French ecologist.

As life goes on, one learns to appreciate these conveniences more and more. It is noticeable how, in England and Australia for example, the edifices housing them always seem to occupy prime sites at tourist resorts. While the situation at the most famous Egyptian pharaonic sites is disgusting, that along French motorways is now of a quality and frequency which is *nonpareil.* Stories of graffiti on and in these hallowed areas abound. There used to be a pub in Estoril, Portugal; the publican's wife was called Mary. Someone had scrawled JESUS IS DEAD above the pissoir; underneath, in another hand were the words DON'T WORRY – MARY'S PREGNANT AGAIN!

In the 'good old days', there used to be regular cocktail parties in Zürich which celebrated the openings of sundry banking institutions. The gathering which many of my generation remember best was the inaugural bash for the new representative of the *Banco Nacional de Cuba.* There were about 100 guests at the party. A political tussle was then going on between the People's Republic of China and the USSR. It was only a few years after the Cuban missile crisis, and Russian Communism was on the wane, although it was still pumping out $1 million a day for Fidel Castro.

China was endeavouring to fill the gap. At the same time, the Chinese were no doubt trying to find out what was going on in the wider world of finance, represented worldwide, as they were in the 1970s, by only one bank, the Bank of China branch in London – though this is now hard to believe.

I knew most of the faces there that evening. The new representative, our host, who went down particularly well with the ladies, was doing a fine job entertaining us. But the floor-show was not of his doing. There were four Chinese representatives there: the Chinese Ambassador, who only spoke Chinese; and someone of senior ministerial rank from Peking, who didn't seem to speak anything. It was the time of the 'cultural revolution' and these two older gentlemen were accompanied – or, better, supervised – by two surly 'red guards'. One spoke French, the other German. They made up a bizarre group, never leaving each other's sides. Whenever anybody went up to address either of the senior gentlemen, one or other of the 'guards' barged in and fielded whatever was said. Inevitably, his riposte was couched in pugnacious, ideological terms.

Very soon, all eyes were on the Chinese caucus. And then – the second act of their very own floor-show – they suddenly formed up in single file and trooped off – left, right, left, right – to the 'Gents'. Conversation died, until they reappeared. This happened regularly during the evening, until it became clear that the red guards – one of whom had a picture of a tank (actually a copy of the Soviet T54A) in his lapel – were not prepared to let their charges out of their sight, when one of the two older gentlemen had to 'go'.

One of our number dared to accompany them in one sortie to the 'john'. We all clustered round him when he came out; he told us that our oriental fellow-guests had spoken not a word while they were waiting for whoever it was to attend to his business. Our host joined in the fun, and, afterwards, we all pruriently agreed – boys will be boys! – that it had been one of the most entertaining parties of the season.

During a reception given by the Zürich Chamber of Commerce, many years later, I spotted the senior Party member from the Chinese Consulate General sitting alone in a corner, facing the wall. Thinking that he was perhaps feeling unwell, I approached him. He looked up and, without rising from his chair or greeting me, said, in fluent German, 'Here I am, a lone communist, in a room with *so many* capitalists.' He looked miserable. But could it all have been for show?

Since my time at McGill, and in the Chartered Bank, when I had many Chinese friends, I became aware of a deviously cruel, xenophobic tendency. For example, Chinese citizens who indulged in too much dallying with non-Chinese were known to their compatriots as 'bananas': yellow outside but white inside. The Party does not discourage this. However, times are changing.

The recently-formed Chinese Cricket Association (CCA) sent their first team to take part in the Asian Cricket Council (ACC) Twenty20 Cup in the United Arab Emirates in 2009. They finished in 12th and last place, having broken the tournament records for low total and high margin of defeat. Against the UAE team's 236 runs, the CCA were bowled out for 27, with 15 of those runs coming in extras. The Chinese were learning how to lose.

That said, the CCA has reportedly set itself some ambitious aims. These include:

- By 2009: Have 720 teams across the country in a well-organised structure
- By 2015: Have 20,000 players and 2,000 coaches
- By 2019: Qualify for the World Cup
- By 2020: Gain Test status
- By (unspecified date): Beat India

Watch this space!

MACDONALD

The Immigration Police were on the phone from the airport:

'Mr MacDonald is with us. He has lost his passport. We are sending him to you.'

An hour or so later, Mr MacDonald walked in. He was a very solid-looking gentleman. Mid-40s; carrying a paper bag.

'How can we help you?'

'I want passport.' Heavy Russian, possibly Ukrainian accent. He handed over a police report.

'Are you British?'

'Breeteesh.'

'And where were you born?'

'Scotland, of course.'

'And what is your date of birth?' I was holding the police report and he, quite obviously, could not remember what date he had entered on it.

'*Sentyabr* born' (the Russian word for September). 1 October was entered on the report.

'And were you born in Edinburgh?'

'Yes, of course.'

211

I felt that if I had asked him: 'Are you the famous Olympic caber-tossing champion?' he would have answered 'Yes of course,' in his stolid Slavic way.

After photocopying the report, I handed him back the original and wished him luck. For an instant, our minds met. Then, with the deep resignation which only a Russian can muster, and without another word, he left.

DIRTY WASHING

'Is that you?'

Pause.

'Good. I need to talk to you. Now listen to me.'

The stage was set.

'I told you last week what was going to happen. I haven't changed my mind.'

Pause.

'No. That is out of the question. (Louder) I have told you that already.'

It was 8.30 in the morning. The passengers in the tram were beginning to look up from their newspapers.

'Are you mad? I never said I would do that. If you want to leave, *you* go. And you can take what belongs to you. The car is mine.'

He was definitely English, with an accent that was slightly short of Kensington. The quacking sound coming from his mobile phone clearly belonged to his estranged spouse. By now all the passengers were pointedly looking out of the windows, the better to hear what was being said.

'No. Definitely not. You can take the fridge if you want to but (louder still) *not* my bicycle.'

Pause.

'I *shall* be going to the authorities. But... No certainly not. It was *your* idea.'

A longer pause. The passengers were now looking at each other as if to say 'these foreigners'. Then, abruptly...

'Don't be such a bloody fool!'

And so it went on ... and on. He was still at it, completely oblivious to his surroundings, and his audience, as I got off the tram.

An hour or so later, the door-bell rang at the Consulate. The same man walked in. And he was still talking into his mobile.

'Must go now; I've got some business to do.'

Then, without so much as a Good Morning, he looked at me and said:

'I've got marriage problems.'

I only just stopped myself from saying, 'Yes, I know.'

REQUESTS AND REQUIRES

- Am I allowed to take my goldfish with me when I take a holiday in Wales?
- May I have your permission to get married, Sir?
- How can I get to see a real cricket match? (under the impression that a Test Match was some sort of preparatory game)
- Under English law, how many times may I get married?
- I have a collection of about 60 biscuit tins with royal motifs: please help me to identify them. (With the help of a colleague at Buckingham Palace and a fax machine, we obliged.)
- Please send me a machine-edible passport.
- I am buying one square foot of land in Scotland; will anybody object if I become an Earl?
- Would you please arrange for this confidential message to be handed to Prince Charles? (a common request)
- 37 years ago, I sold some groceries to Mrs Entwhistle as per list attached. Would you please request her to pay me for them? (a request that came by mail to the Consulate several years in succession: 38 years ago ... 39 years ago ... and so on)
- I should like two tickets for Ascot, please.
- Would you please help me to fill in this application, as I cannot see very well? I need a new passport as I shall be dying soon. (This was arranged for this enchanting 99-year-old lady who genuinely believed she needed a passport for her last trip.)
- Am I doing anything wrong if I marry her – she's Swiss?
- Please settle an argument: what is the English for 'I love you'?
- I worked for two weeks in the British Merchant Navy. I should like to draw my pension. (from a 35-year-old)
- If I have learned English in Australia, may I join the Foreign Office?

- How can I rent a Channel Island? I want to have my anniversary party there.(from an American)
- Can the Queen vote? (a very good question which occasioned a lot of research)
- I have English roots. Please send me proof.
- I was related to a previous consul. Does this give me diplomatic immunity?
- Will you help me to get my cousin out of jail in Zimbabwe? (With the involvement of Consular Division in London, this was successfully arranged, though, a member of the opposition, the cousin was soon detained again, and has since fled the country.)
- Kindly take note of the disgusting conditions on the house-boat we booked last summer.
- (Ex-serviceman:) Sir, should I wear my medals at the Queen's Birthday Party? (Honorary Consul:) 'Yes Sir, you should.'
- Someone regularly drives a motor-cycle with British registration plates through our village so fast that we cannot catch him. Can you help? (from the Swiss village policeman)

THE HOOLIGAN

Father and son had come from the Midlands to Zürich to support their team in a football match. Their team had won. As the father was getting on to a tram to return to his hotel, he was attacked and stamped on from behind by a Swiss hooligan. He was left with serious injuries to one of his legs - so serious, in fact, that he was never able to work again.

I had contacted his family, visited him in hospital and taken care of a number of formalities to do with insurance and repatriation. I only learned later that he was also regularly visited by a Zürich policeman who was so disgusted by what had happened that he went well beyond the call of duty to ensure that the assailant (the son of a well-known local politician) was brought to trial and sentenced, and the victim generously compensated.

214

BAGS CAN FLY

Visited by a very smart young lady who had just had her bag snatched. She was worried about nothing in the bag except her passport, which contained a working visa for St Petersburg that had taken her, she said, 18 months to obtain. She was close to tears.

She was standing at the counter when the phone rang. On the line was a worker at a factory beside one of the main roads out of Zürich, who had left his position to have a quick smoke. While he was there, a lady's handbag, evidently thrown from a passing car, had landed at his feet. As it hit the ground, a passport flew out – hence his call to us.

Your Honourable Consul was never so close to being kissed by such an attractive yuppie, and had never before done so little to deserve it.

DUMB

He was in his late teens, handsome and almost too tall to be Chinese. And he was deaf-mute. What could he possibly want at the British Consulate?

The consular atlas came into play quite quickly and China was the relatively quick answer to question 1. But he also pointed at Australia. When I closed the atlas, the visitor shook his head, looking intently at me. He was opening and shutting his mouth. What could that possibly mean? Had he changed his mind about China? He did not seem to be in an urgent hurry but he kept looking at his watch and looking at me again. I showed him the Chinese code books which we used to consult to help identify Chinese names, but he shook his head. Then he resorted to the atlas again and pointed to the United Kingdom, while glancing repeatedly at me; so there *was* a connection. He went across to the calendar and pointed to a date which was in two days' time. Then he started to run around the office, hitting an imaginary ball with an imaginary racket; and stopped and looked at me as if we were playing charades. Going to England to play some sort of racket game? Knowing that the young visitor could not hear, I mused aloud:

215

'You're a tennis player.'

He beamed as if he could lip-read in English. And it suddenly occurred to me that he *could indeed* lip-read in English. After that it was plain sailing.

Following a process of elimination, with me (now verbally) asking questions and the visitor nodding or shaking his head, it transpired that he was indeed on his way to the UK to take part in a tennis tournament. He had mislaid his Chinese passport, which had contained a residence visa for Australia (where he was living with his parents). He had hoped we might be able to solve his problem. Sadly, we couldn't; and I fear he missed his match. He had come such a long way, too. However, with the addresses of the Chinese Consulate General, the nearest Australian Consular Section and our own Visa Department in Geneva safely in his pocket, he left as silently as he had arrived, smiling in an optimistic, oriental-cum-antipodean way, as if to say 'They'll wait for me!'

WHERE I WAS BORN

They were from Mysore, India, a family of four: father, mother, daughter and baby. It was a very complex subject they wished to discuss, something which, said the mother, a Consul would not have experienced before. Something to do with entry visas, and qualifications. I should listen carefully to her, please, and I would surely be convinced of their case. Suddenly, the father, who was holding the baby, blurted out:

'I forgot to put money in the parking-meter...' and made for the door. Then, realising that his departure would leave his wife alone with me, said: 'My wife will come with me; my daughter will keep us a place in the queue.'

Actually there was no queue. But all three departed, leaving the daughter at the counter. As happens on such occasions, chit-chat developed:

'What's your name?'

'Roneesh.'

'What a pretty name. How old are you?'

'I'm eleven next month.'

'Actually I was born in two places': a facade in Mysore, 2000.

'And where were you born?'

Her answer, after a pause, it seemed, for rehearsal, took me back to what the mother had said: something which a Consul would not have experienced before.

'Actually,' said Roneesh, 'I was born in two places.'

When the parents returned, I could not resist telling the mother what an unusual daughter she had. But somehow (it will never be known) the beans had been spilled; and their plan - whatever it had been - was abandoned. I had never seen an Indian blush before. They left in a hurry and - it seemed - in some confusion.

What a waste, I remember thinking, of a parking-space.

THE VANISHING URN

In the 1960s an Egyptian woman with a British passport came to Switzerland as a dancer, and had a daughter who died in her early 20s. She was supported over the years by a Swiss who was probably the father of the girl. She had mild mental problems and was taken into psychiatric care in the late 1960s. She visited us, saying that she had a heart problem, was devastated by her daughter's premature death and hated everybody. She first wanted to go back to Egypt, but was, she said, disowned by the Egyptians. We offered to try to find her family in Alexandria (?); but she gave us only names - no addresses. I asked a Palestinian colleague to talk to her, but it was to no avail. For a time she wanted to go to the UK but then changed her mind back to Egypt (we had requested a charity to assist her return). She continued to fight with everybody (landlord, neighbours, police etc.) and complained of victimisation following the Luxor tragedy, because she was Egyptian. She refused to let us into her apartment. She was later arrested (we never found out why, as she signed but evidently never dispatched a letter to the police authorising them to inform us) and was committed to a psychiatric institute. She was released unexpectedly and visited us one last time to say she had been asked to leave her apartment and would be looking for somewhere else to live. She was found dead by the police having passed away three to four weeks previously. She could not be buried under Muslim law; the Anglican incumbent here, whom she had visited on our recommendation (in fact she only used the church grounds to dump her rubbish), agreed to officiate at a common gravesite, once the authorities were ready to proceed.

A sordid story, admittedly; but what does not appear in the above report is that this Egyptian woman had the last laugh. Her body had to be cremated and, when most parties had agreed that the best solution would be to put her ashes into her late daughter's urn, it was discovered that she had removed and hidden the urn one month before she died. It was never found.

*   *   *

The 'Luxor tragedy' (see below) alludes to the massacre carried out by Islamist fundamentalists at the Deir al-Bahri temple complex, Upper Egypt, in November 1997. Fifty-eight foreign tourists and four Egyptians, as well as several attackers, were killed; more than 26 were wounded.

A 'SWISSITY'

Portugal, 1974, only weeks before the 'revolution of the carnations' was to begin.

I had driven my Hillman station-wagon from Switzerland and, naturally, it had Swiss registration plates on it. I had made enquiries about Swiss insurance companies represented in Portugal, before our departure; there were none, so I insured the car with a British company, blissfully ignorant of the fact that I was committing a grave crime by doing so.

One day there was a letter in my post-box, headed 'Consulate of the Swiss Confederation'. In it, the Swiss Consul ordered me, in Portuguese, to return my car registration plates to him, without any delay. I wrote back, asking him why. With no reference to my response, and no explanation, he wrote again, an identical letter, but this time in French. I replied, asking him to give me a reason for such a request, and pointed out that, when I had entered Portugal, an official at the small Customs post at Quintanilha had noted the car's Swiss registration plates, and had communicated all details to his superiors in Oporto. The car's papers, now lodged with the authorities there, were completely in order. I had, moreover, over-insured it as, in those days, third-party cover in Portugal was not obligatory; my international 'green card', in any event, covered the whole of Europe. Therefore, would the distinguished Consul, please, explain himself.

A third letter arrived from him, this time in German and registered. This one was different. It threatened me with unspecified penalties if I did not comply immediately; and simultaneously informed me that it was, in any event, too late; that my name had been given to INTERPOL under the terms of some bilateral agreement; and that, next time I attempted to enter Switzerland, I would have to answer for my – still unspecified – transgressions.

I copied all these letters to the Portuguese authorities and, in the hope that they might have seen a similar case, asked them what I should do. I tried to phone the Swiss Consul but he was never there.

As it happened, I was planning a trip to Switzerland, and I thought I had better solve this problem before going. But the Portuguese Revolution was, by then, in full swing, and I could not get an answer from the Customs authorities. It turned out that there had been a fire at their premises; the car's papers could not be found and were assumed to have been destroyed. As a safety measure, just in case the Swiss Consul managed, somehow, to confiscate the plates, I had some new ones made, in the Portuguese style, but with the Zürich numbers, in the full knowledge that I was probably doing something *very* illegal.

I engaged a lawyer – an old friend – in Zürich to disentangle the matter. He discovered that my crime had been to insure a car with Swiss number-plates *with a non-Swiss insurance company*. It mattered not that under Portuguese law I was under no obligation to insure the vehicle at all. I don't know what my lawyer did, but the matter was solved very quickly and, when I next landed in Zürich, the immigration officer, after closely examining my passport, seemed about to say something, but thought better of it, smiled broadly and let me through.

The Swiss Consul, I felt, might have been guilty of an excess of zeal. When I was eventually able to return the plates to him, one year after my arrival, he maintained a diplomatic silence. But I still wonder if there is not a black mark in my file, somewhere.

BATHING BELLE

It was a stifling, hot day, and in walked this tropical brunette, She asked for me, gave her name and handed over a letter of introduction from her cousin who happened to be a personal friend of mine in Teheran; he had sent with her a large tin of golden caviar.

'Would you put in a word for me with your American colleague?'

'In which context would this be?'

'I need a visa to go to America. I have an Iranian passport.'

I explained that under no circumstances could anyone 'put in a word for her' at the American Consulate. It was common knowledge that there was a long waiting-list for entry visas there; she would have to apply personally. I gave her the address and telephone number. She duly applied and was back the same afternoon, in tears.

'They rejected me.'

'What happened?'

'I should have told them about my daughter.'

'You have a daughter?'

'She's five.'

'And your husband?'

'I no longer have a husband.'

She said later that her husband, a doctor, had been executed by the Iranian regime.

'What shall I do now?'

The heat was oppressive. There was a queue at the counter. I had a brainwave.

'Why don't you go down to the lake and have a swim?'

'I can't; I have no swimming clothes.'

We had a small emergency stock of second-hand clothes, including a one-piece bathing costume and a towel which we gave her, and away she went. It seemed a small price to pay for the caviar, which we tucked into with a good conscience.

Some weeks later, she was back, with another tin of golden caviar. She told us she had changed into the bathing costume and gone down to the lake as we had suggested, and within ten minutes had met a young man. He was Swiss. They were to be married soon. There was a good chance that the Swiss authorities would allow her daughter to join her, and her mother too. She would like to keep the bathing costume and the towel, which had brought her luck.

Years later, I spotted her on a tram with *three* little girls.

COUNTING BICYCLES

She was small, chubby and clearly of school age, and she had come to the Consulate with a friend. She seemed quite relaxed.

'Someone has taken my passport. I believe he was Russian...'

'Russian?'

'Yes. That's what the man told me.'

'Which man?'

'The man in the bicycle shop.'

'Bicycle shop?'

'Yes, the one by the Opera House.'

'Tell me exactly what happened, please.'

'Well, I wanted to hire a bicycle and had to leave my passport as a guarantee. Later, when I brought the bike back, the man said that he didn't have my passport any more. Someone else had it. We are leaving for Venice this afternoon.'

As I approached the bicycle-hire shed near the Opera House, it soon became clear that the business was being run by asylum seekers from Kosovo and Somalia; my hopes sank. Although Russian and British passports might look similar to the untrained eye, it seemed likely that the girl might have to say goodbye to this particular document. British passports at the time commanded a very high price on the black market.

A very helpful and apologetic employee of Eritrean origin explained that it must indeed have been a Russian who had the missing passport, as he had one Russian passport over. So where was this Russian?

The Eritrean seemed to recall that the Russian had mentioned a hotel in the *Enge* area of Zürich, within walking distance.

Then luck intervened: as I walked up to one of the most likely hotels on the short-list, someone who *had* to be a Russian walked down the steps.

'Are you Russian?'

'I am indeed. Why do you ask?'

'Would you mind if I looked at your passport?'

'Not at all. It's in my room; come and see.'

The young man seemed quite unworried about a complete stranger approaching him in this way. It was indeed his passport.

'Did you hire a bicycle this morning?'

'I didn't but my friend did; and I am just going to meet him.'

'May I accompany you?'

'Be my guest.'

In a mixture of English and belaboured Russian, as we walked towards *Paradeplatz*, I told him the story. He was amused by it and asked if I would do him a favour:

'Go up to my friend and demand to see his passport; see how he reacts. I will find a place to sit and watch and have a coffee...'

At that moment, a scantily dressed male reveller minced past us on his way to the Zürich Street Parade.

'... you'd be arrested for dressing like that in Moscow.'

We spotted his friend in the square and, as sternly as I could, I went up to him and demanded to see his passport. Without a word, the second Russian reached into his rucksack, took out the passport and handed it to me. It was the girl's. With as serious a mien as I could muster, I asked him what he meant by walking around with someone else's passport. But before he had time to get worried, his friend came up and explained to him what had happened. We all had a good laugh. My new friend confirmed that, in Moscow, even now, it was not uncommon for complete strangers, themselves without any evidence of identity, to demand that one produce one's ID.

Then, of course, we had to go back to the shed and get back the Russian passport. At first the Eritrean was reluctant to part with it as he claimed there was one bicycle missing. Whereupon your Honorary Consul did a re-count himself, and the problem was solved.

Back at the Consulate, where the Pro-Consul had been plying the girls with cups of tea, the young owner of the passport, evidently believing that this was the only possible outcome, looked at her friend and said:

'Good; we will now be able to catch the train to Venice.' And off they scampered.

* * *

Here follow three consular cases typical of those in which I was involved, while working at the Bank of London & South America (BOLSA)/British Consulate in Manaus, Brazil in 1965.

TWO DUTCHMEN

Two charming young Dutchmen visited the Consulate. They were under contract to a large international magazine to take some photographs deep in the Amazon jungle. They duly hired a canoe and disappeared off up the Rio Negro. About a month later, one of them reappeared looking very bedraggled and despondent. He told me that his colleague, suffering from serious depression, had shot himself three weeks earlier. He had wrapped up the body in polythene, loaded it into the canoe and brought it back to Manaus (the temperature at the time was around 30°C).

Where was the body now? It was on the pavement outside the Bank, still wrapped up in polythene.

The steps that had to be taken cannot be related. Suffice it to say that the body was dealt with, next of kin notified, and – most important – the plucky Dutchman was able to return home safely without undue entanglements. In those days, policemen in Latin American countries tended to link the arrest of any connected party with proof of guilt: homicide was always considered a more likely cause of death than suicide.

A KNIFING

We were looking after a native of (then) British Guiana, who was in solitary detention in the two-cell prison at Itacoatiara, some 200 km to the east of Manaus on the north bank of the Amazon river. He had been accused of knifing a shipmate to death on a small cargo boat which plied the river. Circumstances of the alleged crime were obscure and he had never come to trial. Over many months a consensus developed among various Brazilian authorities that the accused should perhaps never have been arrested, as self-defence had been claimed and various relevant documents had, it seemed, been mislaid or - more likely - never been obtained. The case was taking too long to reach the courts and there was no likelihood that any useful progress would be made for the foreseeable future. The prison in Itacoatiara was the only one in that vicinity, and they had other customers for whom they needed to find accommodation. The fact that the political situation in what was becoming known as Guyana was very unstable, added piquancy to consideration of the case.

Certain Brazilian national, state and municipal authorities were content to let it be known (only verbally, mind you) that the unfortunate detainee should be conditionally set free. Nobody was prepared to put his signature to anything, for fear of provoking those other authorities who were frightened that the military junta might insist on a hard line. After a series of radio-telephone calls between various parties in Itacoatiara, Manaus, Rio de Janeiro (still *de facto* the Federal Capital) and London (during which, it was generally acknowledged that misunderstandings, arising from the unstable nature of radio-telephones, might even be beneficial), it was somehow arranged that the main door of the prison would remain open at a specific time and that the detainee would be made aware of this. The guards would be enjoying a game of drafts.

Only one important aspect of this wheeze had been overlooked. Itacoatiara in those days was a very remote place, surrounded by thick jungle to the north and a very wide, inhospitable river to the south. The road from Manaus had been washed away only a few days after its completion and official opening by President Castelo

Branco. Consequently, the alleged killer, after making his break, spent two uncomfortable nights in the jungle before his tum began crying out for its rice and beans, and he asked to be readmitted.

I wasn't party to any further developments of this case and only know that the next time I was in Brazil (in 1971), the prisoner was no longer in Itacoatiara. This episode illustrates the all-encompassing Brazilian word *jeito*, freely translated as 'the art of problem-solving' - even if it does not always have the desired result.

NEEDLES IN A HAYSTACK

Telegram to the Governor of the State of Amazonas and the British Consulate, Manaus, from Rex King II, King Ranch, Arizona:

> YOUR EXCELLENCIES MY ONLY SON REX KING III AND FRIEND CANOEING DOWN AMAZON RIVER FROM IQUITOS PERU TO BELEM STOP POSTCARD JUST RECEIVED STOP IMPERATIVE THEY BE FOUND STOP URGENT PRIORITY STOP END KING

Consulate's reply:

> UNDERSTAND CONCERN STOP MUST INFORM YOU THAT WE ARE NOT RESPONSIBLE FOR THE WELLBEING SAFETY OF US CITIZENS IN THIS CONSULAR AREA STOP HOWEVER AS US CONSUL CURRENTLY ABSENT ON LEAVE WE HAVE CONTACTED US EMBASSY IN RIO DE JANEIRO AND GOVERNOR AMAZONAS STOP LATTER HAS ASSURED US THAT FORÇA AEREA BRASILEIRA FAB BRAZILIAN AIR FORCE WILL KEEP AN EYE OUT FOR THEM END BRITISH CONSULATE MANAUS

King's reply:

> HAD SEARCH PARTY IN MIND STOP PLEASE ARRANGE STOP DOLLARS NO PROBLEM END KING

Before I had a chance to formulate an answer to the father's latest request, I happened to go into a pharmacy in a jungle suburb of Manaus. There was a young American there, obviously having difficulties making himself understood, and he asked me to help. The young man turned out to be the friend of Rex King III, who was himself lying in a primitive shanty some 5km out of town, quite seriously ill with dysentery.

An ambulance was called; it took him to a *Pronto Socorro* (First Aid post), and he made a quick recovery.

After setting out from Iquitos, the youths (17 and 18 years old) had made it across the Brazilian border. They had no food with them and drank water from the river. No maps; no hats; no local currency. Both had become ill and had to beach the canoe. They were badly bitten by insects. A Jesuit missionary happened to find them lying there, in considerable distress, and alerted an FAB detachment nearby, who sent a launch for them and flew them to Manaus, leaving them at the edge of town. They had had a lucky escape.

During a farewell dinner, financed by Rex King II, the friend was constantly looking at his watch as if to say, 'I'm wasting my time in this dump.' Then he turned to me, as if nothing had happened:

'Like ... what other rivers are there round here ...?'

SE NON È VERO...

A woman was filling out an application for a passport. When she got to the space for age, she hesitated for a long time. Finally the new consular assistant leaned over and said:

'The longer you wait, Madam, the worse it gets.'

* * *

I was once visiting an institution for the mentally disadvantaged, and found myself in the wrong place, actually in a line of inmates, during a roll-call. A male nurse was counting:

'One, two, three, four, five, six ...'

When he got to me, he said, 'Who are you?'

I replied, 'The British Consul.'

He carried on, 'Seven, eight, nine, ten ...'

* * *

Nuri al-Said, pre-war Prime Minister of Iraq for seven terms, had a very good command of English. During an audience with diplomats, he was once asked his views on agriculture. Without hesitation, he replied,

'What we need is more missionaries.'

It required an effort on the part of his listeners to grasp that what he had in fact said was:

'What we need is more machineries [i.e. tractors].'

* * *

'What did the brassière say to the top-hat?'

"You go on ahead, while I give these two a lift."'

This riddle was told to Sir Miles Lampson, British Ambassador at Cairo in 1942, by the explorer and authoress Freya Stark. It is recorded that the Ambassador was shocked.

* * *

The Consul was visiting the old-folks' home. He was so put out by the fact that nobody recognised him that he went up to an old lady and asked: 'Do you know who I am?'

She answered, 'They'll tell you at Reception, dear.'

THE OSSUARY

A telephone call:

'Can you help me to find my father?'

'Would you please let me have more details: Is he sick? Has he disappeared?'

'Oh, he's dead.'

'When did he die?'

'In 1950.' That was more than half a century ago. He gave me the exact date.

'Do you have any idea *where* he died?'

'It was in Switzerland. That's why I am calling you.'

'Can you be more precise?'

'In Graubünden.' Graubünden is the largest Swiss canton.

'Do you have any idea where in Graubünden it might have been?'

'Oh, he fell into a river in a place called Mullins, but they never found the body.'

After a lot of detective work, and with the help of a most helpful police officer from *Gemeinde* Mulegns, I discovered that a body had indeed been found some days after the man had been reported missing, in a neighbouring *Gemeinde*. It could not be identified and had been duly buried. Thirty years later, as was customary in Switzerland at that time, the grave had been raked over. I passed this information back to the son and heir.

Some weeks later, I received another telephone call:

'What happens to bones?'

'I beg your pardon?'

'Don't you remember me? I called you about the missing body. What happens to bones after a grave is raked over?'

'Any substantial remains are put in the *Gebeinhaus*...' It was only with difficulty that I remembered the English word: '...in the ossuary.'

'What's an ossuary?'

'That's a place they put bones in.'

'Are they labelled? Are they in boxes? Would you please go down there and find out?'

'What I suggest is that *you* take a trip to Graubünden, which is a very pretty canton to have a holiday in, and see what *you* can find out.'

'But why can't you help? What are consuls for?'

And so on.

Months later, I was contacted by a British citizen who had lost his passport in Graubünden. His voice sounded familiar.

THE CROWN

There was to be a demonstration. The police could not understand what it was all about. But the crowd was definitely heading in our direction. It seemed quite tranquil and the police felt they did not need to give us much cover, at least for the time being. However, with the experience of Dockers and Kurds and other militant groups fresh in my mind, I retreated into the Consulate, closed the blinds, and waited.

Slowly the noise increased; but it was an unusually tuneful sort of noise. Gradually I realised it was Latin-style rhythm, and sneaked a look. The street outside the Consulate had filled up with Central American Indians, covered in spectacular feathers, beating drums. There was an array of hangers-on. There were even hippies who, with their spiked hair, looked uncannily like the Indians. My landlady took some pictures from the top floor. The situation still seemed peaceful and, with the agreement of the police, who were still fielding a modest contingent, I went out to see what it was all about. A man came up to me and shouted (to be heard above the drums):

'You have stolen our crown!'

'I beg your pardon.'

'Yes, you stole our crown and we want it back.' He signalled to somebody; the drums changed their beat and a chant began:

'GEBEN SIE UNS'RE KRONE ZURÜCK, GEBEN SIE UNS'RE KRONE ZURÜCK' ('give us back our crown.')

I must have looked rather nonplussed, and the man continued: 'Montezuma's crown!'

By then my mouth was probably hanging open, and, looking at me as if there couldn't possibly be such idiots in the foreign service, the man went on: 'You know, the crown you have in Vienna.'

Then I twigged: they were demonstrating *outside the wrong Consulate*; the Austrians were across the road. One of the most curious things I ever had to do was to help turn the crowd around so that they were facing the right Consulate, in the full knowledge that the Austrians had taken the afternoon off.

*   *   *

The sacred Aztec feathercrown of Montezuma (minus the gold, which was melted down by the Spaniards, before the feathers were presented in the 1520s to Charles V, Holy Roman Emperor and King of Spain) now resides in the Museum of Ethnology, Vienna.

TROUSERS

He had a misleadingly warm smile, and was quite well known to British Consulates around Europe. He tended to appear at awkward times – just before closing, or when the office was full of difficult cases. Conversations with him were full of pitfalls.

'Hello!'

'Good morning, Sir.'

'May I have a cup of tea?'

'May I ask your business first, Sir?'

'It might take some time as it is quite complex.'

'I must insist that you answer my question first. Just the normal formalities.'

'Oh, I certainly don't want to frighten you. It is about money.'

'About money?'

And, before one knew it, one was conducting a conversation with the man. And everyone else within earshot was interested to see how one would handle him.

Then, without a word of warning, he took off his trousers. He had perfectly decent long-johns beneath, but his action certainly had an effect. He shook out the trousers, folded them over his arm and waited.

'Would you mind putting your trousers on, Sir; there are ladies present.'

'How silly of me; yes of course. Now, where had we got to?'

Trousers safely on again, the conversation continued. 'Ah yes. It's about money…'

By now, all other conversation had ceased. '…I need money.'

Honorary consuls are trained to deal with situations like this. Anything which is not a genuine emergency is sifted out, and such aspects as security are examined.

'You don't believe that I can provide security, do you?'

'Not what I said, Sir.'

'Here is my security!' With a flourish, he produced a large envelope from his bag, and waited. I also waited. Everyone in the room waited. 'Aren't you going to ask me what's in it?'

Silence reigned. I felt that I was at last winning back the initiative. And finally the re-trousered visitor produced a wad of

231

paper from the envelope and, with as much aplomb as he could find, thrust it towards me, and exclaimed:

'It's a symphony!'

Symphony or not, it had been a masterful performance. Quite enjoyable actually. There should have been applause. But it was time for the curtain to come down, and for other customers to be attended to.

Muttering his disappointment, but in remarkably good humour, he left the Consulate, jumped on a tram without buying a ticket, was arrested and was – I later heard – deported.

HIGH FIVE

Visited by two gentlemen from the island of St Lucia in the West Indies, one talker and one nodder. I had seen both gentlemen about town: they were known to be in the drug business, and tended to position themselves in *Paradeplatz.*

After beating about the bush for a few minutes, the talker, who had very distinctive features, and eyes acting independently of each other, abruptly got to the point. Would I arrange UK immigration papers for him? He would be prepared to pay a premium for special attention. This, at the time, was not an unusual request, but it was one which, with the best will in the world, I could not satisfy. And I said so.

The talker exploded: he ranted and raged and shouted and screamed. He left the Consulate, slamming the door behind him. He kicked over a pile of empty Coke cans which someone had obligingly left in his path and, at the top of his voice, he called me by a series of names, each one less attractive than the last, until he reached a category of pejorative phrases many of which began with the letter F. I could imagine windows opening and people stopping in the street.

Still in the office, the nodder, who had taken no part in the proceedings, began to apologise for his friend's behaviour. I told him not to worry; on the contrary,

'When men of my age get called things like that, they tend to take it as a compliment!'

The nodder's face broke into a massive, all-embracing smile and he gave me a 'high five', before following his friend out on to the street, shaking with laughter. Not long afterwards, the talker disappeared from the scene.

But, for months, whenever the nodder spotted me walking past, he would run up and give me a 'high five'. The Zürich police drug squad, who had been discreetly informed, derived some grudging amusement from this eccentric relationship.

SOMEBODY'S PASSPORT

'May I ask you to look at my passport, please?' He was of medium height, self-assured, tanned, and - in his own opinion at least - a real man.

'Yes, of course, Sir; how can we help?'

'Would you say that this is a sufficiently good photo of me?'

'Quite a good likeness. Why? Do you have any doubts?'

'I was just wondering how you distinguish...'

'Distinguish what, Sir?'

'Well, supposing I had a moustache, and the passport photo had none...Supposing I had a good head of hair, and the passport showed me to be - heaven forbid! - bald...'

'What exactly is your question?'

Suddenly he was less sure of himself.

'Well, I was just thinking how difficult it must be for you to tell...' 'Tell what, Sir?'

'Oh, never mind. What I really wanted to know is: this passport, is it good for entry to America?'

'You will really have to ask the US authorities that question. It is machine-readable, which is sufficient at the present time as far as I know. And as long as it is genuine...'

'Could you tell if it were not genuine?'

'Our Passport Section could very easily tell. Would you like me to run a check on it?'

'I don't think so thank you.'

'Were you aware, Sir, that British passports are the property of the British Government, and that tampering with them is illegal? I think I will run a check; then you are less likely to have a problem at the American Consulate.'

'I am in rather a hurry, you know...'

'You are most welcome to do your business and return later; the process only takes a moment or two.'

He left a trifle hastily, taking a state-of-the-art mobile phone out of his pocket as he went through the door. And he never returned.

It turned out to be a case of photo-substitution. The real owner of the passport, who had earlier reported it stolen, was, it transpired, a woman.

THE APARTMENT

The visitor was a handsome young black man with a British passport. He was working, he said, for a large Swiss banking group.

'May I ask your advice?'

'You are most welcome to do so.'

'It's about my apartment.'

'Yes?'

'Every time I leave or arrive home, the police stop me and question me.'

'Have you any idea why?'

'I wanted to ask you that.'

'Where do you live?'

'I live in the *Stauffacher* area, above a Jewish bakery.'

In fact, the area he had named was a very bad one at the time, with many reports of drug-dealing, robbery and attacks on passers-by.

'I am afraid that is not a good part of town at present. I understand that the authorities are trying hard to improve it. But I think it will take a while yet. The police have a very difficult job there.'

'But, what do you think I should do?'

'If, for whatever reason, you are unhappy with your accommodation, you should consider moving.'

'What about discrimination? Do you believe I would have a case?'

'If you are seriously considering taking steps along those lines, all we can do is give you our list of lawyers.'

After a cup of tea, he thanked me and left the Consulate.

A month or so later, one of my sons phoned:

'Hello, Papa. I thought I would give you some good news. I have found an apartment; it's in *Stauffacher*, above a Jewish bakery...'

THE WELSHMAN'S JACKET

'Someone stole my jacket.'

'Tell me how it happened.'

'I was sitting by the side of the road, minding my own business...'

He was Welsh. A very large man indeed. Very fit. And very calm.

'I didn't see it happen, Boyo. One minute my jacket was there. The next minute it had gone.'

'Was there anything in the jacket?'

'I was just going to tell you: my passport.'

We went through the formalities. He was to be in Zürich a few more days and there was no particular urgency.

The following day he was back. 'Good morning. I came to say thank you.'

'May I ask why?'

'Last night I went back to the same café. It is a very nice place. And I sat down in the same chair. And I saw my jacket walking past. So I grabbed it. I didn't hurt the man. The passport was still in the pocket. Thank you for your trouble.'

'You're very welcome.'

He was Welsh. A very large man indeed. Very fit. And very calm.

PRIORITIES

Mrs Smith seemed harassed.

'Are you the British Consul?'

'Honorary Consul, Madam.'

'Thank heavens! I don't suppose you will have noticed but nobody here speaks English. It has taken me absolutely ages to find you. It was all those soldiers downstairs who gave me a clue. We are at war, aren't we?'

'They are Swiss soldiers, Madam. How can I help you?'

'I say: do you have a brandy or a cup of tea or something? I have lost my passport.'

'Have you any idea where you lost it?'

'What a silly question! It fell out of the car.'

'And did you look for it, Madam?'

'What sort of an idiot do you think I am? Of course I didn't.'

'Why not?'

'I couldn't.'

'Why couldn't you?'

'How long are you going to go on asking these questions? I couldn't get out of the car; that's why.'

'Would you please explain, Madam?'

'I couldn't get out of the car because of the accident. Do please get me at least a cup of tea.'

'You had been in an accident?'

'Albert was driving.'

'Albert?'

'Albert's my chauffeur.'

'And where is Albert?'

'Oh, he's quite alright; he's in hospital. They said I should go, too, but I told them: "No, the first thing I always do in these circumstances is go to the British Consul." And here I am. The gentleman sitting over there is the ambulance driver. The soldiers wouldn't let him in to start with but when they found out who I was, they jumped to it. Where's my cup of tea?'

'Perhaps you would tell *me* who you are and give me your date and place of birth.'

'Do you *really* need the date of birth?'

'Yes please. Now, was anybody else involved in the accident?'

'Only Fred; and he wandered off afterwards. He tends to, you know.'

'Who's Fred?'

'Fred? – my husband Fred. You won't have heard of him – even if you've heard of me.'

'Was your husband hurt?'

'He had a bloody nose, but he always has a bloody nose when things like this happen.'

'Do things like this often happen?'

'Oh yes. Albert is not a very good driver but I adore him. We usually drive off afterwards but we couldn't this time because the car wouldn't start; and anyway there was a wheel missing. Rather undignified: a Rolls-Royce without a wheel. Fred used to box.'

'Box? Aren't you concerned about Fred – about your husband?'

Her mobile phone rang:

'Oh Fred, there you are. *Where* are you? Oh not again; which prison? What happened to the driver of the tractor? Oh, poor man; how inconvenient for him. And did they ever find my passport? They caught the man? *You* caught the man? And you hit him? Brilliant. Why did you hit him? Oh I see. But why have you been arrested? Oh, he was a policeman. Fred, I am with a very nice Consul-man who is asking me lots of questions about my lost passport. But, since it has been found again, I am alright I suppose. Let me just ask him what I should do now...'

It all ended well. Nobody had been hurt badly, although Albert had a spot of concussion. He wasn't allowed to drive in Switzerland again, but he was over 80 anyway. All the other admitted incidents had evidently taken place outside the country; Albert had always had difficulty with his lefts and his rights. Fred had indeed struck a policeman, but it had been in the mistaken belief that the man, who was in plain clothes, was stealing his wife's passport which had been flung into the middle of the road at the time of the accident. At the magistrate's hearing he argued strongly that he was not going to stand by and watch British Government property being removed from the scene of an accident by any Tom, Dick or Harry. The policeman had not had time to identify himself and Fred got off with a caution.

Coincidentally (it has been reported), the magistrate was himself a retired boxer. The farmer whose tractor had been involved had had a tipple before he took to the road that morning, but he was able to argue that it had been for a very good reason; his wife had mistakenly topped up a jug of apple juice with some cherry brandy. The muck-spreader was easily repairable. And the Rolls-Royce had indeed lost a wheel; but this was because Albert had not tightened the nuts sufficiently, after another incident. Apart from the fact that, at the time of impact, the fuel feed was dislodged, and the cocktail cabinet jammed open (pinning Mrs Smith behind it), there wasn't a scratch on it.

After the hearing, there was lunch for all parties involved at the restaurant *Rössli* in Zürich at Fred's invitation.

And, at the Consulate, another case could be filed.

GENTLE GIANT

A file note:

Following info from football colleagues and initial police investigation: John Mann from Dorset, 19 years old, 6'4", intended to transit in Zürich on flight from Heathrow to Barcelona for Champions' League Final between Manchester United (his team) and Bayern Munich. During seven-hour transit time in Zürich, found his way to the *Altstadt* and began drinking beer. Got into fight with Bosnian, as a result, it is alleged, Bosnian died. Subject detained for further questioning. Dorset newspaper very inquisitive: passed to London.

Later: Subject claims he cannot remember anything about a fight or getting into a scrap with a Bosnian ('What's a Bosnian?') Remembers someone offering him a cheap ticket to the match but insisting he hand over money first. He was suspicious and declined the offer.

Further police investigations show that subject drank so much beer that it is very unlikely that he could have been violent. Was seen leaving bar with Bosnian. Had difficulty walking. Other witnesses saw them pushing each other. Bosnian discovered later lying on road with head wound; later deceased.

Visited subject in detention. Asked me to ensure that his parents and employer (garden centre) be informed and that his two Golden Retrievers be looked after. He was concerned about the Bosnian's family.

Later still: Full police investigation (ten months) led to trial for manslaughter. Attended trial with parents of accused.

Transpired (from family evidence and police records) that Bosnian was in the habit of offering drunken football supporters cheap tickets, and running off with their money. On this occasion, subject had rebuffed initial efforts but Bosnian had insisted. Subject agreed that he could not deny the possibility of his pushing the Bosnian to the ground. Although nobody had witnessed the whole struggle, pathologist confirmed that deceased's injury was consistent with him falling backwards and striking his head on the edge of a paving stone. Subject's character references read. Known at work as 'the gentle giant'.

Suspended sentence, in view of time already spent in detention; deportation. Case closed.

WATCH YOUR LANGUAGE

It was AGM day for the *Corps Consulaire* of Zürich. There was only one contentious thing on the agenda: language. Actually, this was a very important subject. There were over 80 consular representatives in the city, ranging from professional consuls general (some with ambassadorial rank) right down to mere honorary consuls. Many languages were spoken. Traditionally, French had precedence, and proceedings and all other documents were customarily translated into French. However, apart from the French Consul General, and some South American representatives, who were anxious that this procedure should continue, all of the others felt that there was a serious case for changing the lingua franca to German, with an informal agreement that English or French might also be used if absolutely necessary. In any event, the incumbents of a good number of Zürich consular posts were lawyers, whose first language was Swiss German, and who felt that the choice of High German was already a generous concession on their part.

Opinions had been canvassed; lobbying had taken place; and the subject was firmly on the agenda under Any Other Business. The AGM was opened; the attendance list was circulated, then those present became aware that the French Consul General was not there. No problem: he had already advised the Secretary that he would not be able to make it.

But neither were the South Americans.

The *Doyen* diplomatically slowed his opening address. The attendance list was formally noted. The last proceedings were commented on and corrected – at a snail's pace. The time for lunch approached. The pace increased, and Any Other Business was finally broached.

After a very short discussion, it was proposed and seconded; there was no opposition and the consular representatives present voted unanimously to accept the language recommendation.

Then in walked Argentina and Brazil.

Having learned very quickly what had happened in their absence, they lodged an official objection with the *Doyen* (a career officer, with the rank of ambassador, from another South America country) who summoned up his courage and dismissed the objection, on the reasonable grounds that his colleagues had simply arrived too late. He could, however, entertain the possibility of further informal discussion over lunch. There was uproar. And the two Latin American representatives stormed out of the meeting, before it could be formally concluded.

They *did*, however, return for lunch.

MARRIAGE AFFIDAVITS

It was a beautiful spring morning, and it had been made up entirely of marriage affidavits.

The first to arrive, at 9 o'clock sharp, might have been brother and sister: young, attractive, very much in love; concise and organised. Then came an older pair: he was British but spoke English with a heavy Swiss accent; she was Swiss, and her English was accent-free. We rattled through the short procedure. Both pairs wanted to marry in Switzerland: no problem.

The next to take the oath was a rather conceited motor-racing mechanic, who wanted to get married in Azerbaijan. So be it. Two Hong Kong Chinese were next in the queue; we could issue affidavits for them at that time. Then in came an older lady who wished to marry a young Palestinian in Zanzibar. This had been the first time that we had had Zanzibar as a marriage destination, and it took a little longer to prepare the documentation. Then it was Peru. Then Poland.

Two gentlemen who looked very much alike were the next to walk through the door:

'We should like to get married in Switzerland.'

We began to prepare the same-sex declarations when the telephone went and a female voice asked: 'Are our fiancés already with you?'

We looked across at the two men waiting patiently at the counter, and, just in time, the penny dropped.

'Yes, they are here. Let me put one of them on the line to you.'

All was well; it was just that their two fiancées, who were identical twins, were late. We had already been told of the hazards involved in registering identical twins, and we prepared to take extra care.

It turned out that these two pairs wished to be married simultaneously, somewhere in the *French* Alps (they had believed that the place they had chosen for the ceremony was in Switzerland). We obliged, albeit with a different set of forms.

Just before lunch, two more men came in together. We waited a few moments. We had discussed what to say at a moment like this; it wasn't ideal. But it seemed the most appropriate question to ask:

'Are you alone?'

'We are together.'

That clinched it and out came the same-sex forms again.

After that day, the Pro-Consul developed a very special look which she shot at me, whenever two gentlemen or, for that matter, two ladies came into the Consulate together for an affidavit.

We never got it wrong.

EGGS

Yes, there is no doubt, honorary consuls do meet fascinating people. Very often, at the time, one has to be very shy about details of the visits of distinguished personages; needless to say, security is very important. After the event, however, there is little danger in musing about these chance acquaintances. Various 'Royals' come to mind (Prince Charles, Princess Anne, Prince Andrew, The Duke of Kent); sundry Ministers of the Crown and (inevitably more sensitive still) wives of Ministers; Ambassadors; and so on. Then there are countless representatives of sundry departments, each more important than the last. Not to forget fascinating people from certain secretive services. Then there are 'one-offs' like the Bishop of St Albans, who was visiting Switzerland as a member of a Lord's Select Committee, in consideration of a Private Member's Bill concerning euthanasia and assisted suicide. I was privileged to spend a fascinating hour with him.

One meeting, however, left a lasting impression. It took place at a business luncheon. The conversation began as follows:

'Can you imagine: I got all eggs!'

An Honorary Consul is only a junior member of the Consular Corps, as opposed to the Diplomatic Corps, but he is nevertheless expected to acquit himself adequately in the art of repartee. Sometimes, though, unexpected statements can be quite challenging.

'Tell me about it' (is usually a safe bet).

'I got Hen of course, and Rosebud...'

He had a beard; spoke quite good English, albeit with a detectable Russian accent.

'And I got Cockerel and Orange Tree.'

Yes, he seemed to be Russian: he was leaving out definite articles and auxiliary verbs.

'And Lilies and St George Order and - how do you say? - Renaissance.'

He was listing something important, mainly for his own benefit, as if he was reading a catalogue. And he was beaming with delight.

'And Fifteenth Anniversary...'

'Very impressive.'

He paused as a waitress cleared the plates.

'I even got Coronation.'

'What an amazing achievement!' But he wasn't listening, or so it appeared.

'I got all nine eggs. Yes you right: *amazing*. I proud for Russia.'

So he *was* Russian, and he was talking about eggs.

The penny dropped: there had been an article in the *Financial Times* that morning about a (then) little-known but very wealthy Russian who had privately purchased the whole Forbes collection of Fabergé eggs which Sotheby's was planning to auction; $100 million or so had changed hands. And here he was, sitting next to me!

I happened to have with me a copy of the *Financial Times* in question, complete with the said article about the Fabergé sale; I showed it to him. He extracted something from his own pocket and handed it to me: it was a page from *Commersant*, a Russian newspaper, with an almost identical article. It felt as if we were exchanging passwords. Then, staring at me, as if my position as a consular official of the British Crown had only just dawned on him, he repeated:

'I even got Coronation.'

He then began to look at the *Financial Times* article as if it was somehow an endorsement of what he had done, and, putting the whole newspaper in his pocket, turned to me full face, losing his fluency in his excitement, and continued:

'You not know what means to me...' He was positively glowing with pleasure. 'Rock crystal windows and platinum tyres.'

He was, I later realised, talking about the miniature Coronation coach, which was part of the most famous egg of all.

Suddenly, in the face of his own enthusiasm, his command of English completely deserted him. He lapsed into a jumble of Russian, French and German which was aimed at nobody in particular. Shortly afterwards, he turned to his other side and, I assume, had the same conversation all over again.

Somehow, this brief exchange with oil and gas billionaire Victor Vekselberg ('The religious, spiritual and emotional content captured by these Fabergé eggs touches upon the soul of the Russian people' he was quoted as saying on the BBC web page), was far more compelling than waiting on a blustery aircraft runway for the arrival of a run-of-the-mill VIP.

THE LITTLE BRASS BUDDHA

It had been a harrowing case. And there were all sorts of angles to it. A brother and sister in their 50s had been killed in an appalling car crash just to the north of Oporto in Portugal.

In 1975, I was Manager of the Bank of London & South America (BOLSA) in Oporto and trustee of the Teage Bequest which owned the premises of the British Consulate there. Years before, a Mr Teage had bequeathed the property in perpetuity to the British Government (though I believe that this situation has since been 'unlocked'). It was natural that, in the absence of the Consul (Stephen Lockhart then held the post) I should become involved to an extent with consular affairs.

These were exciting times: we were in the thick of the Portuguese 'Carnation Revolution'. Our day-to-day rhythm was determined by very diverse concerns, such as getting the children ready for the US consular bullet-proof limousine to take them to school; looking for our adventurous black mongrel, which tended to wander; keeping crowds of demonstrators off the scaffolding which we had erected round the Bank for repair work; wrestling with the financial implications of the 'Carbon 14' scandal in the Port Wine industry; and so on.

One of the aspects of this particular case was a legal one. Evidently the arrangement of the separate estates of the accident victims was conditional on one of them predeceasing the other and, although this did not concern the Consulate, there were serious delays in completing the post-mortem examinations; which led to delays in deciding who had died first; which led to further delays in the burial of the brother's body, and repatriation of the sister's body. No family could be traced.

Another aspect of this case was the fact that the brother used to be employed by one of the British Government's secretive services in the Far East, and was assisting a famous author with his next book. An early draft of the book was said to be somewhere in the deceased's house up the Douro, around which some Eastern European types had been seen sniffing. I was asked by the Embassy to put a guard on the building.

Then there was a suitcase, containing a mass of bloodstained clothing retrieved from the wreck of the car, together with a little brass Buddha. I had exceptionally agreed to house these possessions, pending resolution of the case.

In due course, the legal aspects were resolved; and the elusive manuscript was found (in a flat in Andorra). The sister's body was duly repatriated. And I attended the brother's funeral at the Anglican Church of St James in Oporto. The only other person present was an enigmatic, wordless individual from the Embassy in Lisbon. Somehow, it seemed appropriate that the pall-bearers missed their footing as they were approaching the grave, and very nearly dropped the coffin. There was a spine-chilling thud from inside as if the deceased was trying, one last time, to make his presence felt. But balances were regained and he was securely buried.

This left the suitcase.

Two weeks later, a family of three walked into my office and announced that they were there to pick up the personal effects of the deceased pair. They claimed to be cousins and I admit I took their word for it. But I have often wondered if there was anything hidden in that little brass Buddha.

VIP

'Is anybody else listening to this conversation?'

'No. Why?'

'I have to inform you that we are going to have a very important visitor.'

'Can you tell me who?'

Pause and mutterings at the other end.

'The Prime Minister.'

Another pause, as if I was expected to pay diplomatic homage... The conversation seemed to be developing into some sort of formal dance. To break the silence, I asked:

'Is he visiting Berne?'

A longer pause and more mutterings. Evidently the conversation was not going the way the Embassy caller would have wished.

'He is flying to Zürich actually. Zürich airport. And then on to Davos by helicopter. We would like you to meet him.'

'When is he coming to Zürich?'

'Tomorrow evening.'

I consulted my diary. 'I am very sorry; I shall not be able to make it. I am giving a speech at a school inauguration. I cannot possibly let them down now. I am sure the Prime Minister will understand.'

'Giving a speech...'

'Yes.'

'At a school...'

'Yes.'

'...Inauguration?'

'Yes.'

'And you feel you will not be able to meet the PM.'

'No - I mean yes, I will not be able to meet him.'

A much longer pause and, this time, distinctly displeased mutterings.

'Very well...'

The last two words conveyed: 'Your fate is sealed'.

'...I will have to look after him myself then. Fine...'

Clearly, it wasn't fine. However, I felt I could add nothing to the conversation, and signed off.

I had previously looked after the Prime Minister's wife (shuffled off the aeroplane in carpet slippers; charming and polite); the Deputy Prime Minister (took off at such speed, with his coat-tails flying, that I had difficulty keeping up with him); one Secretary of State for Foreign and Commonwealth Affairs whose wife accompanied him (the briefing was entirely about the wife's foibles); and sundry minor political personages. It was somehow ironic that, on this occasion, I could not make it.

The PM duly went to Davos and made his speech. I made my speech. And the following Christmas, for the first and only time, I received a card from the Prime Minister's office, wishing me all the best for the coming year, signed 'Tony'.

I have not been able to work out if I was being slapped on the hand for not doing my duty, or patted on the back for standing up to the powers that be.

FORCED MARRIAGES

This is not a nice story. There is no humour in it, and no happy end. There is, however, a tiny ray of light which is more in the nature of learning and damage containment: if one wants to find treasure, one has to dig for it.

It had been a very full morning, and not an easy one. As well as the usual drizzle of affidavits of various kinds, there were some extremely complex ongoing protection cases as well as a sensitive prison visit which had to be planned for the following afternoon. The Consulate was still full of customers well past closing-time. We were doing our best.

The receptionist phoned to say that three men had arrived and that she was having difficulty understanding what they wanted. So I went down with a selection of forms in the belief that they were probably wanting visas.

'How can I help you?'

'We need to see the Consul.'

'May I ask in what context?'

'Please?'

One man was doing all the talking. He spoke elementary English with a strong Arabic accent. He handed me three Iraqi passports. His companions, it was clear, understood nothing of what was being said.

'Why do you want to see the Consul?'

'Forced marriage. Very urgent. Very bad. We are from Iraq.'

'Forced marriage' sounded ominous.

Security was at a very high level at the time, and we had to be very careful about whom we admitted to the Consulate. However, I felt that the three visitors, all in their mid-50s, looked harmless, and accompanied them upstairs. We had a very small waiting area, and they had to mark time for a few minutes until there was room for them to be seated.

'You were saying you were all from Iraq.'

'Assyrian...'

I had only heard this word in an archaeological context and it took me a while to comprehend that they were from the Assyrian minority in Iraq. The speaker was the chief of an

Assyrian clan in the British-occupied sector. He was accompanied by his brother-in-law and a close friend, on whose behalf he was acting.

The Assyrians (I later read) are adherents of Syriac Christianity; they make up some 3 per cent of the total Iraqi population. Their lives had become almost unbearable after the *Jyllands-Posten* published the infamous Muhammad cartoons, and Pope Benedict berated Islam in his 2006 Regensburg lecture.

In a cruel twist of fate, Britain might be seen as doubly responsible for the Assyrian travails, as she had, in 1918, originally resettled 20,000 Assyrians in Iraqi refugee camps, after the disintegrating Ottoman Empire had violently quelled a British-inspired Assyrian rebellion.

Because of our language differences, the conversation was halting and disjointed. They had only been able to obtain visas to visit Switzerland, and it gradually became clear why they were visiting us.

The speaker's daughter-in-law and another young woman had been 'married' (i.e. abducted and raped) by Iraqi soldiers in the British military sector. The second woman was the daughter of a British/Iraqi dual national who had been unable to leave Iraq.

In such difficult cases, in spite of strict Foreign Office procedures, it is extremely hard to decide how much time should be spent asking questions, in the full knowledge that they will probably be asked again and again at later stages. But there was a logistical difficulty as well: I could not raise any senior people in Berne, and the Duty Officer, I later learned, was out on another complex case. So I went straight to our Desk Officer at the FCO.

On past experience, I had enormous confidence in our contacts there, but on this occasion it very soon became clear that there were no precedents for this type of case, and reactions to my requests for assistance became more and more truculent. The general message was: this must come through normal channels, i.e. not from me, and not at this time of day (London's lunch-hour was, by now, just beginning). Although one of the fathers was a dual national, neither of the women who had been raped were British passport-holders; so there was nothing that could be done anyway.

Not one mention of the three gentlemen who had come through the door of the Consulate, and were still seated there, waiting, at least, for a comforting word – let alone the victims.

It turned into a doubly unpleasant episode, with a reprimand from my immediate superior in Berne, who passed on to me a remark from his line manager in London: 'Can't you control your Honorary Consuls?'

A ray of light shone through the dark clouds of this affair when, some days later, the Iraqi speaker telephoned to thank me for trying; and some six months later, when I accidentally learned that a new section had been created at the Foreign Office, specifically to deal with such cases.

And if one chews through the inherent, time-consuming, cross-ministerial complexities of such affairs, one has to admit that six months was probably very fast indeed.

THE INHERITANCE

We were contacted by a firm of lawyers in the West of England. They were looking for a young British citizen in Zürich, who had inherited a substantial amount of money. They had had no luck with the usual authorities and wondered if we could help tracing him. They believed he might be a hard drug case and were not certain if he still used his real name.

I had a good friend in the Salvation Army who had helped me previously, and went to see him, though not very optimistically.

'Of course I know him. We used him on our latest brochure. But you'll have to find him. He has blown his mind and he's very timid. If he's not in our haven, there are two cafés which he frequents, where he can also get his stuff. He is beyond hope, but I didn't say that.'

During the following week, I went almost every day to the haven, but he never appeared. They knew of him in the first of the two cafés, but he hadn't been there for months. The second was at the top of a lane in the Zürich *Altstadt* – about as shady an address as one can imagine. As I approached, as if on cue, a scraggy, bearded individual came out of the door, put his foot up on the ground-floor window-sill and injected God-knows-what into his thigh. There was no mistake: he was the vagrant pictured on the brochure. When he had finished, I went up to him and, as gently as I could, put some questions to him. He stared at me, unfocused, said not a word, and went back inside.

Yes, I had found him. That was all. Now it was back to the lawyers. This was one of the myriad consular cases which had ended in the middle of the story.

But I still retain the image of the ladies of easy virtue scurrying about at the first-floor windows on the other side of the road, in the mistaken belief that a new customer, in the person of your Honourable Consul, might be looking for *them*.

EXORCISING LUXOR

It was mid-March, and still very hot. Masses of schoolchildren – boys here, girls there – unselfconsciously shouting to each other, and to us:

'Hello English! Where you come from?'

We were with friends in Upper Egypt, as tourists, visiting the Deir al-Bahri complex, just across the Nile to the west of Luxor. It encompasses the remains of the mortuary temples of Mentuhotep II, Thutmose III, and his step-mother and co-regent, Hatshepsut, for whom, it is believed by some authorities, the word *Peraa* ('Pharaoh') became, for the first time, a circumlocution for 'female King'.

There is an enormous arena in front of Hatshepsut's temple, the best preserved and restored of them all, set squarely into the side of the hill, with impressive colonnades and a massive ramp leading up to the first floor. There was speculation at the time we were there, that a mummy, which Howard Carter had left lying on the ground in tomb KV20 in the Valley of the Kings, had been identified as that of Hatshepsut, and 'workers' had accordingly erected red and white fences to keep tourists away from the more interesting parts of the complex, and were sitting there collecting *baksheesh* if anyone wanted to go past (there was nothing very much to see anyway). Except for the general aspect of this famous archaeological site, there was nothing attractive about it at all. The enormous complex of shops near the entrance, selling cheap souvenirs largely made in China, and the many dozens of buses, only added to the ugliness.

It was a grotesque place to go to die.

But this had been the fate of 58 foreign tourists and at least four Egyptians, 11 years previously, when six Islamist terrorists attacked and slaughtered them on this vast arena; there had been very few places to hide. The gunmen, most of them students from Southern Egypt, had been only a few years older than the deliriously happy children surrounding us now.

Thirty-six Swiss and six British citizens were among the dead.

I had become involved in this tragedy when, in the chaos following the event, the body of a British citizen had been erroneously switched with that of a Swiss citizen, and some personal belongings had been reported missing. Press coverage was acute and there was fierce activity at the Foreign Office to ensure that survivors' grief was not intensified.

One month before the event, President Mubarak, still firmly in power, had attended a performance of *Aida* with Hatshepsut's temple as the back-drop, to show how safe the country was for tourism.

One month after the event, four respected Egyptian bodies (the Religious Institutions of Egypt, the Ministry of Endowments, the House of Legal Opinion and al-Azhar University) jointly published a statement on the 'Luxor Affair', hitting the terrorists hard:

> These criminal butchers who murdered innocent tourists who came to Egypt to visit its sights, did not lift their hands to these tourists only. Their evil and traitorous hands harmed all the people of Egypt...

There is something topsy-turvy about a map of *Misr* - as the country is known locally: Upper Egypt is at the bottom, and the Nile appears to flow uphill.

This had been my first connection with a so-called disaster scenario. Involvement of consular staff at the scene must have been quite horrifying. One aspect, however, was common to us all: we had all received training at the Foreign Office; and we were all working as a team. Whatever the circumstances, good team-work induces warm feelings.

This visit, 11 years on, somehow served to exorcise the memories of what had been nothing less than a mass murder...

Life had been cut off in its prime. But a sense of togetherness with our Foreign Office colleagues, with the next of kin, and with the distinguished and courageous Egyptian signatories of the above statement, endured. And the cheerful 'Hello English!' somehow helped.

Cicero had been right: 'While there's life there's hope.'

* * *

Shortly after the Luxor massacre, I became involved at the fringe of the ongoing investigation into the terrorist bomb attack on Pan Am Flight 103 over Lockerbie in December 1988. In this shocking event, no less than 270 people were murdered. Luxor sits among my recollections for its intensity; Lockerbie - during these times when Libya is once again under the spotlight - for its labyrinthine complexity.

Hatshepsut's Temple, Egypt, 2009.

THE YOUNG WOMAN WHO LIVED IN A SHOE

'I want to make a paternity declaration.'

'No problem. Would you fill in this form first please. And may I see your passport?'

'Which passport would you like to see?'

'Your British passport. Thank you. Now this is the actual declaration you will be making so please fill it in legibly; and I will be needing 80 Swiss francs from you.'

'That is more expensive than last time...' (Consular fees varied with the exchange rate.)

'So you have been here before, Madam?'

'Yes, I have... but not as expensive as the time before.'

'So you have been here twice before?'

'Three times actually, but I can't remember how much it cost the first time I made a paternity declaration. That was in the other Consulate. Such a nice man.'

'Now all I need is your signature.'

'Which signature would you like?'

'The one which you have in your passport, please.'

'The same passport?'

'The British passport please.'

'If you insist. Just let me see how I signed then. Ah. Here you are.'

'Thank you Madam. Here's your change. And here is the completed document. You know what to do now?'

'Oh yes, thank you. I am getting quite good at it.'

She came the following year, and the year after that. All the alleged fathers - at least as far back as our files would go - were different. The name in her passport, however, remained the same.

> There was a young woman who lived in a shoe:
> She had so many children and...
> She knew *exactly* what to do.

ONE-UPMANSHIP

The *Dies Academicus* of the University of Zürich is a regular event, to which, as Honorary Consul, I was always invited. There was also an invitation to a small and select drinks party before the ceremony, which allowed me to locate, compliment and formally thank the Dean without too much difficulty. After the ceremony, the Dean was customarily mobbed by dozens of people who wished to pay their respects, and it was quite impossible to approach him.

The art of one-upmanship should be practised very discreetly in the *Corps Consulaire*. One opportunity occurred before the ceremony one year, when I spotted the new French Consul General completely lost in the throng and unable to find his way to the room where the small party was to take place. I offered to show my colleague a quick way up the back stairs which enabled us to arrive just ahead of the Dean, and be at the front of the queue to greet him.

'*Volontiers*,' said the Frenchman.

The timing was perfect. I shook hands with the Dean first and, as promised, introduced the Frenchman. Whereupon the latter turned his back on me, and began to harangue the Dean on the necessity for the University to intensify the use of the French language in all fields.

I felt that my French colleague, in his *revanche*, should have practised the art of one-upmanship more discreetly than that.

* * *

One-Upmanship is the title of a book by Stephen Potter, published in 1952.

4-1-9 SCAMS...

Once a month or so at the Consulate in Zürich, we would have a visit from someone who had received a communication (by letter, by fax or by email), announcing that he or she had been selected as a likely candidate to receive millions of dollars (or pounds or Swiss francs) on behalf of an African potentate (or central banker or politician), if he or she would only send exact details of his or her bank connections as well as, say, $5,000 (or $10,000 or $20,000 or $50,000) in advance, to cover administrative expenses.

These attempted frauds were known as '4-1-9 scams' after the article in the Nigerian penal code relating to financial fraud. In most cases, our visitors were simply curious about these approaches and, because there was often some alleged connection with a UK institution in the blurb, they came to see us. Having obtained clearance from the FCO, we simply advised them to throw the letters away. In a small number of cases, our visitors had already fallen for the trick and, not having received the promised millions, wanted their money back. These people we advised to go to the Swiss police who, we knew, had documented many thousands of such attempts at fraud.

Then there was the 'lottery' scam, where, using the same principle, tricksters would send thousands of certificates out to potential fall-guys, confirming that the recipients had won (say) the United England National Lottery and needed only to contact, for example, Mr So-and-so at the International Bank of Great Britain (on such and such a telephone number), and give him full details of their bank connections in order to qualify for receipt of some enormous sum of money which represented their winnings; they should also make 'deposits', of the above order, to cement their claims.

We were once visited by an unremarkable Swiss gentleman. The conversation went something like this:

'I am waiting for a letter from the International Bank of Great Britain.'

'What did you say the name was?'

'The International Bank of Great Britain.'

'I don't believe such a bank exists, Sir; I have certainly never heard of it.'

'Oh it definitely exists (produces lottery certificate); look here...'

'Ah. The lottery scam.'

'Pardon?'

'The lottery scam. Did you receive it in the post?'

'Yes I did: addressed to me personally. Here is the envelope. If it hadn't been *meant* for me, why was it *addressed* to me?'

'If I were you, Sir, I would throw it out. But, if you have any doubts, go to your bank or your lawyer or the police.'

'But I cannot possibly throw it out. It is the proof of my winnings.'

'Up to you.'

'And it *is* a sort of receipt.'

'Receipt for what, Sir?'

'Well, it says here that I have to send £1,000 to this address for administrative expenses so that I can claim my winnings.'

'Throw it out, Sir. Now, if you don't mind...'

'What would happen if I were to send £1,000 to that address?'

'I wouldn't advise it, Sir; now I really have to ask you to...'

'And if I had already sent the £1,000?'

'Have you in fact sent these people money?'

'Actually, yes. And I thought that since I sent it to the International Bank of Great Britain, and since you are the British Consulate, you would perhaps let me have my money back.'

'I regret that we cannot help you, Sir. I have already advised you what you should do.'

'I am not leaving until I get my money back.'

'Very well. I will call the police on your behalf.'

He was out of the door before I could reach for the telephone. But this wasn't the end of the story: a week or so later, we had an email message from the said unremarkable gentleman, in which he thanked us for the advice we had given him. He had told Mr So-and-so of the International Bank of Great Britain that he had received this advice from the British Consulate in Zürich. He had, in a separate registered letter, demanded his lottery winnings (if my memory serves me right, the amount was £22 million). Failing that, he expected to receive the £1,000 by return of post. He hadn't (the email concluded plaintively) received anything yet.

...AND A STING

During his career, the manager of a bank is bound to be exposed to fraud from time to time; and in my previous incarnation, I was no exception. Very often these fraudsters would appear on a Friday, just before lunch, in the belief - apparently - that the Big Banking Boss would be away playing golf with a customer, and that his stand-in might be more gullible. As conformity officer, I recall a number of incidents, such as my refusal to negotiate a commercial letter of credit for several million dollars, covering the export of rubber gloves to Cambodia; and my refusal to sanction an application to negotiate another letter of credit, for an even larger amount, covering the shipment of submachine guns to the Costa Rican Army: quite apart from the fact that the financing of weapon exports was frowned upon, it was common knowledge at the time that Costa Rica *had no army*.

In most such situations - particularly the successful heists - bank secrecy is common sense; but there is one story, faintly relevant to the theme of this book, which bears telling.

In 1990, non-negotiable Bank of England bonds with a face value of £292 million were stolen from a City of London messenger.

One year later, just before I retired from my banking job, I was contacted by a North Korean diplomat - let us call him Mr Hu Pinch Dat - who was trying to find a market for some sterling bonds which, it transpired, were from the missing lot. Mr Hu foolishly agreed to leave me a copy of one of the certificates and come back the following day.

After hectic negotiations with the Bank of England, the Swiss Federal Banking Commission, another institution in the City of London (the nominal owner of the bonds), sundry lawyers and other parties, which led - in this case - to the breaking of bank secrecy, a 'sting' operation was set up by the police in my office. The offending diplomat (who could not claim diplomatic immunity, because, as it turned out, he was not accredited to Switzerland) was arrested and deported, and a quantity of the missing bonds was returned to the rightful owner.

This experience took me back to the trainee course, 30 years previously, during which we had learned how to handle bribes; not to finance perishables; and *never* to advance money to diplomats.

HELICOPTERS

Some consular protection cases are bizarre.

I had been contacted by a psychiatrist in the Bundnerland. He told me that he was treating a Briton who had come to him in a very unusual way. His was a case of split personality. In his normal life (happily married, with children), he was a successful engineer, with a business near London. When his mental state metamorphosed (for want of a better word), he began to run, and he ran, and he ran - until he dropped.

On this occasion, he had found his way on to a plane at Heathrow, reached Zürich airport, somehow got through immigration, and set off. He ran through the Canton of Zürich and via Schwyz or St Gallen or Glarus - nobody knows - into Graubünden, where he eventually collapsed and was found by the Cantonal Police and taken to hospital, having run through his shoe leather and, to an extent, through his feet.

He had now almost fully recovered, and would I please make certain he got on to the plane to return to the United Kingdom? There was only one thing which I should look out for, said the psychiatrist, and that was: should the engineer suddenly start talking about helicopters, this might signal the beginning of one of his absent moments, and he told me what I should do.

I duly met up with the engineer, a charming young man in his late 30s, took him to the airport and accompanied him through to air-side. We chatted for half an hour or so in the departure lounge, and, just as he was about to embark, he suddenly said:

'And then, of course, there are the helicopters...'

Happily, I had been well briefed, his diversion only lasted a few minutes, and then - so smoothly that I hardly noticed it - he was normal again. We hadn't left our seats.

We said goodbye like two old friends and he flew out of my life.

The *really* odd thing about this story is that, some three weeks later, we were visited by a destitute vagrant (very few of these ever reached Zürich). He was a cheerful, energetic type who owned nothing but the clothes he stood up in. He was well known on the consular circuit. Harmless but persistent. On one occasion, I saw him in the road outside the Consulate, turning his grey tee-shirt inside out, and brushing himself down, as if to say: 'Right. I am now smart enough to try again.'

A short chat we had on the occasion of his visit to us went something like this:

'So, where are you off to now?'

'Oh. France or possibly Germany; but I would prefer to go to Spain; it's warmer.'

'You seem a cheerful sort of character. Don't you have any worries?'

'Oh. The money...' And, after a short pause,

'...Then, of course, there are the helicopters...'

Once we had aired the office, Yvonne and I both admitted that we were sad to see him leave.

THE WETBACK...

'I'll send you a postcard as soon as I arrive.'

'I'd rather you didn't.'

We were sitting together in the visitors' room in a Zürich prison. He had been given a surprisingly lenient sentence for bringing a large amount of cocaine into the country. It had been accepted, apparently, that he was just a 'mule'. His parents lived in the United States. He had asked to see me in order to facilitate his repatriation, after a successful plea-bargaining process. Following the usual formalities, our short conversation had gone as follows:

'Can you arrange for me to be sent back to America?'

'You are British so I can only arrange for you to return to the United Kingdom.'

'No exceptions?'

'No exceptions.'

'But what about my Green Card?'

'What about your Green Card?'

'Will you tell anyone about my prison sentence?'

'We are keeping the Foreign Office informed.'

'Yes, I know. But you won't be talking to the Americans?'

'About what?'

'About my Green Card.'

'Why should we?'

'That's what I'm asking you.'

'All I am here for is to arrange for you to be returned to the United Kingdom.'

'And you don't care what happens after that?'

'You are of age. Why should we?'

'You don't mind if I go to America?'

'That has nothing to do with us at all.'

'Then, how I get back to America is my business?'

'It is.'

'Good. Then I'll send you a postcard as soon as I arrive.'

'I'd rather you didn't.'

We never heard from him again.

BIGAMY

'Date and your full name here please, Mr Wolf.'

'Initials do?'

'Your full name please, spelt out.'

'Have I been married before?'

'Yes, you will need to fill that in. If you are divorced, please let me see a copy of the Decree Absolute.'

'So...single?'

'If you have not been married. And may I see your passport please.'

'My full address?'

'Your full current address please.'

'Telephone number?'

'Yes please. Have you ever been married?'

'No.'

'Then who is the Mrs Wolf mentioned on the "emergencies" page in your passport?'

'That's my sister.'

'You're sure it is not another Mrs Wolf?'

'It's my sister.'

'Mr Wolf, were you not at this Consulate about two weeks ago for us to certify a will?'

'Yes, but...'

'Were you not the sole beneficiary of your mother's estate, or is my memory playing me tricks?'

'My sister was cut out of my mother's will.'

'So, you are not an only son?'

'No. I have a sister...had a sister.'

'Mr Wolf you came here this morning to make a marriage affidavit. Were you intending to swear that you had never been married before?'

'Yes.'

'May I ask you then why you were removing a ring when I picked you up from Reception this morning?'

'That wasn't a ring. I mean it wasn't a wedding ring.'

'Mr Wolf, perjury is a serious offence. I am acting this morning as a Notary Public and it is my responsibility to take oaths which I am reasonably satisfied reflect the truth. Would you mind coming to the next room with me?'

'Why? You can say what you want in front of *her*,' he nodded at his fiancée. 'She doesn't speak a word of English.'

'In that case, I must invite you to leave and only come back here when you are absolutely satisfied that all formalities regarding your planned marriage have been completed. You may take a copy of the form along with you, to remind you what still has to be done.'

'If you say so.'

He came back some months later - with another girl.

POIGNANT EPHEMERA

• The enormous Australian who needed nothing more than comfort after he suddenly learned of his father's death in Vancouver. The value of a cup of tea.

- The look of apprehension on the faces of Chinese citizens of Hong Kong when they were told that they had to approach the Chinese Consulate General to replace lost identity cards.
- The strange man from one of the newly independent 'stans' in former Soviet Central Asia, who brought with him an authoritative epistle (or so he claimed) on the misdeeds of the clan in power.
- The general relief which was felt when a British husband and father brought his young son back from one week's holiday in the Far East after his estranged wife had claimed that he had abducted the boy and taken him to China for good.
- The preponderance of lawyers in the Zürich Consular Corps.
- The nationalistic Scotsman who refused to accept assistance from a British Consulate.
- Each passport which was returned to the Consulate, accompanied by a death certificate with an imprecise time of death, indicating euthanasia.
- The boundless capacity of some citizens of the Indian sub-continent - outdone only by some Chinese - to tell whoppers.
- A wide-ranging drug case, which had come to light when the fiancé of a girl in Trinidad died after drinking from a bottle of rum laced with cocaine concentrate, which she had innocently purchased, after it had escaped from a consignment.
- The persistence of Sudanese, Somali and Eritrean refugees, determined, by hook or by crook, to reach the shores of Blighty.
- The interview in a Zürich prison, with a 20-year-old, born into drug addiction, who told me that her hardest challenge was knowing that she must have objectives.
- The Swiss authorities who have difficulty believing that the United Kingdom does not have a central register of all its citizens, which can be neatly closed at time of death.
- An intervention, together with the incumbents of two Zürich churches, in an unpleasant case of child-molesting.
- The gentle Fijian, jailed for harassing his estranged Swiss wife, and, on release, being deported 16,650 km back to Fiji because he could not keep up welfare payments for his daughter.
- The Sri Lankan terrorist, jailed for murder, who kept writing to us, in the hope of asylum.
- Perpetual reminders of the extraordinary complexity of British citizenship, the result of a colonial history which is both fascinating and - for a consular officer - extremely demanding.
- The large young man, who visited us regularly with his modern, custom-made *Laufmaschine* ('dandy horse': a bicycle without pedals), spent a few minutes looking wordlessly through brochures at Reception, 'walked' his vehicle back into the lift, and departed.

- The relief we felt in the case of a convicted British murderer when it turned out that he was a dual national, and therefore the responsibility of the Swiss authorities.
- The anonymous would-be letter-bomb addressed to The British Consul, containing the iconic white powder, which, when opened by the police bomb-squad, played Happy Birthday to You.
- The popularity of Gretna Green among Swiss (and Japanese) citizens.
- The sang-froid of the British steeplejack who had fallen over 20 metres from the roof of a warehouse, having accidentally grabbed a live wire, and sustained terrible compound fractures to both legs.
- The long-drawn-out repatriation of a Welsh manic-depressive and his dog.
- The haunting, expressionless eyes of the international criminal, who told me, while I was visiting him in prison (behind glass, for my own safety), that he was to be extradited to a Latin American country to face drug charges.
- The insouciance of the Russian/British dual national, detained by order of the Russian justice machinery in Moscow for alleged financial crimes, who believed that extradition, conviction and jail for an indefinite period were inevitable. He was right.
- The famous orchestral conductor, with all conceivable details of his life on his website, who still had to fill in a passport application by hand.
- Sundry Libyans with dark glasses, who sidled into the Consulate with confidential information on Colonel Gaddafi.
- British mothers, estranged from their professional soldier sons, but desperate for news.
- The load off our minds when it was established that a British youth, first believed to have died in suspicious circumstances, had in fact succumbed to a weak heart.
- The extraordinary experience of Desk Officers at the FCO. Don't ever think it has never happened before.
- From the Foreign Office instruction jingle: Note It; Date It; Time It; Sign It. A wag once suggested that all that was missing was: Do It or Bin It.
- Tales from other Honorary Consuls from around the world, many of which put my own experiences firmly in the shade.

THE CRIMINAL

'I'm not a criminal.'

'Is anyone suggesting that you are a criminal?'

'Why have I got to fill this in then?'

'Did you not tell me you had to sign a criminal affidavit?'

'Yes, but...'

'Do you have a problem with the text?'

'No, but...'

'Please tell me what your problem is.'

Before the bilateral agreements were signed between Switzerland and the member states of the European Union, the Swiss authorities insisted that all foreigners wanting to work in Switzerland should supply proof that they had no criminal records. In the case of the United Kingdom, which had no central criminal register, the Swiss had agreed that British citizens should be allowed to make a so-called criminal affidavit at the Consulate. In those days, criminal affidavits were the documents which we issued most. The discussion with Mr Green continued:

'My problem is that I am being asked a very personal question here.'

'You are being asked to confirm, under oath, that you do not have a criminal record.'

'What about my rights?'

'You have every right not to submit this document, if you feel - for whatever reason - that you are unwilling or unable to do so. And that will be the end of the matter. But it will also be the end of your job application.'

'What happens if I have had a parking ticket?'

'If you feel that you should mention your parking tickets, there is space on the affidavit for you to do so. It could be counterproductive though.'

'And what happens if I have done something more serious? Had an accident or...?'

'Mr Green, please remember that this affidavit is concerned with criminal activities.'

'...or something more serious than that? Supposing I was a bank robber...'

'Mr Green, we have talked enough and I have other customers waiting. Please fill in the affidavit if you intend to go through with this. It will cost you Sfr. 75.- and I will need to see your passport.'

At this point in such a discussion one had to keep reminding oneself of the cultural divide between Switzerland and the United Kingdom. Mr Green might have been a bank robber. But he was far more likely to be showing the beginnings of truculence simply because he was not used to being asked questions like these so directly. And being asked to swear something can suggest to a Brit that someone somewhere doesn't believe him. The Swiss too can suffer from such a culture gap: I recall one lady being amazed when she ran across our use of the phrase 'British subject', which, to us, simply means something like a British national. If translated literally into German, the word becomes *Untertan*, which has the sense of subjugation or submission – definitely not the same thing!

On this occasion, Mr Green looked over his shoulder at the queue forming, filled in the affidavit, took the oath, paid and left, thanking me profusely.

THE COMPANY

'I need signature.'

'Good morning, Sir. How can I help you?'

'I need signature.'

'Would you be good enough to give me your name?'

'Not necessary. This new company. I need signature.'

Unsmiling. Mafioso. Probably Russian or Ukrainian.

'I regret I cannot continue this conversation unless you identify yourself.'

Not a word. Produced a Ukrainian passport. And placed a bulging wallet on the desk.

'Thank you, Mr Ivanov. Now what is it that you want?'

'I need signature. New company.'

'May I see the documents please?' Still silent. Handed over a wad of paper.

'Please show me the document you need the signature on.'

Scowling. Took out one page and put it on the desk. 'British Consulate General Zürich', already typed, stood out. I read it.

'If I understand correctly, you are setting up a new Ukrainian company in the island of Nevis, and you need some sort of certification.'

'I need signature.'

'Do you own this company? Is it your company?'

Angry now. Unaccustomed to not getting his way.

'I need signature. Give me signature. How much?'

'We are not a British Consulate General here. And we do not sell signatures. I suggest you contact our Embassy in Berne or your lawyer, before you visit us again. And, in future, kindly do not type our name on your documents before first contacting us.'

He picked up the papers and his passport and his bulging wallet, and stalked out.

NAME-DROPPING

Sir Edward Heath was never known as a shy speaker, and on the occasion in September 1998 when he addressed the 27th Churchill Symposium in Zürich, he took the subject firmly in hand. The last time he had been in the city, he said, was in 1971, on the 25th anniversary of Winston Churchill's famous 'Let Europe Arise' speech on 19 September 1946.

I attended Sir Edward's presentation with other officers from the Embassy in Berne, and heard him make the point that it had been Georges Pompidou, after de Gaulle's abrupt resignation, who had resolutely supported the idea of European integration. Switzerland, continued Sir Edward, had been materially responsible for his initial meeting with Mr Pompidou. A junior Swiss diplomat in Geneva had approached Sir Edward after an EFTA meeting there, having heard that Heath was proceeding to Paris.

'Are you going to see Mr Pompidou?' asked the Swiss diplomat.

'Pompidou? Pompidou? What a funny name, I thought,' said Sir Edward: 'Who's he?'

And the Swiss diplomat told him who Pompidou was. Heath then approached the British Embassy in Paris to arrange a meeting with him - no easy task as the Embassy hadn't heard of Pompidou either. But the die was cast.

Heath got along very well with Pompidou, who later, after a lightning political career, became Prime Minister and then President of France. And Heath, ten years after de Gaulle's veto, following only two years of talks, succeeded in negotiating Britain's entry into the European Community.

Sir Edward never forgot his debt to the Swiss.

In one part of his speech, I felt that Sir Edward had been a little hard on the Americans, and later told him that the American Ambassador was present. Sir Edward's reaction was:

'Silly woman! Why didn't she tell me she was here?' And off he went to make amends.

A few weeks later, Angelika and I happened to be at Glyndebourne where we saw a notoriously bloody production of *Don Giovanni.* I walked into Sir Edward during an interval. Without a moment's hesitation, he said

'Hello. You here too?'

It gave me a really warm feeling: the great man hadn't known who Pompidou was, but he had remembered me...

BYE BYE

To His Majisty British Consul general Zorach (Swiss) 2002

Respected Sir,

I undersigned Rehmat Bye Bye Widow of No,14454 L/NK Ramsat Shah resident of village by Chilianwala Gujrat Pakistan beg to state that a Emergency Certficate was issued to my husband on his transferred to penrion establishment but unfortunately misplaced some where in the house and could not availed the oppurtunity mentioned in the Emergency Certificate [dated 1944] to settle himself in swiss and joined the professional of Drawing a private van which he is carried out up to his death leaving back two daughter and one adoplid son named Ramsat also who presently to look after my all affairs and also giving financially help and tallerate all sort of expenses.

Near about a month gone I shifted my self to another village and at the time of packing my house hold goods I found your issued emergency certificate along with the documents of property.

Now I approach to your kind honour with this petition and request if the above said chance may please be given to my adopled son which was given to my husband (Late) and I shall be highly thankful to your kind honour for this act of kindness.

I hope a favourable action will be taken into my case and a hopefull replay will be given to me.

Thanks
(Signed)

I asked for guidance from the Consulate General in Geneva and wrote back, telling Mrs Bye Bye that she should contact the British High Commission in Islamabad. Three months later, another letter arrived, addressed to the British Consulate, 'Zürich Miner Vastrasse' (correctly: Minervastrasse). The adopted son had had no luck at the High Commission. The letter continued:

It is request in the light of the above circumstances please guide and help me for the further step which will give a fruity result because of the fact I am too much worried about the further of my adopled son and it is mine desire that he should be establish himself in your country according to the opportunity which was given to my husband (Late) etc etc

Above, verbatim (except for names which have been changed), are the texts of two letters I received, by special delivery, from Pakistan.

This was an interesting case not only in the light of the charming Indian-English style of the text (typed evidently by a village '*babou*' or scribe). The adopted son (if he really *was* the adopted son) was conducting it on the basis of a curious 'emergency certificate', purported to have been issued at the British Consulate General, Zürich, in September 1944, which authorised Mrs Bye Bye's late husband, a 'British Subject by birth' to travel to the United Kingdom and reside in Switzerland for two years – a scenario which is unlikely to have been sanctioned by the Swiss.

THE SWISS WATCH

A telephone call.

'British Consulate, how can I help you?'

'I am calling to report a theft.'

'I think you should call the police...'

'No. Please listen. I have tried the police, but they are unable or unwilling to help me.'

'Right. Are you British?'

'I am. Would you like my passport number?'

'Not at this stage, Sir. Your assurance will do for the time being. Now what is the problem?'

Mr Black had a pleasant voice. He was calling from the West Country and I felt he probably had a good reason to do so.

'I have spent my business life abroad, in various countries, and have just retired. My wife and I feel we can just about survive on my pension. But I could do with a little more...'

I had a small qualm at this stage of his explanation but - rightly, as it turned out - let it pass.

'Twenty years ago, I invested in an expensive Swiss watch. It was then worth some 20-30,000 Swiss francs. I bought it in Zürich. I was working in Argentina at the time and didn't want to take it with me; so I left it in the shop against a receipt, telling them that I would pick it up in due course.'

He gave me the name of a well-known jeweller in *Bahnhofstrasse*, and continued:

'About a year ago, I sent them the receipt and asked them to let me have the watch as I had retired. They wrote back and told me that they could not find any trace of the watch in the safe, retained the original receipt, and told me they considered the case closed. Can you advise me what I should do?'

Although I knew that an Hon. Con. should not get involved in this sort of affair, Mr Black sounded like a decent sort of chap. What had happened to him was not correct and I admit that I did bend the rules: I have a very good friend, an ex-policeman, who is an expert in insurance fraud, and had a quiet word with him. He kindly agreed to take on the case without charge and I asked Mr Black to call him. My friend worked patiently at the case for about six weeks, exercising pressure on the jeweller to investigate it more closely.

It turned out that an employee who had been sacked some years previously, had run away (oddly enough, to Argentina) with some expensive items from the shop, including, it seemed, Mr Black's watch. Under continuing pressure from my friend, the jeweller agreed to indemnify Mr Black to the full current value of the watch.

Mr Black wrote to express his thanks and added that he had had two small silver items (a bill-fold and a card-case) engraved to AM and to MB, my friend.

FCO rules about accepting gifts are very rigid. I had to phone Mr Black to thank him but tell him that I could not take them. Bizarrely, he became quite annoyed and asked me what I could suggest he do with something which had already been engraved. Knowing that I should not have become involved in the first place, I had to exercise my brain considerably, before I came up with a formula for the application form, which gave only the barest essentials of the circumstances in which I had earned these souvenirs. After all, it wasn't quite as straightforward as the bottle of whisky from the football team. But it had still been worth it.

DRUM AND TRUMPET

I was often asked why on earth the Consulate had to spend so much time on football matches. Here is a typical memo regarding a visit of Leeds United in November 2001.

- A useful meeting was held this morning with those gentlemen mentioned in an earlier fax, plus three officers of the Zürich City Police, one private security man, two from Kuoni Travel, the Grasshoppers Event Manager and the undersigned.
- At this stage, 1400-1500 fans are expected, absolute maximum 2000. Most of these will be identifiable members of LU; all personal details are on a disk with Smith. Of these some 200 will be on 1 night stopover arrangements at 3-star or 5-star hotels. There will also be 2 x day returns of 250 each; late flight departure permission has been obtained for the latter up to 23.55 (match will end 22.00). 10-15 coaches are expected.

Football endorsed by Pelé, who used to be Angelika's neighbour in Santos.

- 50 to max. 150 classes 'B' and 'C' troublemakers may appear. They tend to arrive late without tickets and try to surge through the gate; the Zürich Police assured us that such tactics will not succeed at the GC ground. (At Troyes last week, a large horde of last minute arrivals including hooligans managed to get hold of tickets which were obtained locally and sold on at a 4x mark-up by the Independent Travel Company; this increased spectators by 25 per cent and led to standing room only. Zürich Police have taken note.) West Yorkshire Police have been tipped off that a gang will be arriving by Easyjet from Luton on Thursday, returning on Saturday. These troublemakers, in their late 20s and 30s, tend to look quite tidy and wear designer clothing (Armani jeans etc.) not club colours.
- Smith suggested – and I strongly endorsed – the presence, at LU's expense, of his superintendent and two intelligence officers, as well as himself at the game. The intelligence officers know the heavies well and are known to them; their presence with a video camera generally has good results. The Zürich Police had no hesitation in agreeing (as long as the officers are not armed!)

- Security arrangements will not permit alcohol, cans, air-horns or fireworks; GC usually bans large flags which obscure the view and advertising hoardings, but, at Smith's request, are reviewing this. No problems with phones, cameras, small videos; you may also bring your drum or your trumpet!

MISSING PERSON

A memo to the Consulate General in Geneva, responsible for such cases at the time.

ELAHI, Maqsood, Stateless, DoB 1.1.71 Afghanistan

As briefly reported by phone earlier today, I was visited yesterday by the wife of the above, who was with her young daughter.

Mrs Elahi, who is of Afghan extraction, speaks a little German and was assisted by her daughter who is at school here. She told me that her husband had left her on 15 November last and had since gone to the United Kingdom with the help of a *Schlepper* (people smuggler). She reported him missing a week ago. She asked for my help in finding him. I regretted that I almost certainly would not be able to help her; but she left with me photocopies of both Swiss 'F' permits and a recent colour photograph of her husband and her telephone number.

A mutual Pakistani friend called Hali indicated to her that her husband had gone to England and gave her a telephone number there. This may well be an invention. She believes that Hali knows more but does not want to tell her.

KURDS

A note to the Ambassador about a demonstration at the Consulate, by a group of Kurds who were (according to the document they handed over) protesting the closure of an unlicensed Kurdish television station in the UK.

Herewith the document which I agreed to accept from a Mr Amojgar, representing the approximately 60 Kurdish demonstrators here this morning.

Mr Amojgar complained, through the police, that I had not shown much interest in their cause. In my reply, I reminded him

272

that he had not shown much courtesy. It is true that, when he began to talk, in Kurdish, into his state-of-the-art mobile telephone in the middle of our conversation, I curtailed the meeting. I had expressed no objection to the handover - outside the door of the Consulate - being photographed, but when the photographer whipped out a note-book, moved too close for comfort, and made as if to write down everything I said, I judged it was time, very politely, to cut it short anyway. Mr Amojgar also told the police that he felt it was humiliating (*erniedrigend*) not to have been allowed into the British Consulate.

Short of the nailing of some posters to our fence, there was no unpleasantness.

LUCIEN

I never met him; but, by all accounts, Lucien was a remarkable young man.

An uncle had smuggled him, at the age of 12, out of Rwanda, after Lucien had witnessed the murder of his mother and sisters. Judging by drawings he made years later for the psychiatrist, they had all been decapitated. Then he had crossed Africa to the west. All he remembered of that trip was being submerged in a mass of bodies, inside an enormous truck, and occasional periods of quiet, with a curious sense of motion: he had never been on a river-boat before. He recalled strange, disjointed names like Kisangani and Bolobo, which suggested that he had travelled the Zaire river for weeks; Franceville, Douala, Enugu and Ibadan. But the psychiatrist didn't know if he was making this up to keep her happy: he was an imaginative young man. After that, he was in a tent on a beach for a month or so. Here he saw his uncle for the last time. Then he was in a big tin trunk with many others, in the pitch dark, feeling hungry and nauseous. The trunk also seemed to be moving. He had never been in a container before. Or on a ship on the ocean. And then there was noise and unfamiliar smells. He had never been in a city before: São Paulo, Brazil. Here he was let out of the big tin trunk and put into an old bus. He was definite about this, as he had once been on a bus back to his village in Rwanda. They drove through some big iron gates under a sign which said ASILO DE SÃO JOSÉ. He clearly remembered the squiggly mark over the A.

There, he had a room and a bed, and good food. He lived in an enormous house, behind a wall. When he looked over the wall from his window, he could see a tunnel with masses of cars and lorries coming out of it at great speed. In the distance he could also see the words HOSPITAL DE and FÁBRICA DE written on big buildings in the distance. They asked him to write his name, and his address: he wrote 'Lucien' and 'Kanzi'. People were nice, particularly his guardian, who wore the white robe of a religious man, and had a cross hanging from a rope around his waist. There were people of all colours from pale white to dark black. And there were girls: he had never seen such girls. Then he met Lenny from Nigeria, who wanted to talk to him; but he couldn't understand what Lenny was trying to say.

One night Lenny came to him and indicated that he should put his things into a plastic bag and go with him. He didn't want to leave. He had just been given a piece of paper on which there was the word *Autorização*. He didn't know what it meant but it seemed to be important. Lenny snatched it from him and dragged him out of the house. There was a large car waiting, with some of Lenny's friends in it. They drove him down to where the ships were, and forced him back into a big tin trunk. There were less people in it this time, and they were given fruit and bottles of water. He was there for a long time. A long long time. Occasionally there was cold rice and black beans. When they let him out of the container, everyone was black.

The Swiss social worker who somehow coaxed the above tale out of Lucien, then worked out that he had been taken across the desert from Nigeria to somewhere in North Africa; boarded an open boat to a small Italian island, probably Lampedusa, and was then taken by the Italian Navy to the mainland.

On arrival in Italy, he was given a bath and the biggest meal he had ever seen, before being driven up into the mountains, furnished with a rucksack with more food and drink and a blanket in it, and told to walk - and keep walking. He was eventually picked up by the Swiss frontier police and taken to an open prison, just outside Zürich.

Lucien's story was almost impossible to believe. But one of the reasons that he was taken seriously was the fact that he spoke several languages. The psychiatrist, together with an interpreter – actually several interpreters – pieced together parts of his story from those languages. He spoke a few words of Italian and some North African Arabic expressions; some other words which, with great difficulty, they identified as Berber and Chadic; a little English, mixed with Hausa; fluent Brazilian Portuguese; quite good French and fluent Kinyarwanda, which is spoken throughout Rwanda.

He hadn't done anything wrong in Switzerland, except come over the border without papers, and the authorities were keen to send him back. But where to?

He was thought to be about 18 years old, well into the age of consent. It seemed that his odyssey had taken him five to six years, including one year or so in Brazil. He couldn't be returned to Rwanda: the Hutu had stopped slaughtering the Tutsi by then, but revenge killings continued. Repatriation would have been, logistically, all but impossible. Lucien did not want to go back there anyway: he desperately wanted to return to Brazil. He believed, in any event that he had permission to be there and to remain there. The only friends he had were in São Paulo. His best friend worked at the *asilo* (a home for poor immigrants and refugees). His name was José.

The Swiss social worker assigned to Lucien heard by chance that I was flying privately to São Paulo for two weeks or so. We both knew that the case had nothing whatsoever to do with the British Consulate, but he asked if, as a friend, I might be able to make some enquiries on his behalf. He talked French with Lucien but couldn't speak Brazilian. I agreed to do my best.

Diógenes, with whom we were staying in the city, used to be a taxi-driver in his student days, and knew São Paulo like the back of his hand.

We had the name of the *asilo*, and we knew it was near a motorway, a factory and a hospital. After scouring maps and the telephone book, we found four suitable candidates; one was out of the question as it was nowhere near a motorway. We visited the other three. I asked about Lucien as well as Lucio and Luciano, possible translations of his name. In the last one, in the Baixada do Glicério, I got very close: there used to be a receptionist called

José, but he had resigned three months previously. In the card-register of previous guests, his successor found mention of a Lucien from Africa. Tantalisingly, there was also a note of some correspondence with the Immigration Department. A hospital ('HOSPITAL DE...') and a textile factory ('FÁBRICA DE...') were visible in the distance. The fact that the institution was run by Jesuits, who wore long white robes, seemed to clinch it.

José's successor agreed that I pass on the name and address of the *asilo* to the Swiss authorities. We went home that evening, feeling that we had accomplished something.

* * *

But this whole exercise came to nothing when, only days after my return to Zürich, Lucien absconded from the open prison and disappeared.

JOHN SMITH

The reader will have gathered that consular sections' primary function is to look after British nationals abroad, and that, in the absence of ID cards, passports are their point of reference. A lost passport is an extraordinarily common occurrence. It can happen in a number of ways. They can be mislaid ('I *know* where I put it, but it wasn't there this morning'), dropped somewhere, or stolen (while the holder is, say, on holiday abroad). The number of British passports which expire in washing-machines is impressive. Other obscure circumstances abound.

I was once visited by a British woman of Indian extraction. Our dialogue went like this:

'Good morning, Madam.'
'Good morning. I need a new passport.'
'May I see the old one please?'
'I don't have it.'
'Did you leave it at home?'
'I don't know where it is.'
'You mean, you have lost it?'

'Not exactly.'

'Well...what happened to it?'

'My husband needs it for his sister.' The truth, straight out: not a trace of remorse – albeit a smack of revenge...We inhabited different worlds.

Consulates have always addressed the matter of lost passports very seriously. My own tenure at the Consulate straddled the period from the phasing out of the old blue passport and the phasing in of the modern electronic type, with a chip in the cover. Nowadays, if you are stuck abroad with no passport, Big Brother definitely helps: your biometric passport details can be swiftly located.

However, it was not so much the issue of an emergency passport (a temporary document, designed to get you back to the UK) which was complicated. It was, rather, the initial identification of the applicant. People might have a new-style driving licence or credit-card, containing a photographic likeness or signature; but, as often as not, such identity documents had disappeared with the passport. And the most challenging age-bracket was 55- to 70-year-olds, particularly British citizens with a name like John Smith. The details of new issues were automatically fed into the new space-age system. Particulars of more mature passport-holders were not gathered and recorded so rigorously in the past. There were gaps in the system.

'Mr Smith?'

'That's right.'

'Any forenames, Christian names?'

'John.'

'No other names?'

'Just John.'

'Your address in the UK please.'

'We've just moved. Shall I give you both addresses?' He did so.

'Where was the passport issued?'

'That was the time I went to Liverpool, I believe, about five years ago. Or London?'

'Never mind. Can you recall approximately when it was issued?'

'Certainly in the last eight or nine years. Perhaps more recently.'

'Thank you, that will do for the time being. Now, who can vouch for you?'

'Jane can.' He looked across at his companion.

'Thank you. May I just take your personal details, Madam? You are Mrs…'

'Miss, actually, Jane Smythe, with a y and an e.'

'Then you are not related to Mr Smith?'

'Oh no!'

'But you would be prepared to confirm that Mr Smith is who he says he is? No offence, Sir.' 'Of course I would be prepared to do so.'

'Thank you. Now, how long have you known him?'

'We met last night. In a pub.' She flashed Mr Smith a smile.

'Ah. I understand. May I see *your* passport?'

'I was going to tell you, mine was stolen too.'

And so it went.

On the old passport applications, one had to know the applicant's height, colour of eyes and colour of hair. And there was another section which asked for 'Special Peculiarities', which was later changed to 'Distinguishing Marks'. Young men proudly entered the positions of their scars, and so forth. On one occasion, a lady I was tending got to that section and turned scarlet. She asked if I would mind if she talked confidentially to Yvonne, the Pro-Consul. After whispering something into Yvonne's ear, and hearing the reply, she seemed much relieved. I never found out what made her blush. I never asked.

ACCOMPANIMENT

The young man came through the door first. He was of medium height, oriental and effeminate, in his late teens or early 20s. He wore a flowered shirt and white silk slacks. I guessed he might have been from the Philippines. His companion, who followed him into the Consulate, was quite different: white shirt with the sleeves neatly rolled up above the elbow; grey trousers. He was slightly built, dark-skinned, large-nosed, unsmiling, sinister. But the most disquieting thing about him was that his right hand had been amputated at the wrist. Every time he talked – he did *all* the talking – he waved the stump in the air; he flourished the stump;

he brandished the stump; he *flaunted* the stump. There were no introductions.

'He is going to Britain.' He pointed with his stump at the Filipino. 'I need to go with him.'

'May I ask your name, Sir?'

'You don't need my name.' Almost perfect English: Middle Eastern?

'Do you have your passport with you?'

'You don't need my passport. He...' He pointed again with his stump...'*He* is not going with *me*, *I* am going with *him*.' The emphasis was unmistakable, but still baffling.

'So this gentleman is travelling to the UK and *you* wish to travel with *him*? I could accentuate too. He nodded. At that moment, the Filipino wandered round the end of the counter and, staring intently at a signed picture of a young Queen Elizabeth which I had on the wall, began to push past me into the office area: security was not very good in those days. 'You cannot go in there.' He stopped and smiled at me but did not withdraw. I wondered if he spoke English, steered him back to the reception area and said slowly and clearly '*Not* in *there*.' The Arab pointed with his stump at a chair and the young man went over and sat down.

'Exactly...' said the amputee, and waved his stump, '...It is urgent.' Yes, Middle Eastern.

Trying to collect my thoughts, I addressed the Filipino: 'May I see *your* passport please?' He stared vacantly at me. Then I turned to the Arab: 'Until you give me *some* idea of your identities and nationalities, *neither* of you is going *anywhere*.' With his left hand, the Arab gave me a passport. It was the Filipino's, except that he wasn't a Filipino - he was a Thai. In those days, there were no visa requirements for citizens of Thailand to enter the UK. Somehow, the Arab was trying to take advantage of this. But conversation stalled and we got no further. I handed the passport back to the Thai, and, shortly afterwards, they both left, without exchanging a word.

I thought long and hard about this case. How had the Arab (if that is what he was) lost his hand: had he lost it in an accident? Or had he perhaps been punished for stealing in some orthodox Middle Eastern country? How had he got into Switzerland without papers? How had he met the Thai? Had he really believed that he could enter the UK as a sort of chaperone for an alien who needed no visa? Was he waving his stump in my face in an attempt to provoke me to do something, or say something? Or was he simply looking for sympathy? Or was it an involuntary gesture? In what language did the two men communicate? And finally: *Who had rolled up the Arab's left sleeve so neatly?*

I was in no position to help them, but then: *savoir, c'est pouvoir.*

SILENCE IS GOLDEN

Every first Monday in the month, the Zürich Consular Corps traditionally had a get-together in the bar of the Storchen Hotel. It was a very informal affair, with a glass of wine, some *Bündner-fleisch* and nuts; it gave us a chance to relax together and talk, off the record, about whatever we felt like discussing. Sometimes ten Consuls turned up; sometimes only three or four. On one occasion, the Honorary Consuls of Sweden and Norway came, as did a representative from the Chinese Consulate General. They were having a very cordial discussion about various aspects of the international scene, and I just sat there, enjoying the friendly atmosphere, musing about history in general, and about Alfred Nobel in particular. Nobel, a chemist and engineer by trade, was fluent in several languages and wrote poetry. He was awarded 355 patents, the most famous of which was for the manufacture of what he called 'blasting oil', the precursor of dynamite.

Until 1814, Norway had been regarded as a backward possession of Denmark. In the later nineteenth century, it was bound into a union with Sweden. True, it had its own parliament (the *Storting*) and government. But the King and the Foreign Ministry in Stockholm embodied Swedish hegemony over its smaller neighbour to the north-west.

In 1895, war between the two countries was only averted by the demeaning withdrawal of Norwegian demands. Months after these traumatic events, Alfred Nobel made his will.

The main reason for this near-conflict had been Norway's request for its own consular service. This became a battle of the cultures, with the Swedish Kingdom, its privileged nobility and its courtly cabinet politics, standing against a young nation which had introduced parliamentary democracy and had banned the aristocracy. European monarchs, particularly Oscar II, were aghast at Norway's push for independence. 'Starve them,' Kaiser Wilhelm II is reputed to have demanded.

While Sweden's soldiery had once been feared throughout Europe, Norway could boast no significant military tradition. Moreover, the Peace Movement, towards the end of the nineteenth century, was developing into a meaningful force. In 1890, the *Storting*, in Oslo, called in vain upon the king in Stockholm, to sign arbitration treaties with other countries. The *Storting* was also the only parliament which financed the trips of its members to peace congresses. It was the work of these congresses, the pledge of brotherhood between nations, and the reduction of standing armies which caught Alfred Nobel's eye. In his last will and testament, he left much of his enormous wealth for the establishment of a prize fund, with a Nobel Prize in each of five categories: Physics, Chemistry, Medicine, Literature and Peace. Moreover, he laid down that the Peace Prize - unlike all the other Nobel Prizes - should be awarded 'by a committee of five persons to be chosen by the Norwegian *Storting*'. The gold medal for the said Peace Prize should be produced at the Royal Mint in Norway. His action did not go down at all well in Sweden.

Oscar II did all he could to contain the damage. He summoned Nobel's nephews to the palace, told them that their uncle had been unduly influenced by 'peace-fantasists' and 'women's lobbies', and demanded that they contest the will.

In short, the Swedish king's behaviour was comparable to that of a large oriental country which objected to the Peace Prize being awarded in 1989 to the Fourteenth Dalai Lama, and in 2010 to Liu Xiaobo, 'for his long and non-violent struggle for fundamental human rights in his native land'.

At the Storchen Hotel, Zürich, on that Monday evening, the representatives of the Kingdoms of Sweden and Norway and the People's Republic of China were still cordially chatting together. I did not interrupt.

* * *

There is a curious 'prequel' to this story:

Children, it is well known, love bonfires, and, in 1953, I was throwing twigs on to a roaring blaze in the garden of Les Lumières, Jersey, the home of my stepfather-to-be. He, his two daughters and his two sons were about to move to Le Ponterrin, where we McCammons lived, on the other side of the island. David and I were looking forward to their company.

While staring into the fire, I spotted two rectangular, seemingly carved wooden panels, which I felt might come in useful in my carpentry ventures. They were already smouldering but I managed to get them out of the fire before serious damage had been done, and stored them in a cupboard for the next 30 years, with some other souvenirs. Pressed by my mother to 'get rid of all that junk,' I gave them a good brushing and brought them back to Zürich, where I examined them properly.

They turned out to be beautifully carved Tibetan book-covers, dating back to the fifteenth to seventeenth centuries. I have never been able to understand how such works of art landed up on a bonfire. Many years later, some circumstantial evidence came to light that these artifacts may have been brought back by a member of the Younghusband expedition to Lhasa in 1903-4.

On the smaller panel, a single deity is surrounded by stylized lotus flowers, with traces of colouring, gold leaf gilding and the ash of the bonfire; the back of it looks as if it has been used as a breadboard. The larger panel features five deities in a more traditional surround, and has three lines of Tibetan script on the back. In 1970, after quite a search, I located a Tibetan refugee in Zürich, Losang Chodak, who was kind enough to provide a translation of these lines:

> Oh! This wooden cover from the book of such a holy man also gives the Work brilliance and beauty. These show an extraordinarily fine quality which would gladden the eyes of a connoisseur! May this cover (together with the Work) bring luck and prosperity to all living beings!

* * *

One of the many readings of the history of Chinese intervention in Tibet, puts the blame squarely on the British, who, in the early 1900s, were concerned only by the Russian threat. The arrival of the Younghusband expedition in Lhasa, and the subsequent flight of the then Dalai Lama to Mongolia - goes the theory - gave the Chinese the opportunity they had been waiting for.

FLIGHT FROM MINSK

'Good morning, Sir. Good morning, Madam.'

She was in her 40s, not unattractive.

'Vee veesh get married.'

'Are you British, Madam?'

She nodded at her companion, 90s, vacant expression, two hearing aids.

'He Breeteesh.'

'And you, Madam?'

'I not Breeteesh.'

'Are you British, Sir? Do you hold a British passport?'

'I said vee veesh get married. You marry us?'

'I was talking to the gentleman, Madam. Your passports, please.'

She handed me two passports: one British, one from Belarus. I addressed him.

'Do you wish to get married to this lady, Sir?'

'Vee veesh.'

'Please allow me to talk to the gentleman.'

'Hee veesh get married.'

'I repeat my question, Sir. Do you wish to marry this lady?'

'Hee veesh get married. You not understand?'

This banter continued. It seemed that she would not allow him to say one word. In the end, I had to ask her to leave the room, while I talked to him.

'Do you wish to get married to this lady?'

He smiled for the first time and nodded resolutely. His British passport was in order as was his birth certificate; he was 91 years old. He firmly signed the marriage affidavit and paid the fee. *He pocketed both passports.* He smiled at me again. He could not speak, but his look said it all: I had done exactly what he had wanted me to do.

I invited her back into the room. She addressed him nervously. 'Vhat you do?'

He ignored her.

When they left, there was a spring in his step.

SAILING OFF GUYANA

A telephone call: 'British Consulate; good morning.'

'I'd like to ask you a question...'

'Go ahead.'

'I want to take a group of teenagers sailing off Guyana. I am the sports teacher at...' (He gave me the name of the school.)

'What is your question, Sir?'

'Would you advise it?'

'Have you looked at the Foreign Office Travel Advice website?'

'Seems to be no problem...'

'Have you looked at the website, Sir? If not, I strongly advise you to do so.'

'Yes, but what do *you* think? Everyone in the class knows how to sail...' (I had in the meantime accessed the website.) '...and I will be in possession of my Swiss sea permit...'

'Are you aware, Sir...?' He interrupted: 'All the parents have signed letters of indemnity and have confidence in me. Money has been invested in the planning of it...'

'I am looking at the website now, Sir, and I repeat: you should study it too - very carefully.'

'What have you got against my going to Guyana? The trip has already been decided...'

'Armed robbery; shooting; multiple murders; dangerous drug problems; heavy rains; endemic Dengue fever; inadequate medical facilities: I am reading from the website, Sir.'

'...But there's no terrorism and no hurricanes. I am an accomplished sailor. I know what I am doing. What more do you want?'

'How do you intend to travel with your group to Guyana?'

'*I* was going to ask *you* that...'

'Read the website, Sir.'

He hung up.

THINGS PEOPLE LEAVE BEHIND

...Pens and car-keys and passports and cardigans and wallets and umbrellas and hats and spectacles and mobile telephones and the odd coat: most items were later reclaimed.

He was thick-set, quite smartly dressed, and he was wheeling a trolley full of brochures. He was sweating profusely and he didn't smile. I put it down to nervousness.

He was definitely British, but I couldn't place his accent.

'I'd like to ask you a favour...may I leave some of these on your counter?'

'Let me see one, please.' He obliged.

'You know...' he was blushing slightly '...we are not very popular at the moment.'

I looked up. 'Who do you mean by "we"?'

'Scientologists...' His face was like a question mark.

The brochure was indeed about 'dianetics' and Ron Hubbard: quite often, in *Bahnhofstrasse*, salesmen from this organisation had tried to thrust one into my hands.

He did not seem at all surprised when I declined his request.

After he had gone - without saying goodbye - we found a well-thumbed Bible which he had left on a chair: we knew it was his because he was the only visitor we had that day.

He never came back for it.

GILES

He was an elderly gentleman. Well turned out. English-style tweed jacket. Smart tie, polished shoes. And he carried with him a Giles Cartoon Annual for 1980. There was a crowd of people in the Consulate, and he found himself a place in the corner, opened his book and occasionally chuckled as something seemed to tickle his fancy. His turn eventually came, and I asked him how I could be of assistance.

'Do you like Giles?'

Something in the way he asked the question told me I should be cautious, and I answered guardedly:

'Yeeeeees – I used to look at his cartoons occasionally.'

'Don't you think his wit is extraordinary...'

Swiss. Very polished.

'...and the way he draws?'

I looked at the clock on the wall, and at the queue behind him. 'How can I help you?'

'I have a complete set of Giles Annuals...'

'Very interesting but how can I help you?'

'Would you like to buy the set?'

'No. Thank you. Is that what you wanted to ask?'

'Yes.'

'I am sorry. I really have no space...'

'No problem. I am in no hurry to sell. But it's a bargain...'

'No thank you. Now I must ask you to make way for this lady. Goodbye.'

'Goodbye.'

The following day, he was back, with another Giles Annual.

'Good morning. I thought I would try again.'

'Try what?'

'Would you like to buy the set?'

We had no customers at the time. 'Did you say you had a complete set?'

'I do indeed.'

'And how much do you want for them?'

'Two hundred francs.'

'Yes, you are right: it is a bargain. It is a pity I cannot buy them.'

'What do you mean?'

'I've told you I am not interested.'

'Yes, but you told me it was a bargain. What do you mean by that?'

'I mean that you should ask more if it is a complete set. Can you get them to an auction company in London?'

He thought for a moment. 'No. I cannot possibly do that. I have just moved out of my house and I now live in a retirement home. I have got rid of everything except my Giles set. I have no room for it...'

At that moment, a group of British tourists arrived; two of them had lost their passports.

'...Don't worry. I'll be back next week.' And, on Monday morning, back he came.

'How much do you think I should ask for them?'

'I have no idea. But it just seems to me that 200 francs is rather little for a full set of Giles. I may be wrong.'

'Shall I show you my favourite?' He had brought it with him. He was actually a charming gentleman and we had a good yarn. 'If you would drive me home, you can pick the set up...'

'I have already told you...'

'I would be really pleased if you would take them off me; I feel sure they would be going to a good home; and you yourself said they were a bargain.'

On our way to his home in my car, he told me how, just after the outbreak of the Second World War, his father had sent him out to Argentina as a salesman in the textile machinery industry. His ship had been torpedoed and he, and only one other passenger, a young girl, had survived. Towards the end of the war, he made his way to the West Indies, and eventually, after being torpedoed again, back to Switzerland. He loved the British and their culture. He was so proud of his collection. We arrived at his house, now completely empty but for two piles of Giles annuals in the hall, all wrapped up.

I reached into my pocket and gave him two banknotes. He looked at them sadly...

'But you said they were worth more...'

So I gave him another 100 and we shook hands. He was a good salesman. But, with the story he had told, it had been a bargain for both of us.

It was a real pleasure to drive him to his new abode.

When I unwrapped the two packages at home, it was by no means a complete set...

But I always did like Giles...

287

DIS-APPOINTMENT

I have a rule of thumb about honorary positions. This once, I broke it.

I had resolved that two periods of five years each would be about right as Honorary Consul at Zürich. It had been Richard Blandy in Madeira who advised me not to go any longer. 'Do not, under any circumstances, exceed this.' And: 'Do not expect to be remembered.'

They were shrewd words, and I remembered them when I was chatting in Jersey with Nigel Broomfield, just retired from the post of HM Ambassador to Germany. I recalled Richard's words again, while showing Chris Patten, former Governor and Commander-in-Chief of Hong Kong to a lecture room at Zürich University. He told me the story of his retirement from Hong Kong, his departure in a black, chauffeur-driven limousine, after the lowering of the Union Jack, and his arrival home in the UK in a taxi, which he had to pay for. These were very different worlds to mine, but, after hearing about them, I felt I was well prepared for my withdrawal from this very public world.

I agreed to stay for one year more than my statutory ten, so as to help in the arrangements for the UEFA European Championship 2008. Thousands of British supporters were awaited in the two host countries, Switzerland and Austria.

In the event, not one British team qualified. So the title of this short, anti-climactic essay refers to British football fans – not to me. On the contrary, I had had the benefit of extra time.

END-PIECE

Not three years after retiring from the Post, I have just learned (February 2011) that, buried among FCO budget cuts and the reciprocal whims of the Swiss Federal Department of Foreign Affairs (themselves in the midst of a drastic cut-back), a decision has been taken that the British Consulate in Zürich be closed.

There is to be a new network of 'consular wardens', the appointment of whom seems to fly in the face of the Vienna

Convention on Consular Relations (1963), under which a host country - Switzerland, say - might choose not to recognise such officers as consular agents.

But to some, Vienna's sister Convention on [sovereign] Diplomatic Relations (1961) might be seen as even more seriously impugned, since the European Commission appointed its first, very own, ambassador - ironically an Austrian - to Switzerland in 2007. Do the duties of this new Post complement or impinge upon those of Her (merely Britannic) Majesty's envoys?

Whatever the answer to this question, it is my privilege to have learned from four seasoned British ambassadors that the E of politics equals the MC^2 of diplomacy. They are different sides of the same equation. One will not function without the other. *Ergo*, for every political problem, there will be a diplomatic solution.

* * *

Apart from the rhinoceros, the rhinoceros beetle, the marmots, the sitatunga and the skunk, mentioned above, I have seen sandfish (also known as skinks) disappear into a Tunisian

The women of Baly Bay, Madagascar, home of the ploughshare tortoise, 2008.

Last days of the Consulate, with Angelika, 2008.

dune in less than a second. I have tasted sea lamprey at Factory House in Oporto; I have sighted a thorny devil strutting, in slow motion, down the highway near Geraldton, Western Australia; stromatolites at Shark Bay; a train of processionary caterpillars (*Ochrogaster lunifer*), scampering around in a perfect circle one metre in diameter, near Cook (population: four) in South Australia; a porcupine, which rose up from under our feet near Morin Heights, Quebec, climbed up a five-metre pine tree, and hung there absurdly; sloths creeping about high up in the evergreens of the *Praça da República* in Santos, Brazil; six-foot Amazonian manatees, and a seven-foot pirarucu. I have viewed ploughshare tortoises in Madagascar, cycads in Madeira and Livingstone's fruit bats in Mayotte.

But it is my contention that *not one* of these creatures is as exotic as some of the human specimens whose habitats lie in the territory of the average honorary consul abroad.

That said, I confine myself now to the observation of Farmer Burkhard's small herd of Brown Swiss cattle, which I can see from my study window, overlooking the Zürich *Oberland*; and Farmer Houzé's Jerseys, which decorate the green fields around Le Ponterrin on our visits there, as they follow each other, in procession, to and from their pastures.

* * *

On the subject of farewells, Colonel Etherton, 'late HM Consul-General in Chinese Turkestan', recorded that, in Tibet, instead of saying 'Goodbye' the host speeds his guest by saying 'Go slowly'; to which the guest replies, 'Sit slowly,' implying that he does not wish to be forgotten too soon.

Finally, a *Haiku* of Matsuo Bashō on 'Coolness':

Japanese: *Hiya-hiya| to| kabe| wo|fumaete| hiru-ne| kana*
Literally: Cool-cool|thus|wall|[acc.]|putting-foot-on|noon-sleep | *kana*
Translated by Henderson:
How very cool it feels
taking a noonday nap, to have
a wall against my heels!

ACTE FINALE

Among the consular officers, diplomats, ministers of the Crown, and sovereigns, who have played noteworthy parts in the above memoirs, are (in chronological order):

- William Duke of Normandy, Count of Maine, King of England, who was ultimately responsible for the Jersey connection (1066–87).
- Edward I, King of England, Lord of Ireland and Duke of Gascony, from whom both my paternal grandmother's family, and my maternal grandmother's family claim descent (1272–1307) Although he spent a lot of time in hard negotiations with the Scots and the French, Edward was definitely no diplomat; the word had, in any event, not yet been invented. Nevertheless, it was he who summoned the Model Parliament in 1295, which evolved into the Upper and Lower Chambers (1485), and became Lords and Commons (1544). This political structure, in turn, gave rise to the appointment of the first secretary of state for foreign affairs (1782) and what is now called the Foreign & Commonwealth Office (FCO).
- Sir Charles Bankhead (a great-uncle by marriage of my paternal grandmother), HM Minister Plenipotentiary to the young Republic of Mexico (1843–47), who helped to lay the basis of a solid commercial relationship with Central America, which

Great-grandfather's passport from 1857.

led in turn to the establishment of the London Bank of Mexico and South America, a forerunner of the Bank of London & South America (BOLSA), my employer for over a quarter of a century.

- George William Frederick Villiers 4th Earl of Clarendon, once Lord Grey's Envoy Extraordinary and Minister Plenipotentiary at the Court of Spain (1833), who signed my great-grandfather's passport (1857).

- Ernest Huelin, my mother's second husband (1953-72), Honorary Vice-consul in Jersey for Denmark, Finland, Norway, Portugal and Sweden, who helped to plant an idea.

- Leonid N. Bobkhov, Second Secretary and Consul of the Union of Soviet Socialist Republics at Ottawa.

- Jasper Cross, British Trade Commissioner at Winnipeg.

- David Brower, at the office of the High Commissioner of the United Kingdom at Vancouver.

- Jan Solecki, who after the war spent some time with the Foreign Office in London, Switzerland and Germany, later moving to Canada. Jan and the above three gentlemen helped me materially to travel on the Trans-Siberian Railway from Nakhodka to Moscow and onwards (1961).

- Sir Herbert de Vere Redman, Counsellor at the British Embassy, Tokyo, who may well have facilitated the issue of an important visa (1961).

- Wilfred Thesiger, famous explorer, formerly of the Sudan political service, who, during a brief interview in the City of London (1962), told me to change my tack, or I would end up in a shed on a tea plantation in Burma. I changed it.

- Minou Hamidi, Assistant Cultural Attaché at the Iranian Embassy, London, and

- Denis Wright, HM Ambassador to Iran, who offered me sound advice for my stint with the British Institute of Persian Studies in Teheran (1963) and my sally to Afghanistan.

- Bob Allstone, Second Secretary at the British Embassy, Kabul (1963), who sorted out my repatriation in an unusual way.

- Joseph Richard Duffy, HM Vice-consul at São Paulo, who not only signed our Lex Loci marriage certificate (1965), but also saw to it, by tactical replenishment of a whisky glass, that the addition of a counter-signature by the officer from the local civil registry, on a document written in a foreign language (English), was not, after all, an insurmountable problem.

- Sir Geoffrey Wallinger, HM Ambassador to Brazil and non-executive director of BOLSA, who held my hand during a short but important stint in London as PA to Sir George Bolton, chairman of the Bank (1967).

- US Ambassador Vernon Penner, with whom, over the years, I have successfully found solutions to most of the world's problems (1974-2010).
- Richard Blandy, British Honorary Consul at Funchal (Madeira) and a connoisseur of good wines, who furnished me with some opportune tips about how long I should remain in the post (1995).
- John Nichols, Deputy Head of Mission and later HM Ambassador to the Swiss Confederation, and Michael Hannant, HM Consul, who backed me in my early days as British Honorary Consul at Zürich (1997-2008).
- Richard Reeve, Counsellor at the Embassy in Berne, and his successors, who introduced me to the twilight world of international security (1997-2008).
- Paul Dunn, drugs liaison officer with NCIS, who took me into his confidence (1997-2000).
- Sandra Darra MBE, British Honorary Consul at Montreux, who gave me some timely words of advice (1997-2008).
- Charles Garrett, Head of the Political Section at Berne, who instructed me in the fine tuning of his métier (1997-98).
- Christopher Hulse and Simon Featherstone, HM Ambassadors to the Swiss Confederation, who gave me their complete support (1997-2008).
- Arthur Martin, Tony Bates and Mike Doig, Management Officers at the Embassy in Berne, who put up with the unruly disposition of their Honorary Consul in Zürich (1997-2008).
- Kurt Ricklin of the *Sicherheitsdienst, Stadtpolizei Zürich,* a specialist in diplomatic and consular protection, who looked after my physical wellbeing (1997-2008).
- Basil Eastwood, HM Ambassador to the Swiss Confederation, who showed his support for a conference on the environmental future of aquatic ecosystems (2003).
- Jesús Carlos Riosalido Gambotti, Consul General of Spain at Zürich, who taught me about the Arab world, and Iraq in particular (2004).
- Clare Douglas, HM Consul at Muscat, who explained the intricacies of the Omani royal succession (2005).
- Nenad Hölbl, Consul General of the Republic of Croatia at Zürich, who enlightened me about Balkan history (2006-8).
- Marcel Studer, Honorary Consul of the Republic of Ireland at Zürich, who has as fine a sense of humour as any in the Corps Consulaire de Zürich (1997-2010).
- Nigel Broomfield, Former HM Ambassador to Germany and
- Chris Patten, last British Governor of Hong Kong, who, in their own ways, forewarned me about retirement (2008).

* * *

The vast majority of the stories in this book are based on the truth. Of the rest, one is a composite story, made up of real events which took place on different occasions; one is allegorical; one is a parable; one is a child's history lesson; and two are fictional but based, respectively, on the Old Testament and on historical records. Of the five little tales told in '*Se non è Vero*' the third and fourth are believed to be true; readers are invited to make up their own minds about the other three.

Seven essays, 'Bombay at a Glance', 'Saints Alive...', 'Atlantis in a Wink', 'Playing at God', 'The Baobab and the Thumb-piano', 'Valentine's Day' and 'Snoring' were first published in *Search*, the journal of St Andrew's Anglican Church in Zürich. 'Playing at God' also appeared in *Kontakt mit Albanien* (an Albanian periodical for Germany and Switzerland) 7 (March 1995).

The drama of Canute's birthday ('Roots') can be found in William Buchanan of Auchmar's *History of the Ancient Surname Buchanan* (Glasgow, 1793) p.14. For the 'Most Recent Common Ancestor' theory, see Professor Joseph T. Chang's 'Recent Common Ancestors of All Present-Day Individuals', *Advances in Applied Probability* 31/4 (1999), pp.1002-26.

The Reverend George Hill's *In Memoriam* ('Pop') was published in the *Ulster Journal of Archaeology* 6/3 (July 1900).

Some details of the life of Lewis Davies ('Gwynneth') are taken from David Jenkins, 'Cardigan, Liverpool and Sydney: the Career of Captain Lewis Davies', *Cymru a'r Môr/Maritime Wales* 20 (1999), pp.16-36.

Currencies of the Anglo-Norman Isles ('Cod') was published by Spink, London, 1984; *Robin Frères* is mentioned under reference JN100.

Much of what Professor Honda told me ('One Old Man') is documented in a booklet which he gave me on his Harvard Lectures, which had first appeared in the *Mainichi Daily News* of 1 and 2 January 1961.

Translations from the Japanese ('Back to the Hive' and 'End-Piece') are from *An Introduction to Haiku* by Harold G. Henderson (Doubleday, New York, 1958) pp.35, 49.

Robert Woodd-Walker and others ('Afghanistan') published 'The Blood Groups of the Timuri and Related Tribes in Afghanistan' in *The American Journal of Physical Anthropology* 27/2 (September 1967), pp.195-204; Clare Goff described her experiences in *An Archaeologist in the Making* (Constable, London 1980).

'The Rupununi Savanna' of Robert Goodland, MSc (McGill) was published in *The Journal of the British Guiana Museum of Natural History* 41, pp.15-23 ('Roraima').

The novel by Julian Fellowes, *Past Imperfect*, was first published by Weidenfeld & Nicholson, London, 2008 ('David').

I am indebted to the late John Delaforce, author of *The Factory House at Oporto* (London, 1979), for some of the historical details which appear in 'Speaking in Riddles'.

The story of the Tatlock family ('Atlantis in a Wink') is told in Rodney Bolt's *Madeira and Porto Santo* (Cadogan Guides, 2007).

The conference of November 1991 on Banking and the Environment ('Greenery') was reviewed in *Environmental Conservation* 19/1 (Spring 1992) pp.86-87. 'Banking Responsibility and Liability for the Environment: What Are Banks Doing?' was published in *Environmental Conservation* 22/4 (Winter 1995) pp.297-305.

Swift's maxim ('Microcredit') is recorded in Thomas Sheridan's *Life of the Rev. Dr. Jonathan Swift* (2nd ed., 1787) p.234.

Aquatic Ecosystems ('Water'), edited by Nicholas Polunin, was published by Cambridge University Press, 2008.

'UNCED' was published in *Environmental Conservation* 19/4 (Winter 1992), pp.372-73; all 'National Reports' appeared in *Nations of the Earth Report* (3 vols, United Nations, Geneva, 1992).

Arthur Clark's 'The Silver Ship' ('Oman') appeared in the March/April 1997 print edition of *Saudi Aramco World*, pp.20-27. The story of the B-flat clarinet score is told, with many other compelling tales, in *Diplomatic Bag: An Anthology of Diplomatic Incidents and Anecdotes from the Renaissance to the Gulf War*, edited by John Ure (John Murray, 1994).

Quotations ('Ambassadors and Consuls') from Sir Ernest Satow's *Guide to Diplomatic Practice* (Longmans, Green & Co.,

London), are from the 1st edition, 1917, pp.2-3, 229-30, and the 5th edition, 1979 p.211; the story of the Transvaal maps is told in Robert Durrer's *Heinrich Angst – Erster Direktor des Schweizerischen Landesmuseums [&] Britischer Generalkonsul* (Glarus, 1948) p.347; for Arnold Lunn's note see his *Switzerland and the English* (London, 1944) p.53.

I could not have written the chapter headed 'Honorificabilitudinity' without frequent reference to and liberal quotation from S.T. Bindoff, M.A., F.R.Hist.Soc. 'The Unreformed Diplomatic Service' in *Royal Historical Society Transactions* (4th series, vol.XVIII, 1935) pp.143-72. Sir Douglas Busk's *The Craft of Diplomacy: Mechanics and Development of National Representation Overseas* (London, 1967) was another useful source, as was Sir Neville Henderson's *Water Under the Bridges* (London, 1945).

The Tibetan salutation ('*La Diplomatique*') and farewell ('End-Piece') are quoted by Colonel P.T. Etherton, *The Last Strongholds* (London, 1934) p.75; Samuel Johnson's comment ('*La Diplomatique*') was reported by Boswell in his *Tour of the Hebrides*, under the date 18 September 1773.

My thanks are particularly due to John Nichols, who not only revised the draft, but also kindly agreed to write a foreword; David Roscoe, who gave me some invaluable tips on style; Michael Sternberg who was responsible for my trip to the 'Holy Mountain'; Michael Morgan who assisted me in reconstructing the service of our grandfather ('Pop') with the Royal Army Medical Corps; Anthony Rock Cooper, with whom a lifetime of expeditions was first plotted on his parents' living-room floor; and Lester Crook of I.B.Tauris for his sound advice during the publication process.

A lot of what has been written here is subject to the fallibility of memory. In February 2010, I was eavesdropping over a glass of wine in the bar of the Ghan, somewhere between Adelaide and Alice Springs, when I heard a lady exclaim, in a thick Aussie accent: 'Damn it all; seen it all; heard it all; just can't remember it all!'

Says it all.

Index